# wogfood

*For Gloria*

AN ORAL HISTORY WITH RECIPES

# wog food

## by John Newton

### photography by Grenville Turner

RANDOM HOUSE
AUSTRALIA

Random House Australia Pty Ltd
20 Alfred Street, Milsons Point, NSW 2061

Sydney   New York   Toronto
London   Auckland   Johannesburg
and agencies throughout the world

First published in 1996
Copyright © John Newton 1996
© Photographs Grenville Turner

National Library of Australia
Cataloguing-in-Publication Data

Newton, John 1945–   .
Wogfood: an oral history with recipes
Includes index.
ISBN 0 09 183134 2.

1. Cookery - Anecdotes. 2. Gastronomy - Anecdotes.
3. Cookery, Australian - Anecdotes. 2. Cookery, Australian -
Foreign influences. I. Title.

641.30994

Edited by Julia Cain
Designed by de Luxe & Associates
Typeset by Midland Typesetters, Maryborough, Victoria
Printed in Singapore by Kyodo Printing Co (S'Pore) Pte Ltd

# Contents

A venerable Carlton institution, the Lygon Food Store. From left: John Peluse, Joe la Greca and Tony Pollo.

# Thanks

To the International Olive Oil Council and the Brown Brothers of Milawa for financial assistance with airfares. Claude Forrell for invaluable help on the restaurant history of Melbourne. David Dale for allowing me to quote from his Walkley Award-winning article 'The Italian Waiter Conspiracy'. Stefano Manfredi, Vince Trotta and George Haddad for planting the seed. Everyone at Anticos, especially Joe, Sam and Michael, for a lot more than just the garlic on the cover. George Koolis for sharing his memories of the early Sydney restaurant scene. To a patient publisher, Margaret Sullivan. And finally, as always, to my wife, who has only to read something in a certain tone of silence to send me scurrying to change it.

# A *few words about the recipes*

The recipes included in this book are from professional and home chefs, have not been laboratory tested, are included for both historical and practical reasons, and on the assumption that anyone trying them will be sufficiently skilled not to need measurements to the last millimetre (with the obvious exception of pastries). I assume commonsense.

For reasons of space, I was forced to make selections from a number of recipes sent to me. The choice was made based on the story told in the book. The author has tried several of the recipes and they are damned good.

WRITERS' BLOC

THE READER IS ALWAYS RIGHT

# *Introduction*

THE STAR HOTEL on the corner of Goulburn and Sussex Streets in Sydney is an adamantly Australian pub on the very edges of Chinatown. It's the pub for the left-wing factions from the Trades Hall across Goulburn Street—has been so for years. Foster's bar towels, blokes smoking Winfields, even a little room out the back that looks suspiciously like a Ladies' Lounge. Surrounded by Hokkien, Chiu Chow, Szechuan, Cantonese and Singaporese restaurants, the Star is making no concessions.

Walking past this cultural bastion, while working on and thinking about this book, I noticed, leaning against the tiled outside wall, a tall blackboard covered with white painted words. At the top it read AUSSIE FOOD. Below it was a menu. The first item on the menu—lasagne.

But this casual acceptance of what is and isn't genuine Australian munger (in itself an interesting word, being, according to the Oxford *Australian National Dictionary*, First World War services' slang corrupted from the Italian *mangiare*, to eat, which arrived here via England) depends, really, upon when you were born, on whether you grew up alongside the migrants who flooded in after the Second World War, or whether you are a member of the pasta generations.

On another occasion, when flying back from Melbourne, I was seated next to an elderly woman in a brown woollen coat and cap who clutched her handbag nervously to her lap during the entire flight—until lunch arrived. I lifted the foil flap on my serving and found it was airline lasagne. I noticed my neighbour, having placed her bag beside her, cautiously lifting hers, peering in and poking at it apprehensively with her fork, as one would at a slug in the lettuce. 'What's the mystery?' she asked, perhaps to no-one in particular, but I answered anyway. 'Lasagne,' I said, 'a layer of pasta, cheese, tomato sauce and probably mince.' She continued to poke at it before pushing it away with a sigh, adding, 'I'm too old.'

Such an incident underlines the importance of food to culture. None of the ingredients of that lasagne would have been unfamiliar to my flying companion—flour, water, eggs, minced meat, tomato and cheese—but it was the way in which they were put together and served that was foreign to her. Nowhere is this clash of cultures more obvious in the stories in this book than at the Bonegilla migrant hostel.

Bonegilla wasn't the only migrant hostel in Australia, but it seems to have been the one that processed most of the people I spoke to. About 15 kilometres from Albury, Bonegilla was opened in 1947, and closed in 1971. Its major purpose was to house non-British migrants. The naive intention of the authorities was that they would be familiarised, Australianised, and placed in employment in six weeks. Nothing better illustrates the gap between the cultures of most of those new arrivals and the hosts than memories of the food.

In *Fresh From Italy*, Stefano Manfredi remembers, even as a little boy, recognising that something was wrong with the food at Bonegilla. It didn't occur to him until later what it was: 'We had left behind more than a country when we got off the boat from Italy and went to live in that migrant hostel—we'd left behind an entire culture. And in daily life, that culture was expressed in the preparation and eating of food.' At Bonegilla, the preparation of food was left to the Army. 'Rotten old mutton for lunch and dinner,' remembers migrant journalist and writer Pino Bosi in Glenda Sluga's invaluable book *Bonegilla, a Place of No Hope*.

Miraculously, our relationship—by 'our' I mean that between Anglo-Australians and these new arrivals—survived those days. It survived the incidents reported to me during the course of gathering these stories, when two people speaking in their native tongue in public would be told to 'speak English or get back to your own country'. It survived the gibes, the taunts and the unconscious and conscious racism to the point where I can write a book like this—and call it Wogfood.

From being predominantly a term of offensive racist abuse, it has become, even among themselves (probably especially among themselves), a term of affection, a tribal word to reaffirm common backgrounds and experiences. On the side of an Italian-Australian farm outhouse that I visited was scrawled this riddle: Question—what's green and drives a Valiant? Answer—Kermit the Wog. If different ethnic and racial groups of people are going to be able to live together in peace and harmony anywhere in the world, I believe it will be in Australia.

And, it should be reported, the terms of abuse were not all one way. We may have had wog and wop and dago, but the Italians were calling us *testa quadrata*, square head; or *morti fami*, die of hunger (look at what we ate!); and *doppio ciglio*, two eyebrows. Calabrians had some words for us in their own dialect: *culuo rutto*, broken arse; *salami*, dope; and *kaka sices*, deadshit to name just three.

One of my favourite foreign pejoratives is the one used by the Greeks, *alathotos* (pronounced ala tzo sos), a word meaning unanointed with olive oil, and so not a member of the Greek Orthodox Church—sort of like saying 'ungreasy wog'.

Nowadays, as I understand it, the universal term for all Anglo-Australians is skip—short for Skippy, and, to be really offensive, its use is accompanied with a kind of short-armed nibbling and hopping motion.

One of my Italian informants, after telling me a few of these words, said, 'Jesus, John, it's taken us 40 years to get accepted—now you're going to blow it by telling everyone what we used to call you.' On the contrary, bringing it all out in the open is, I believe, a gesture of reconciliation.

But who is a wog? This is a decision I had to make before I started this book. And, I discovered, the word has very different meanings in different English-speaking countries. When I told a table at lunch in London what the name of my book was to be there was a horrified intake of breath. 'I don't think,' murmured one well-bred pom, 'you could call it that over here.' Wog, in England, is still a very nasty word: it means nigger. In America, on the other hand, it means nothing, the preferred terms there being spic, wop and dago, and still offensive.

I decided, before compiling a list of people to interview, that for Australians, wog means just about all those whose countries share a shore with the Mediterranean, except the French, who are frogs, and the Yugoslavs and Albanians, who used to be balts.

Usage apart, *The Macquarie Dictionary* defines the word as applying to '1. a native of North Africa or the Middle East, esp. an Arab. 2. a person of Mediterranean extraction or of similar complexion and appearance'. For etymology it offers '(? short for Golliwog)', although I have also read, somewhere, that it derived from First World War services' slang used by troops stationed in Egypt, being the initials for 'worthy oriental gentleman'. A little heavy-handed racist irony.

My own etymological preference is that offered by my friend Jan Power, the Brisbane food writer, philosopher and wit: 'I've always thought it stood for wine, olive oil and garlic.' And so it does.

The idea for this book came from one cook whose story is in this book, George Haddad, whose assertion that Australians are infinitely more open to new food ideas than most of the wogs of his acquaintance set me to thinking, and two others whose stories I haven't told here: Stefano Manfredi and Vince Trotta. Stefano because, while working with him on *Fresh From Italy*, I began to wonder about everybody else's story; and Vince, who didn't have a restaurant when I started (he was too busy getting established), who, when I asked him what sort of food he cooked, told me, 'Well, I'm a New Australian, so I guess you'd call it New Australian food.'

And isn't it what. The changes have occurred so quickly, so profoundly, it's occasionally necessary to check our bearings by looking over our shoulder. The 1970 edition of *The Australian Women's Weekly Cookbook*, edited by Ellen Sinclair, does indeed have a pasta section—with eight recipes (including lasagne). But look at the ingredients for spaghetti bolognaise: '1 large onion, 1 lb minced steak, 8 oz can tomato paste, 1 pint water, salt, pepper, 2 beef stock cubes, ¼ teaspoon oregano, ¼ teaspoon thyme, tablespoon oil, ¾ lb spaghetti, grated Parmesan cheese.'

The word 'olive' is mentioned once in 257 pages, in a caption for a page of photographs of canapés: 'creamed blue cheese with stuffed olives.' Not one recipe suggests the use of olive oil.

Even as late as 1982, the relatively sophisticated *Australia The Beautiful Cookbook* (Weldon Owen) offers scant evidence of what would have been called, in those days, 'ethnic dishes', sprinkled throughout the text, yet there is a separate section entitled 'Our cosmopolitan cities: recipes including French, Italian, Balkan, Spanish, Middle Eastern, Chinese and South East Asian.'

For the first 150 years of white settlement in Australia we lacked the peasant class that would have given us a solid culinary tradition, and the middle class that would have given us a dining-out tradition—the restaurants that existed were for the 'upper classes', a relative handful of Australians in the two major cities.

Until recently, what most of us ate at home all over Australia (of course, there were exceptions) was very much the food that my wife remembers from her own childhood: 'charcoal chops, cremated kidneys, mushy veggies'. The food Gay Bilson told *The Sydney Morning Herald*, in 1983, she ate at home was: '. . . three cuts of meat: mid loin chops which were grilled, rolled beef which was roasted, and leg of lamb which was roasted too. All were cooked and cooked and cooked until any trace of blood disappeared.'

It is obvious that those who arrived here after the Second World War preaching the gospel of wine, olive oil and garlic did so into a culinary vacuum. What is fascinating is that the message has been taken up with such evangelical fervour.

This book ignores competing academic theories on the existence or otherwise of an 'Australian cuisine', or the sources of what we eat, in favour of recording the directly remembered and even misremembered foodlore of that group of non-Anglo-Australians (all but three from a post-war migrant family) who came here with their culinary cultures intact. Because, however the academics choose to interpret it (and choose they will), there is no doubt that these people have had a profound influence on the way we eat and live in Australia today. Especially in the last ten years, as the second and third generations have grown up so comfortably Australian that they have become increasingly curious about their origins and their roots—and discovering the food of their homelands.

Wogfood's contribution to what we are eating in Australia today is only one part of the story—yet it is a very important part of that story, because it has to do with more than food. It has to do with our adoption of a way of life far better suited to our climate than that first imposed on us by the original colonists. It often seems to me that, just as you have to live in a house for some time to understand how it works, to appreciate its spaces and idiosyncrasies, it has taken us 200 years to understand how best to live in this 'wide brown land'.

And it took a bunch of migrants from the Mediterranean, arriving with their rolling pins and mortars and pestles, and with absolutely no intention, like Rosa Matto's mother, of 'falling into whatever the natives of the new land ate', who taught us, finally, how to be comfortable here, and how to eat. Three cheers for the wogs. Where would we be without them?

Peter behind Cosmos in Darlinghurst.

*'If I had to choose one ingredient, I'd say that wild greens are the essence of Greek food.'*

# CHAPTER ONE

# Peter Conistis

IN 1993, I remember taking two Greek friends—one Australian-Greek, one Greek-Greek—to lunch at Cosmos, Peter Conistis' first restaurant in Sydney. For those of you who never went, it was tiny, a 40-seater, with peculiar plastic chairs, a Minoan wave frieze on the walls and a kitchen smaller than most home kitchens. From this kitchen, Peter and his mother Eleni would produce Greek food the like of which has not been seen in this—or perhaps any other—city.

That day we ate a selection of their usual brightly coloured, boldly flavoured dishes. As usual, I just asked Peter to 'bring food'. There was sure to have been a *moussaka* of eggplant, *taramasalata* and seared Coffin Bay scallops; there were roast king prawns with spinach, herbs and fetta; a duck and black olive pie, of that I'm sure; and a mastic and raspberry ice cream with red fruits in rosewater syrup.

At the end of two and a half hours of this, I turned to my two friends and said, 'Well, what do you think?' 'It was wonderful,' they said, 'but it's not Greek food.'

Peter Conistis was both pleased and frustrated when I reported this response. He recognised that they were, at the same time, right and wrong. Any discussion of his food has to become an analysis of what exactly it is we're talking about when we talk about 'Greek food'.

Peter was born in 1967. He grew up in Newtown and Marrickville, at that time (the 1970s) the two most Greek of Sydney's suburbs. Peter has one older brother, John. Although his father, Kyriacos, met his mother, Eleni, in Australia in the early sixties, they both come from the same part of central Greece, Roumeli—Kyriacos from a family of olive growers who still owns land in the mountains in the village of Efpalio, and Eleni from the town of Agios Polikarpos.

Like a lot of Greek families, the Conistis' travel back and forth, spending time in Greece. All of Kyriacos' brothers but one came to Australia, and all but he returned, eventually, to Greece.

To hear Peter speaking of his early life, it was one long series of crowded family dinners, parties and picnics, occasionally interrupted by work and schooling. It was the Conistis family—or one very similar—that I remember as an Anglo (only) child at the beach with my parents. The children were noisy, hungry, continually having food that smelled delicious shoved at them by an army of chattering mothers up to their armpits in pies and salads and delicious meats barbecuing and turning on spits.

'My first memories are all around family,' he told me, 'going to the beach with three or four families, everyone packing the station wagon—all the mothers and the fathers and the kids stuck in the back. Mainly we'd go to Cronulla, then a huge Greek community beach. They'd put down the blanket and have their picnic and everyone would bring food out and you'd go for a swim and then you'd eat more.'

I told Peter that I used to sit alone with my parents (we never took picnics to the beach because we lived close by and went home to eat) and smell their food hungrily and envy them their crowded, noisy, smelly chaos. He was amazed and said, 'I thought you all used to laugh at us. When we got older we got embarrassed about the food and the way it smelt and we said why can't we just go and get some Kentucky Fried Chicken like everybody else? But it was a big deal. The mothers would cook all morning. They'd find out who was doing what and they'd pack these huge baskets of food.'

What kind of food? 'Lots of cold finger food they could chase us with when we were running around. Greek spinach pies—where my mother comes from they're called *hortopitas*. Basically pies of wild greens.' This triggers off a significant food memory.

'We'd go and gather wild greens. We'd travel at least an hour out of Sydney, out Penrith way and they'd gather all these wild greens from the fields. Some were variations of the Greek ones. We'd also grow our own—from seeds brought back from Greece. That's a very important part of the Greek diet. I was talking to someone about what Greek food was all about, and I thought hard about it and its ingenuity—especially with wild greens, one of the staple ingredients. If I had to choose one ingredient, I'd say that wild greens are the essence of Greek food.'

Wild greens are what we would call weeds. Edible weeds. In Greek, *horta*. They have been utilised in Greece since ancient times. In Australia, Peter uses as many as he can find: amaranth, chicory, purslane, dandelion and pigweed. In her book *Honey From a Weed* in the chapter entitled 'Edible Weeds', Patience Grey lists sixteen species including—and I'll use their common English names—comfrey, fat hen, wild fennel, broom rape, field sorrel and rock samphire. The Greek collective word for these wild greens is *radikia*—indeed radicchio is one such. Closer to home, Irini Germanos' book *A Taste of Greek Life and Cooking* lists 22 species, with photographs, Greek and English names, and their various culinary and medicinal uses.

But what does Peter mean by saying that wild greens—edible weeds—are the essence of Greek Food? The meaning is simple. And I mean simple. Simplicity as opposed to complexity. Further defined as ungarnished. Unembellished. Innocent. And natural. This is indeed a radical (in the original sense of the word, from the Latin *radix*, root, and perhaps beyond to—*radikia*) reappraisal of Greek cooking which, if most of us had thought about it, we would have said was more about *taramasalata* and a *moussaka* of eggplant, meat and bechamel sauce—although, after a moment's contemplation, we'd have to agree that bechamel is hardly Greek.

'I know from my Mum,' Peter told me, 'about twenty different dishes to make using these wild greens. They'd either boil them as a salad and dress them with olive oil and lemon juice, or braise them with garlic and onion, or bake them into a pie (*hortopita*), or when they really had very little money they'd make a flour- or cornmeal-based soup and add the wild greens to it. They'd never eat that these days. It reminds them of that poverty.'

These food expeditions—visions of hordes of Greeks with bulging picnic baskets ravaging the countryside for food— didn't stop at wild greens. 'In the same way we'd go into the Blue Mountains and gather wild mushrooms. We'd come back with boxes full.'

Many European mushrooms now grow in Australian forests, the spore presumably having been imported along with seed and seedlings from exotic plants and trees. Orange produce broker Rob Robinson forages for several different types of mushrooms—including Saffron Milk Cap (*Lactarius deliciosus*) and Slippery Jack (*Suillus luteus*) in the Canobolas State Forest. Some of these varieties are today finding their way into specialty fruit and vegetable shops under the generic name of 'pine mushrooms'. But back then we Anglos ate only one mushroom—the common field mushroom (*Agaricus campestris*)— or, occasionally, if very bold, the champignon (*Agaricus bisporus*), usually from a tin. Everything else, we were warned, was a toadstool, and would kill you or send you mad.

As I listen to Peter Conistis' rapt memories of family picnics and food gathering expeditions, I suspect I've found one of the sources of my own Mediterranophilia. Even though my mother did cook spaghetti bolognaise, it was with butter, not olive oil, and based on half a pound of best—grey— mince. We didn't gather food, we shopped. And as much as I enjoyed going with her to Reg at Household Supplies in Double Bay for a tasty wedge of Epicure—it didn't rank with family mushrooming expeditions. These wogs have taught us to enjoy gathering our food. The gathering, as well as the cooking of our food, should be joyful.

When he was ten, Peter went to Greece for the first time, a trip that would prove to be a major influence on his life, and the first of many such trips. What does he remember of that first—at least spiritual—homecoming?

'The smell. The smell was the first thing I remember getting off the plane. I mean, I know there's congestion in Athens, but I swear I could smell food miles in the air—congestion and food. They told me to prepare for meeting a lot of relations. We got out of customs and there was this crowd. I thought, it's just a crowd—but this was my family! I was introduced to all these people and then suddenly we were in a car and driving along the main road and I remember the men selling those little pretzel rings on a stick [*pasteli*] so we bought some and munched on them all the way, and from that day I remember, wherever you'd go there'd be food. Everyone's house, everywhere.'

On that first trip, Peter stayed mainly in Athens, but at Easter he was taken to his father's village. 'That was a real experience for a ten-year-old, going to this village, and walking down the street and having herds of goats pass you, and using my grandmother's toilet, which was a hole in the backyard. But it all seemed natural, like this was how it was supposed to be.'

After finishing school, Peter completed a dutiful six months at Sydney University doing law. 'Hated that. My parents' idea, lawyer or doctor. I tried it and thought, this is ridiculous, I don't know why I'm here. So I went to Greece and spent four months there. We [his friends and cousins, this was now his third trip] got on a ferry and went straight to Santorini. We spent time hanging around the islands, Mikonos, Naxos, Ios.'

'When I came back I studied Communications at the University of Western Sydney. Three years. Then I went to the Film and Television School at Ryde, and did a year's production course and made a couple of student films.' Neither film—*Deadlock*, which he describes as the story of a hate/hate relationship which stared Kerry Fox 'and some Indian guy', or *Looking Through a Glass Window*, about schizophrenia—had much to do with food.

While he was studying, Peter moved out of home. He first lived in one of his childhood suburbs, Newtown ('which by now is groovy!'), but he discovered that he needed a job to pay the rent. Like so many students, he drifted into the entertainment/hospitality industry. As he used to 'party a lot' he knew a lot of people in the nightclub world, so got a job managing Spago's. 'That was interesting. Finish uni, go home, do a little study, get a couple of hours sleep, go to work at 9PM, finish at 6AM, go home for a shower and back to uni. That went on for a whole year.' Deciding that it couldn't go on much longer, he found a job in the bar at Merrony's (Merrony's, a French/Australian restaurant owned by chef Paul Merrony) where he worked for a year and a half. 'That's when I started getting serious about food.'

He started cooking at home, using recipes from *Vogue Entertaining* and *Australian Gourmet Traveller*, inviting friends over for dinner, and becoming well known for his dinners. 'I remember one dinner party I did for my twenty-third birthday. I decided to do risotto for 26 people—not just any risotto, this was a saffron risotto with seared quail breasts and fresh peas and so on. Everyone ate at 2AM. We had dessert at 5, and by 6 we were falling asleep.'

'After I'd finished the student films, I knew this wasn't what I wanted to do. I was inching towards the restaurant business. I liked the buzz of going into (Paul's) kitchen and watching it all happen. I had a long chat to Paul one night about restaurants. By then I was seriously passionate about food.'

That passion took him back to Greece. Not once, but several times, like a latterday Archestratus (the fourth century BC author of 'The Life of Luxury', an epic poem on the subject of food) of whom it was written '. . . travelled over every land and sea with precision, in a desire . . . to review with care the things of the belly'.

Peter certainly travelled with precision. 'I couldn't just open up "a" restaurant. I had to do something I could cook. I knew if I just did "modern Australian" style, it wouldn't work. So I did a lot of reading. I read a lot of Greek cookbooks, went to Greece a few times, and ate a lot of Greek food. First, I went to the Peloponnisos and a few of the islands.'

He spoke to his Greek family, asked questions, became a culinary detective. Because Greece isn't a restaurant culture, this made the search more difficult. 'I'd speak to people and say where can I get something that typifies the food of this region, and they'd always say, well, it won't be as good as if you come to my house, but go here.' Very rarely was he invited home. 'A lot of people tell me how generous the Greeks are, and they are, but they just don't often say come to my house and eat.'

This is a curiosity that I have noticed in Spain, and in discussing it with Peter, we decided that at least those two cultures are similar. In both Spanish and Greek houses there are 'formal' entertaining areas, where guests are confined. But the inner sanctum of the house—the kitchen and eating areas—are kept for family. In Greece, Peter told me that, 'In the country they might have just one room with bedrooms off it, but in the city, there's a formal sitting room and further back the family room. I remember going to visit people we didn't know that well, distant cousins and family friends, and we were invited into these really lovely sitting rooms, and given coffee and a sweetmeat and it'd be all nice and proper. Then you'd go to your family and they'd take you straight to the kitchen and the food'd be coming out of the oven—and as a kid I'd wonder why they took me to this room and not the nice rooms. I could never work that out.'

When he came back to Australia he was sure he wanted to open a Greek restaurant. But a Greek restaurant unlike any he'd seen. He spoke to his mother who was, as always, encouraging. 'I spoke to a few friends and said this is what I want to do and they said, look, it doesn't matter what you do, it'll work. So I thought, it's time to do this.' He returned to Greece. 'I was concentrating a lot more this time. I think I went back looking for any restaurant that was doing what I wanted to do. To see if it works. But there was nothing. Modern Greek food (in Athens and the cities) is French food with a little bit of Greek flavour to it. They're still stuck in a terrible cordon bleu period.'

At the beginning of this chapter, you will remember that my two Greek friends said of Peter's food that 'it was wonderful, but it's not Greek food.' So what exactly is—and was—Greek food?

Peter told me that, on one of his trips to Greece, he found an unleavened barley bread being made in the villages in Northern Greece, and that in certain parts, they drop this bread, dried, into a water-based soup called *katsamaki*, which sounds very similar to an Hellenic Age dish of barley gruel.

These are the foundations of Greek food. Bread is still central and important to this day. In *The Foods of Greece* Aglaia Kremezi writes: 'I know of no other culture in which bread plays such an important role at all stages of people's lives. Bread is so much linked with our existence that, instead of saying that a person is about to pass away, we say "his bread is finished" or "he has eaten all his bread".'

Add wheat, barley, fish, cheese, figs, wine and olive oil, and you have the basics of Greek food, then as now.

The olive was being grown on Crete in the time of King Minos, 2500BC. In the fifth century BC, Herodotus described Athens as a vast centre of Greek olive culture. Today, Greece has over 100 million trees planted, is the third largest olive oil producer in the world and supplies 20 per cent of the world's oil. The olive tree is important for many facets of Greek life and culture.

And then there are the external influences. For 1100 years Greece was a part of the Byzantine empire—from 330 to 1450 AD—and for 400 years under Ottoman domination, from the middle of the fifteenth to the beginning of the nineteenth century.

The Byzantine court developed an elaborate cuisine with roots in ancient Greece. Later, the Ottoman rulers adopted this cuisine, and sent their cooks to study in Europe, so when they returned, they invented new dishes. Aglaia Kremezi gives as one of these *moussaka*—a bechamel sauce added to eggplant and lamb.

And, let's not forget, as Martin Bernal reminds us in *Black Athena*, that the classical civilisation of Greece—including, of course, its cuisine—has deep roots in Afro-Asiatic cultures—Pythagoras himself studied in Egypt and in Babylon.

Alas, politics, war and nationalism interfered. The Greeks came to abhor the Turkish influence in their food and language. Memories of the occupation are, after all, a lot more recent than, say, the Spanish memories of Moorish occupation. Turkish sounding words were—and still are—being denied or expunged. Turkish coffee became Greek coffee. In many cases, the Turkish names attached to Greek dishes were merely the result of Greeks being forced to use a Turkish word to describe a Greek dish.

The most successful attempt to rid Greek food of unwelcome Turkish flavours and influences came in the 1920s (with the memory of Turkish occupation still very fresh) at the hands of one Tselementes, a Greek from Siphnos who grew up in Constantinople, worked in Europe, and saw it as his mission to 'refine' Greek cooking, in much the same way that we 'refine' sugar, and 'refine' flour.

It was Tselementes' rather strange theory that French cooking had its origins in ancient Greece, and that, under Turkish rule, it had become more eastern. He detested the 'barbaric' spices which he believed were a remnant of those days, and banned them from his dishes.

As Kremezi reports, to this day, the name Tselementes is synonymous with cookbooks in middle-class Greece. 'What most Greeks of my age and younger have known as "Greek" food is the "neither Eastern nor European" dishes that Tselementes promoted.'

The proof of his success in diluting a rich and ancient cuisine can be seen in the number of Thai, Chinese, Indian and other restaurants in Athens—which also now has its first McDonald's and Wendy's. Look for ethnic restaurants in Rome and Paris.

And then there was—and still is—most Greek restaurant food, the Greek food that we Anglo-Australians (and tourists in Greece) were served for so long. *Souvlaki. Tsatziki. Taramosalata.* Lamb with beans, lamb with okra, lamb with everything. An unimaginative and limited canon of good, solid food, inspired by Tselementes, and set in aspic around 1950—when most Greeks came to Australia.

And now, in our time, in our place, one of those strange accidents that can change the course of culinary history. In 1993, a young Australian film school graduate decided that he would open a Greek restaurant.

Before he did so, he took several trips to Greece. He wandered in the countryside, around the islands, in the mountains, talking to village women, professional and merely locally renowned cooks, gathering recipes, noting ingredients, listening, and eating, eating, eating.

He came back and worked on these recipes with his mother, Eleni, always a fine home cook, and now the keeper of the spirit in the kitchen at Cosmos.

No. It's not the Greek we know. It's not the Greek that many Greeks remember from their middle class mothers' kitchens. It's not the Greek I remember from Sydney's Hellenic Club restaurant—or even the Greek I remember from Xinos in Athens.

It's no less Greek food than Steve and Franca Manfredi's (The Restaurant Manfredi in Sydney, an Italian restaurant with another mother and son kitchen combination) is Italian food; than the dishes invented by George Haddad and Kathy Witbreuk at Ali Akbar in Hobart (see Chapter 5) were Lebanese. Peter is the latest in an increasingly long line of inventive and creative Australian cooks who are making late twentieth-century adaptations which change the form, but retain the spirit.

It is interesting that such a seemingly clearly defined cuisine has been so obscured. Is it that Greece was such a poor country, that the average Greek didn't move around inside their own country, and that, as there was no restaurant culture outside the big cities, dishes were private, family-owned creations?

The answer to these questions is yes. It's the reason why any claim to an 'authentic' recipe or an 'authentic' cuisine from any of these Mediterranean cultures is so much tosh. What's authentic in one village is risible two kilometres down the road. At first, when Peter came back and told his parents about some of the dishes he'd discovered, they laughed at him. 'When I told them I'd had this amazing eggplant pie, they said, what are you talking about, no one uses eggplant in a pie.'

Peter's wanderings turned up some real surprises. 'The second time I went up to Northern Macedonia, it was winter. It was then I realised that Greeks used chillies in their food, which I'd never heard of before. Around Voulos, I had this one dish, a layered braised casserole thing of leeks and sardines and chilli, slices of leek, slices of fanned out sardine, sprinklings of oregano and chilli and baked in the oven. Serious winter food. And cabbage leaf stuffed with pork and veal and chilli, but not with the traditional egg and lemon juice but lots of chopped up herbs like parsley with lemon juice squeezed over it.'

And others. 'In Corfu and Kephalonia, you find an Italian influence. I had some food there I told my Mum about that she'd never heard of—that's where the rabbit pie comes from—they do an artichoke pie too. Whole artichokes braised with tomato and mixed with crushed cinnamon and eggs and cheese and made into a pie. And lots of pasta dishes—in Corfu they braise meat really slowly and stuff it inside this tubular pasta and pour it into a dish and put cheese over it and bake it in the oven.'

'On a few of the islands,' Peter reported, 'I remember they'd make the *skordalia* with walnut meal or almond meal, no potato,' betraying pre-Columbian, even Medieval, origins.

Peter made three or four of these exploratory trips, each of around six weeks' duration, and returned with a pocketful of recipes, and a well-defined attitude towards Greek food today. While critical of much of the restaurant food, he is full of praise for the Greek way of cooking and eating. 'They're not out to show off. They're not out to say we can do this amazing sauce. [Greek food] is about really good fish or meat or vegetables, and letting them stand on their own. Having a fresh red mullet just grilled on charcoal and served with a wedge of lemon and olive oil, or vegetables sliced and roasted in the oven with some olive oil. Food is important to them. They know good food.'

And the produce, he insists, is wonderful. 'I could cook the food that I do here in Greece and it wouldn't taste the same. I still think we have a long way to go before our fruit and veg have the flavour they have there.

You still can't get a decent tomato here. We make amazing roast tomato sauce out of the Romas, but for a Greek salad you need a really good tomato. And we buy the most expensive we can find for our salads, and they're nice . . . but.'

Armed with this knowledge, having worked on the recipes with Eleni, having found a hole in the wall site in Darlinghurst ('I wanted to do it all on my own—no help from Mum and Dad, I didn't want to go to a bank, I didn't want to be in debt, so if it didn't work, it was my own money') he opened the doors in April 1993. And it was a success from that very first night. At the end of his first year of operating, he had gained a hat in *The Sydney Morning Herald Good Food Guide.*

This is quintessentially Greek-Australian food. Created by a Greek boy born in Australia and his Greek-born mother, a conscious blending of local produce, Greek technique and personal taste. 'I know what I like in food. If something wasn't what I enjoyed eating, I'd change it, play with it, until I enjoyed it. I've always been very selfish in that way. If I don't like it, I don't serve it.'

I asked Peter why what he and other young chefs are doing is happening here. 'Because we have some very imaginative young people out there. Because we haven't the barriers—like in France and England where you're taught this is the way it's done. We don't have those restrictions. We don't have Michelin Guides.' Like a lot of Australia's new chefs, Peter is entirely— and proudly—self-taught. During one of our conversations when I asked him when he'd decided on cooking as a career, he replied 'about two and a half years ago.' Later he told me, 'I didn't know any techniques until I opened the restaurant. I didn't even know how to do a veal stock. But within six months, I'd taught myself how to make a pretty good veal stock.'

The other difficulty, surely, was working in the kitchen with his mother. 'We get on. We get on really well. When we work, most of the time it's not like mother and son, we respect each other. It's amazing. The moment we walk out of the restaurant, immediately I'm her son again.

In his next venture, Peter plans to move 'more into Middle Eastern food— I want to do Lebanese and Egyptian and Turkish food and I don't care about the politics.'

Then, of course, people can walk away shaking their heads saying, 'It was wonderful, but it wasn't Turkish/Lebanese/Egyptian food.' By then, Peter Conistis will be used to it. For him—and for us—it'll be just another strand in the intricate weave that will, one day, become Australian food.

# Eleni's Wild Greens Pita

SERVES 6–8

I know from my Mum about twenty different dishes to make using these wild greens.

## PASTRY

4 cups (500 g) bakers flour plus extra
1 teaspoon salt
150 mL chilled water
4 tablespoons olive oil
a little olive oil (extra) as needed

## FILLING

1 small bunch English spinach
1 small bunch purslane
1 small bunch sorrel
1 small bunch amaranth
2 handfuls of very young vine leaves and tendrils (if you have a vine leaf handy)
1 tablespoon sea salt
2 medium leeks, cleaned and white parts thinly sliced
1 small bunch dill, leaves chopped
1 tablespoon rice
200 g sheep's milk fetta, crumbled
1 egg, lightly beaten

To make pastry, sift the 500 g flour and the salt into a large bowl. Make a well in the centre of the flour and add the water and 4 tablespoons olive oil. Stir quickly with a metal spoon, until all the ingredients are combined.

Turn out the pastry onto a lightly floured surface and knead until smooth and elastic. If the mixture is too doughy, add extra flour as needed. Cover with plastic wrap or a damp teatowel and set aside for 30 minutes.

Divide the pastry into four equal balls. Keep each dough ball covered until you are ready to roll it out.

Take one of the balls and place it on a lightly floured surface. Roll out into a thin sheet, making a circle of about 30 cm diameter. Brush with a little olive oil. Repeat the process with another ball and place the pastry sheet on top of the first sheet of pastry. Set aside, covered. Repeat this process with the other two dough balls, so that you have two circles of double layered pastry when you are finished.

Preheat the oven to 180°C (355°F). Oil a 26-cm springform pan. Set aside.

To make filling, pick and wash the leaves of all the greens. Shred the leaves and toss them with the sea salt. Leave to wilt for 1 hour. Drain under cold running water and squeeze very dry. Combine with the remaining ingredients.

To make pita, line the prepared pan with the first two pastry sheets. Spoon in the filling and cover with the remaining two pastry sheets. Gather and pinch the edges of the top and bottom pastry sheets.

Brush the top liberally with olive oil. Bake in the oven for about 45 minutes or until golden. When it has cooled slightly remove from the pan.

To serve: cut the pita into wedges.

**Peter Conistis with his mother Eleni at the original Cosmos.**

## Tomato Roasted Ocean Squid filled with Pickled Eggplant and Roasted Red Capsicum on Olive Orzo

SERVES 4 AS A MAIN MEAL; 6 AS AN ENTREE

The pickled eggplant needs to be prepared 24 hours before you wish to use it. Orzo is a rice-shaped pasta.

PICKLING SOLUTION
2 cups (500 mL) white wine
 vinegar
100 g white sugar
1 teaspoon salt
½ head garlic, cloves
 peeled and roughly
 chopped
1 bay leaf, crushed

To prepare pickling solution, place all the pickling ingredients in a saucepan, bring to the boil and simmer for 10 minutes. Remove from the heat and allow to cool. Store in a non-corrosive 2-litre container.

Sprinkle the eggplant generously with salt and stand for 2 hours to disgorge the bitter juices. Rinse in cold water and pat dry. Heat some olive oil in a frying pan and fry the slices on both sides

EGGPLANT
2 medium eggplants, thinly
  sliced lengthwise
salt
olive oil for frying

TOMATO SALTSA
1 kg very ripe Roma toma-
  toes, halved
2 large brown onions,
  chopped
1 head garlic, cloves separated and peeled
1 tablespoon Greek oregano
1 teaspoon ground
  cinnamon
1 pinch saffron threads
1 teaspoon white sugar
¼ cup (60 mL) extra virgin
  olive oil
⅓ cup (90 mL) white wine
salt and freshly ground
  black pepper to taste
2 tablespoons tomato paste

STUFFED SQUID
3 large red capsicums
olive oil
60 g kefalotyri cheese,
  grated
black pepper
2 ocean squid (also known
  as arrow or sea squid)
  about 800 g weight, external layers and beaks
  removed, tubes cleaned

OLIVE ORZO
500 g orzo (or risoni if you
  can't get orzo)
200 g kalamata olives,
  pitted and chopped
¼ cup (60 mL) extra virgin
  olive oil
1 tablespoon Greek red
  wine vinegar
salt and freshly ground
  black pepper

until they are golden, about 1–2 minutes. Drain on paper towel, then place the eggplant in the cold pickling solution and refrigerate for at least 24 hours before using it to stuff the squid.

To make saltsa, preheat the oven to 180°C (355°F). Place all the ingredients in a large baking dish and stir. Roast for about 1 hour. Remove from the oven and allow to cool slightly then blend in a food processor for 1 minute. Pass the mixture through a sieve. If it is a little thick, reheat the sauce and adjust the consistency with white wine or water. Set aside.

To make stuffed squid, preheat the oven to 240°C (465°F).

Rub the capsicums with olive oil and roast in the oven until their skins have blackened and blistered, about 20 minutes. Remove from the oven, cover with a damp cloth and set aside for 1 hour. Remove the blackened skin, cut each capsicum into quarters horizontally and discard the seeds. Pat dry with paper towel and set aside.

Divide the capsicum, the cheese and the drained and dried eggplant into two.

Repeat the following process twice. On sheets of plastic wrap, spread the capsicum out to just under the length of the squid. Sprinkle over the cheese and a little black pepper. Cover the layers with the eggplant slices. With the aid of the plastic wrap roll the slices into a roulade and carefully place inside the squid, first removing the plastic wrap. Secure with several toothpicks.

Place the two filled squids in a baking dish, cover with the tomato saltsa and bake in a 180°C (355°F) oven for 35–40 minutes.

To cook olive orzo, bring a large saucepan of salted water to the boil. Add the pasta and cook until tender, about 15 minutes. Drain and toss with the remaining ingredients.

To serve: slice the squid and arrange it on top of the olive orzo. Spoon over the tomato saltsa.

# Lemon Clove Kourambiedes with Lemon Ice Cream and Candied Green Walnuts

SERVES 6

Kourambiedes are shortbread. The candied walnuts need to be prepared ten days before use.

CANDIED GREEN WALNUTS
100 immature green
 walnuts
1 tablespoon whole cloves
4 cups (1 kg) white sugar
1⅓ cups (500 g) honey
2 cups (500 mL) water

KOURAMBIEDES
1 cup (250 g) butter
¾ cup (125 g) icing sugar
1 teaspoon vanilla extract
2 egg whites
zest of 2 lemons
2 cups (250 g) plain flour
1 teaspoon baking powder
¼ teaspoon ground cloves
¾ cup (90 g) walnuts (not
 the candied walnuts),
 lightly roasted and finely
 chopped
icing sugar for dusting

LEMON ICE CREAM
(You'll need a 10-cm loaf
tin with two lids to mould
the ice cream, otherwise
you can scoop spoonfuls of
ice cream between the
biscuits but you will have
to balance them carefully.)
1 vanilla bean cut in half
 lengthwise
800 mL thickened cream
juice of 2 large lemons,
 strained
10 egg yolks
1¼ cups (250 g) caster
 sugar

To prepare walnuts, with a paring knife remove the outer green husks of the walnuts, then make a tiny slit into each walnut. Place them in a bucket of water. Change the water daily for 10 days.

Place the walnuts in a large, cast iron enamel pot and cover with water. Bring to the boil and simmer until tender—test them with a skewer. This could take from 1–3 hours. Drain the walnuts and set aside overnight.

Place all the ingredients into a large, cast iron enamel pot and bring to the boil. Simmer until the syrup reaches 110°C (225°F) on a sugar thermometer. Alternatively, test if it is ready by dropping a little syrup into cold water. If it forms a soft ball when cool, it is ready.

Remove from the heat and leave the walnuts in the pot overnight. Pour the walnuts and syrup into two large (1-litre) sterilised preserving jars.

To make kourambiedes, preheat the oven to 160°C (315°F). Grease 2 baking sheets and set aside.

Beat the butter in an electric mixer for at least 10 minutes until very light and creamy. Add the icing sugar, vanilla, egg whites and lemon zest, and beat until smooth.

Sift the flour, baking powder and cloves together into the butter mixture and fold through until well combined. Fold in the walnuts.

Roll out the dough and using a 10-cm pastry cutter make 18 circles of pastry. Place on the baking sheets and bake for 10 minutes until golden. Dust with icing sugar. Allow to cool and dust again.

To make ice cream, scrape the seeds of the vanilla bean into a saucepan. Add the cream and lemon juice and bring to just below boiling point. Remove from the heat.

Beat the egg yolks and caster sugar together until creamy. Add the cream mixture, whisking all the time.

Return the mixture to a clean saucepan and stir over a medium heat until the mixture coats the back of a spoon.

Strain the mixture and refrigerate until cooled.

Churn in a domestic ice cream maker following the manufacturer's instructions.

Line the loaf tin with silicon paper and pour the ice cream into the tin with the base lid on. Place the other lid on top and freeze for about 3 hours.

Dip the tin into warm water and remove the ice cream from the mould. Place back into the freezer until required (this process makes it easier to slice).

To serve: for each serving, you need three kourambiedes. Place one in the centre of a plate and top with a 1-cm slice of ice cream, slice the candied walnuts and add several thin slices of candied walnuts.

Repeat the process then top with a freshly dusted kourambiede and drizzle with a little of the walnut syrup. Serve immediately.

Tiberio Donnini.

*'People just want to eat a nice piece of bread with a nice pasta and a glass of red wine. That's a meal, isn't it?'*

# CHAPTER TWO

# *Tiberio Donnini*

TIBERIO DONNINI is the only one of the people I spoke to for this book who I'd hesitate to call a wog. We met, of course, in Lygon Street, or rather on Lygon Street, outside Ti Amo, the Donnini family's adopted cafe: they don't own it, they use it. Lygon Street is the most Italian street in the most European city in Australia. Although I've been told that many of the coffee shops and pizza joints are now Lebanese-owned, Ti Amo is Italian to its upside-down coffee spoons.

Around us sit men with that air of permanence that says—I'm not going anywhere. I'm happy to be where I am, with the people around me, talking about what we are talking about. Sit down, have a coffee, tell me the story of your life—we have time, all the time in the world. They will not move, these men (and it is always men sitting around outside these cafes, here and in Europe), not unless the earth moved and shook them free. Melbourne knows this. Melbourne does this much better than Sydney. When Sydney people sit outside cafes, you can see them fidgeting, worrying about where they have to be next. But then Melbourne has been doing it much longer than Sydney. And this is due, in part, to the families Donnini and Milani and their University Cafe.

'See this table here,' Tiberio speaks softly, pointing behind us to a table of five elderly gentlemen on the kerb, 'when I was a baby, they used to knock around the University Cafe—they're all still here. Come here in ten years' time and they'll still be here.'

But let's go back to the word wog. Tiberio remains uncomfortable with it. 'That word. In Sydney it's meant in a ... to me it's a word that will always be derogatory. Some people say it in jest, and I know it's in jest. But inside it's like a trigger ... when we were kids, that's the word that really said, I don't like you, we're ready to tango. It's funny you called the book that. But I can understand why.'

Tiberio Donnini has something to get off his chest. I'm not going to stop him. 'What a lot of people don't understand is that my generation (he was born in 1958) paid the price. Our parents didn't speak the language. We were thrown into the Anglo schools, but our fathers, all men in their twenties, could hang around outside the University, and look at the girls walking past. It was our generation, with names like Tiberio Donnini, that was thrown in at the deep end. We're the ones who take offence more than they do.' Later—and we returned to this theme several times during our talk—I told Tiberio that he is the only person among those I interviewed for this book who reported serious racial problems, what would today be called vilification. Was it Carlton? Was it the massive intake of Italians post-war into an Anglo-Australian working-class suburb? There had been Italians in Melbourne since the nineteenth century, but they were mainly middle-class, and scattered. Carlton was the first Italian ghetto. The trip from working class to cafe class has happened in just 40 years.

Tiberio's father, Fernando, is from Rome. He came to Australia in 1951 with a group of friends for an adventure—they were going to stay for a couple of months, then go back to Italy. The family, Tiberio told me, was 'a working-class family, his grandfather was a bricklayer, my father used to work for Cinecitta [the Italian film company with large studios in Rome]. When I say working class, not a big worker, the old man. I mean, not many Romans are, they've got a touch of rebel in them.' Almost as soon as he arrived in Melbourne, Fernando met Elena Milani, Tiberio's mother, married her and began work at the University Cafe, her family's business. They met at the Catani Gardens, a dance hall in St Kilda. 'St Kilda was the only place that was—let's use the word—cosmopolitan. A lot of Italians knocked about the beach when they arrived.'

His mother's family, the Milanis, had come out earlier from Modena. It was Ero Milani who began the University with his son Gianni, Tiberio's uncle, and Fernando. Ero was a political refugee from Fascism. His wife, Eros, Tiberio's grandmother, was 'involved in food in Italy. She was a pasta maker and seamstress, and made money out of making tortellini and various things.' At the time of writing, she is still very much alive, at 85, 'I love talking to her, they get to the age where they don't care what they say. When Ero was alive, he was diplomatic.'

'She can seriously cook. There are not too many people who can. Most haven't the basic ingredients: a set of genuine taste buds. If we were to sit down in 100 Italian restaurants, I would walk out and say five of them know what they're doing. I suppose it's the difference between Michelangelo and a local artist. When is it going to get to the stage in Australia when you can sit down anywhere and have a fair dinkum meal? When you don't have to pick and choose?'

Tiberio Donnini is Italian, and, for him, there is only Italian food—and most of it just isn't good enough. 'If you want a plate of pasta, you want a plate of pasta. Some places you go it's as hard as this, somewhere else as soft as that.' Acompanying this are descriptive, and somewhat obscene, gestures. 'Australians are very good at being innovative, using new things and new ingredients like emu and crocodile, but the basics are what people want. People just want to eat a nice piece of bread with a nice bowl of salad, and a nice pasta with a glass of red wine. That's a meal, isn't it? You don't need all the bullshit.'

At home, the big dishes were lasagne and tortellini, the specialities of Modena. And not just any tortellini. 'We've never eaten tortellini in anything other than chicken broth. There's probably no restaurant in Australia that specialises in *tortellini in brodo*. The delicacy of tortellini is the taste within the meat and anything you put with it will kill it. It's like having an oyster with 5 kilos of tomato poured over it.' Another early food memory is *gnocco fritto*. 'Gnocco in Modena is like a pita bread, but a little bit higher. They make the same dough as you would for pita bread but they roll it out incredibly thinly and deep-fry it, and it puffs up, and you put a bit of prosciutto on it. I don't make it. When it comes to frying and doughs I leave it to the ones who can.' Tiberio's a restaurateur, not a cook, but he loves to watch. 'To watch my grandmother make something is like watching a surgeon. She's so precise.'

The Donninis lived in Nicholson Street and young Tiberio first went to school at St George's, a Catholic school in Carlton. 'There were a fair few Italian kids—there were also a few Italian nuns, the Catholic religion was smart enough to set up a kindy with Italian nuns.' Although even here, there are school lunch memories. 'Most of the Italian kids would eat their lunch in the toilet. I'll never forget this one kid, his mother used to bring him his lunch and she'd sit him on the front step and feed him. It was frightening, poor guy.'

He left St George's because, 'My Dad wanted to turn me into a gentleman and tried to send me to a private school—Ivanhoe Grammar, very straighthead—in year 8. You can't put brains in monuments, they say, and by that stage I was already pretty much formed. I was the only Italian in the school, so you can imagine what a great time it was.'

'The first day, three guys belted me. I went into the tuckshop—we never even had a tuckshop in our school—I saw this big bottle of soft drink, beautiful. I bought this drink and I went outside and sat under a tree. These three guys walked up and literally started on me, grabbed me by the shirt-front—wog, dago, little greaseball, the usual things. As it turned out, I eventually dealt with the three of them. I got one of them ten years after. I saw him on a beach and I said, do you remember me, son? And he said no, and I said, well, I remember you. Bang.'

Eventually he went to his father and told him, 'I don't like school too much, I want to leave. He said you start tomorrow. That was at the University Cafe and I worked there from 1973 to 1977.'

'The University Cafe opened on Lygon Street in 1952. It wasn't the first cafe—the Cafe Sport was already there—but it was the first place that fed the migrants.' The important thing about the University Cafe was that it opened before the Olympic Games in 1956. 'Lygon Street started to come good after the Olympic Games, my Dad said. A lot of people never mention that. All the European teams that were here were coming into Lygon Street because it was one of the few places where there was somebody here at eight or nine in the evening. The pubs closed at six. A lot of them used to head down this way and I think that's where the popularity began.'

At this point, with impeccable but accidental timing, we are joined by Gianni Milani, son of Ero and Eros, and his brother-in-law Fernando Donnini, father of Tiberio. After introductions and another round of coffee, I was to get a first-hand account of the early days at the University Cafe—which the families sold in 1977.

But first, a historic aside: the true story of the Great Bonegilla Pasta Riot of 1951. In common with most post-war migrants, the young Fernando was sent first to Bonegilla migrant camp. The riot was in the news—just before we spoke there had been mention of it on the SBS television series, 'The Italians'. But they hadn't got to the bottom of it. Fernando fills me in—he was there—and, of course, it was set off by food.

'There were 200 Italians in block 9. In the whole camp were 3000 young Italian men, unemployed. They put in charge of the kitchen three Russians, who put on top of the pasta 1 kilo of sugar. You can imagine—sugar on the pasta for us is like poison! We told the man in charge why don't you

**At Ti Amo coffee shop in Lygon Street, Carlton. From left: Gianni Milani, Tiberio and Fernando Donnini.**

get an Italian cook, and he said no, no. After the riot they sent in soldiers and tanks. I was in a group of Sicilians, I was the tallest one—they got me straight away.'

There were, to be fair, other causes mooted for this riot. The lack of work for the inmates was one, and the mere presence of Harold Holt in Albury another, cited by Glenda Sluga in *Bonegilla, A Place of No Hope*. But as Richard Beckett wrote in *Convicted Tastes*, of a 1982 ABC radio series on migrant hostels: '. . . the horror that remained engraved in the minds of most Europeans was the food. Insults from officials, refusal to accept qualifications, terrible accommodation, and an English language that was incomprehensible to anyone but a native-born Australian; all these paled into insignificance in comparison with the food.' And so it was with Fernando: that riot was, indisputably, sparked by sugar on the pasta.

The fascinating thing about Carlton Italians is that after 40 years, so strong is their own community, they still have accents. Fernando tells the story of his father-in-law, Ero: '45 years in this country and he never learnt a word of English. A guy walked into the University and said I ate here last night and I left my wallet. Ero said yes, and then walked away. This bloke is still at the counter. Ero walked back a couple of times and eventually the bloke says excuse me, if I left my wallet here, where is it? Ero says yes. After the fourth time, the bloke starts to get dirty. Eventually somebody said to him, in Italian, he's telling you he lost his wallet. Wallet, Ero said, I've seen no wallet!'

Lygon Street in the fifties might as well have been another world: it was Australian, and Australians didn't go out much at night. 'There were hardly any lights,' Gianni Milani told me, 'between here and the police station (a little over a kilometre away), maybe eight. Look at the street now,' he gestures around to an endless line of tables and chairs with people eating and drinking coffee in the sun, 'back then you were not allowed to stand on the footpath, by law. More than three [people together] they would arrest you. The police would come by, they'd line them up and they had to stand against the wall. I learnt quickly. I spoke English straight away, I married an Australian girl.'

'He's a turncoat!' interjected Fernando.

'We started serving at 5.30PM,' Gianni continued, 'and we finished by 7.30PM.' But things got better. By the time the Olympic Games came to Melbourne in 1956, the University was staying open later, and serving later.

'In '56 we had all the soccer players from Italy,' Fernando remembered. 'The manager came to our restaurant and he said give me a little bit of *brodo* because in this country you can't get anything to eat after nine at night—I finish at eleven and there's nothing to eat!'

'The Victorian Government gave us special permission to serve wine— we were unlicensed—but only to the Italian Olympic Committee,' said Gianni. 'We were allowed to open until 10, 11, because the sports finished late, so the journalists and the committee came late. The very day the Olympics finished, the permit finished.'

The University is one of those places around which stories and rumours in Carlton swirled. The National Trust's publication *A Walk Through Italian Carlton* reports that the University Cafe was frequented by Italian soccer players and boxers, was renowned for selling wine illegally, and, although often raided by the police, no wine was ever found. Ero Milani bought an espresso machine in 1952 which is still housed (but unused) in the present-day University Cafe—it wasn't the first, but it was the first licensed machine, and Gianni was the first operator. Mention of that machine causes scowls in the Milani and Donnini families: the present owners refuse to sell it to them.

Gianni Milani still works, running Donnini's, and importing foodstuffs from Italy. Fernando Donnini has retired, spends half his time in Italy, half in Melbourne. He is pleased that Australia has changed. 'Today Italians are at the top of the tree. After 45 years, they discover we're not bad. We mix better and we give something back.'

And the younger generation is also discovering who they are. When the University Cafe was sold, Tiberio also went back to Italy, to Modena, where his mother's family lived. 'I was eighteen. I lived there for two years. But I rented my own place. We say in Italian that family are like shoes—the tighter they are the more they hurt. It's nice to have a loose pair of shoes.' Young Tiberio walked into a fresh pasta shop—he'd never seen one—and asked for a job. 'I asked the guy whether I could work there for free.' He got the job, became friendly with the owner, and 'learnt everything I thought I had to know about fresh pasta.'

I asked him about being an Italian-Australian in Italy. 'I was lucky that Dad forced us to speak Italian— I felt at home that way. Where I didn't feel at home was with all the things I was used to—stupid things. Like going to the station to buy an English newspaper to get the cricket results or ringing the Australian Consulate in Milano to see whether they could send me a Melbourne newspaper.'

He kicked around at various jobs, and then woke up one morning and decided to go back to Australia. Before he left, he met one Signor Giacobazzi, the largest producer of Lambrusco in the world and the

Salami (one salami, two salami . . .).

largest exporter of wine to America: he was sending Lambrusco to America in tins. 'I suggested they bring Lambrusco to Australia, and I fluked the trip back for free. I did place the product. That was an experience. Lambrusco is a wine that does not travel well.'

Once back in Melbourne, he decided against the life of a wine merchant, 'I'd had enough of that sort of bullshit,' and toyed with the idea of opening a delicatessen, again without much enthusiasm. 'Then one day I was walking past a restaurant owned by a Greek friend and he said do you want to buy it off me and, in the end, we agreed on a price.' 312 Drummond Street had begun life in the 1940s as Cohen's Kosher restaurant, was briefly Italian in the 1950s before going Greek as Byzantium, and then, in 1978, took on its current guise as Donnini's. He hired as chef a woman who had worked for Ero, Lina Briscuso. 'She was a godsend, just like a mother to me.'

'We did things differently from what everybody else was doing. We provided genuine pasta—handmade—with sauces that didn't exist. Nobody used to pan toss the pasta with the sauce for you. We did all those things which were second nature to us but nobody else was doing. We were doing *tortellini in brodo*, ravioli with ricotta and spinach—real lasagne and real tagliatelle— unheard of then.'

It was here that Tiberio invented the famed *'tris di pasta Donnini'*. 'A lot of people claim that it takes brains, but it's just making do. We had a menu with seven or eight different types of pasta—and three gas jets. I remember walking up to a table, and I think they ordered six or seven different types of pasta. I went into the kitchen and Lina said this is ridiculous. I said don't worry, just make three types. And I went out the back and got a big silver tray, warmed it under the grill and we put on it tortellini, tagliatelle and gnocchi. I remember walking into the dining room with seven bowls, this tray and a pair of tongs, and I started to give them a serving each. The next table that walked in saw the big tray and said we'll have that. It blossomed from there. It became an institution.'

Donnini's was remarkably successful. 'It was crazy—we'd have queues, we were booked out for months in advance. We won awards from the Italian Government, the Australian Tourist Commission. It's still respected.'

But even in Italian Carlton, the custom was mainly Anglo-Australians. 'The Italian is nowhere near like the Chinese. Walk into a Chinese restaurant and it's full of Chinese. Not many Italian restaurants in Australia are full of Italians. The first time I really understood why was when we opened the pasta shop. We were making tortellini. I bought this machine in Italy, a new system of filling the pasta with meat or cheese so the consistency was firmer—we were able to sell real tortellini. An Italian woman walked in and she said how much the tortellini? I said $5.00 a kilo. She said, but I can make them cheaper than that. And I said to myself, well, there it is. They compare all the time.

Tiberio opened one of Australia's first fresh pasta shops in Lygon Street in 1981, followed by Donnini's Pasta Bar, a bistro-style eatery in Spring Street, Melbourne. The family still owns and operates its Drummond Street restaurant. In 1993 Tiberio went to Cairns and opened a restaurant called Donnini Ciao Italia at the Pier Marketplace, and has never looked back. 'First impression [of Cairns] not so good. I went back, and warmed to it. I think it's the best decision I've ever made. It really is a different Australia up here. It's like going back in time—people leave their doors open, you walk outside and there are no footpaths, there's something about the sun that reminds you of holidays.'

'It's like going back in time in other ways too. Recently somebody used the expression you fucking wog, which I hadn't heard for . . . people use that when they don't know what they're going to say. It was an argument about something. I didn't deck him. The last thing I need is that sort of drama in my life. I really can control myself a lot better than I used to.'

(The recipes printed here are reproduced, with permission, from *Donnini's Pasta. Favourite recipes from Australia's premier pasta maker, Tiberio Donnini*.)

## *Gnocco Fritto*                    Fried Gnocco

SERVES 4

Not to be confused with gnocchi, these delicious fried pasta shapes are quick and economical to make as a filling snack, an accompaniment to a meal or a cocktail party nibble. Children relish them.

4 cups (500 g) plain flour
1 tablespoon salt
200 mL milk
1 cup (250 mL) olive oil

Mix the flour and the salt in a large bowl. Form a well in the centre of the flour and add the milk slowly, combining with a fork. Now work the dough with your hands to form a cohesive mass.

Turn out onto a lightly floured board and knead the dough for 10 minutes, by rolling the dough over onto itself with the palm of your hand. Form the dough into a sausage shape and cut it into four equal pieces.

Knead each segment for 5 minutes, then form each piece into a flat patty shape, about 10–12 cm wide and 1 cm thick. Cover the dough with an inverted bowl or soup plate and allow to rest for at least 5 minutes.

Pass the first patty through the wide roller of your pasta machine ten times and lay it out to dry on a cloth-covered tray. Repeat this process with the remaining pieces of rested dough. Change the machine rollers to number 4 thickness and run each sheet of dough through the machine twice. Put each sheet back on the cloth as you roll.

In the order in which you rolled the strips cut them with a sharp knife into any shape you want— such as triangles, circles or squares.

Prick each shape thoroughly with a fork, making sure that the prongs of the fork fully penetrate the dough. This is the secret to perfect gnocco as it allows the oil in which you cook the gnocco to penetrate each piece of dough and cook each piece very quickly.

Shallow fry the gnocco in the olive oil in a frying pan over a high heat. They will cook very quickly, puffing up sometimes so much they turn themselves over in the oil. The gnocco are cooked when they are puffed and golden brown. Remove the gnocco from the oil and drain them thoroughly on brown paper or paper towel.

To serve: gnocco are delicious hot and unadorned or you can top them with prosciutto or other ham or meats, cheese or jam.

Gnocco dough can also be prepared enclosing a sweet or savoury filling of your choice. In the former case the cooked gnocco can be rolled in caster sugar and cinnamon immediately prior to serving.

Cold, the gnocco deflate but are no less delicious. They are good to mop up pasta sauces.

# Tortellini in Brodo

Tortellini in Broth

ALLOW 15 TORTELLINI PER PERSON

There are many weird and entertaining stories about the origins of tortellini. They're frequently called Venus' Navels because it is said they were originally formed in their particular shape to honour Venus and her beauty. Another story concerns a chef to a rich nobleman who was having an affair with the nobleman's wife and had created tortellini in honour of his lady's charms. Even though the nobleman surprised the chef in his wife's bed, he could not dismiss him for fear of losing the maker of the extraordinarily delicious tortellini.

A more practical version is that tortellini were developed as air-tight packages. In pre-refrigeration times, meats and other perishables were wrapped in pasta as today we use plastic wrap and aluminium foil.

**FILLING**
50 g lean pork
50 g lean veal
1 tablespoon butter
3 slices ham
3 slices mortadella
3 slices prosciutto
50 g chicken breast, poached
½ nutmeg, freshly grated
salt
black pepper, freshly ground
1⅓ cups (150 g) Parmigiano cheese, freshly grated
2 eggs

**PASTA**
2¾ cups (350 g) plain flour
3 eggs

**BRODO DI POLLO**
1 large chicken, trussed, plus neck
2 celery sticks, cut into 7-cm lengths
8–10 peppercorns
2 bay leaves
1 onion left whole and unpeeled (optional)

To make filling, cut the pork and veal into pieces. Lightly fry the pork and veal in the butter. Allow the meat to cool. Put all the remaining ingredients and the cooled meat in the bowl of a food processor and mix until well-blended. Put the mixture aside until you are ready to make the tortellini.

To make pasta, put the flour in a large bowl. Make a well in the centre of the flour and break the eggs into this cavity.

Beat the eggs with a fork inside the well, gradually incorporating the flour. When the fork becomes clogged, clean the mixture off it and continue mixing with your hands until the flour and eggs are well incorporated.

Form the dough into a ball and, still working in the bowl, knead the dough with the heel of your hand, adding an additional sprinkling of flour until the dough doesn't stick to your hands or the bowl. Push your finger into the dough. It should bounce straight out and be quite clean.

Turn the dough onto a floured surface and knead for 10 minutes, pressing the dough over on to itself, pushing the mixture together with the heel of your hand. Knead the dough until it has a definite velvety consistency. Any crusty bits of dough should be discarded—if you try to incorporate them they will cause the pasta to break up when you are rolling or cutting it.

Cover the dough with an inverted bowl or a clean cloth and allow it to rest for 30 minutes. Cut the dough into four sections, leaving three sections covered with the cloth or bowl.

Roll the remaining dough through a pasta machine until it is paper thin. It can then be cut into rounds with a biscuit cutter or a liqueur glass or into 5-cm squares with a sharp knife.

Place ¼ to 1½ teaspoons of the filling mixture in the centre of each circle or square. Fold the pasta in half and press the edges together to seal the tortellini. Turn the sealed edge back towards the filling edge to make a sort of cuff. Wrap the tortellini around your forefinger and press the edges together. Lay the tortellini out neatly on a cloth covered tray.

Repeat the process using the three remaining pieces of dough. The tortellini may now be cooked in the brodo.

To make chicken broth, arrange the chicken, neck and other ingredients in a large pot and cover with water. Bring to the boil and cook at a fast rate for 15 minutes, reduce the heat and simmer, covered, for 2 hours. Carefully remove the chicken and neck and reserve for later use.

Discard the herbs and vegetables and strain the broth several times through a fine sieve lined with kitchen paper until the liquid is quite clear.

Cook the tortellini in the brodo for 8–10 minutes.

To serve: serve tortellini with plenty of freshly grated Parmigiano.

Lorenzo Garcia Villada wearing a Galician hat.

*'Finally, when I'd answered all their questions, one of them said—but what about the blind people?'*

# CHAPTER THREE

# *Lorenzo Garcia Villada*

THESE POST-WAR Australians brought with them more than luggage and recipes. What has been popularised by the gourmet press as Mediterranean food is a lot more than that: it is a Mediterranean way of life. For example, public space and where you sit as well as what you eat can re-define a community's relationship to its environment.

Take the case of Lorenzo Garcia Villada (another who shares the kitchen with his mother), whose family business Casa Asturiana is in Sydney's Little Spain, that block of Liverpool Street between George and Sussex Streets. To assess the full impact of his cultural influence on the people of Sydney, I have to introduce another character, a bit player admittedly, but one who illuminates the story.

When I met Marta Angulo Santamaria she was the *Jefe del Departamento de Productos Agroalimentarios Transformados Direccion General de Promotion* with ICEX, *Instituto Espanol de Comercial Exterior*. In other words, she worked for the body that promoted the export of Spanish food products: but doesn't it sound better in Spanish?

We had been at a conference together, and I had offered to show her around some of Sydney's better food stores. We visited David Jones Food Hall, the showroom of Simon Johnson Purveyor of Quality Foods in Ultimo, and a handful of other fine food retailers.

At the end of about three hours wandering, Marta had two questions. 'Where are all the children?' was the first. 'Well, they're in school,' I said. 'Yes,' she said, 'they go to school in Spain, too, but you see children on the streets going between home and school. I have seen no children here.' Of course. We had been in the city and the inner city, and, unlike Spain, where cities are residential, children are not much in evidence. And, as I also explained, we do not have a siesta so there are not children returning home in the middle of the day. That was an easy one to field.

The second was a lot harder. 'Where are the *terrazas*?' In other words, where are the people sitting outside cafes enjoying the sunshine, drinking, chatting and watching life being lived around them. I had to tell her that they were few and far between, and that it wasn't until the early 1980s that we, in Sydney, were allowed to sit outside and drink a cup of coffee. This took some explaining.

I told her we did have isolated pockets of this sort of behaviour, and I took her to one of my favourites, Parmalat in Victoria Street, Darlinghurst. She sat down, crossed her legs, lit a cigarette (Spaniards still smoke) and ordered a Cinzano. At the end of this third explanation—why she couldn't have a Cinzano—I could see her mentally packing her bags in preparation for the flight home to civilisation.

I have already pointed out that Melbourne is far more advanced in the question of outdoor eating and drinking than Sydney, and, in spite of being climatically challenged, the people of Melbourne have taken to lolling around on pavements with a vengeance.

But at last, thanks in no small part to Lorenzo Garcia Villada, we in Sydney are on the way towards having a little public life that does not revolve around the public house. The outdoor cafe is, if not as common as the pub, becoming so. And, who knows, if we can loosen the iron grip of the Australian Hotels Association (on licences to sell alcohol without food), Marta may soon be able to have her Cinzano on the pavement without frightening the horses.

When his family left Spain for Australia in 1962, Lorenzo Garcia Villada was five years old, his brother Manuel was two.

In spite of having left at such an early age, Lorenzo has a collection of powerful—and formative—memories of his time in Spain. 'I remember my first birthday vividly. I recall this massive cake with one candle, and sharing the cake with my friends. It was a sponge cake with lots and lots of cream. We all wore party hats.'

His mother, Maria, comes from a family of restaurateurs and bar owners. 'One of the strongest memories of food is the aroma of fried calamari and beer. From the age of two, I had three favourite foods; *mejillones escabechadas* (mussels marinated in vinegar and white wine), *salsichon* (a kind of spicy sausage) and fried calamari. They used to tease me with it. My mother would take me down to the bar that serviced the apartments we lived in at the time. It was a new building. They had a cinema complex underneath, a patisserie, the bar which was also a deli, a central fountain and a plaza.'

'I'd put out my hand and they'd fill it with fried calamari. Then I'd put out my other hand, and they'd fill that one. Then I'd open my pockets and when there was no more room, I'd open my mouth. These are still my favourite foods today, what I'll eat when I'm sick. They're all on the menu in the restaurant.'

This plaza is important to the story. Lorenzo describes the birth of his brother Manuel: 'I was riding around on my three wheeler in the plaza. I remember my father sticking his head out of the window [of their apartment above] to say I had a bro-ther. I ran upstairs to check out this kid, I looked at him and thought, that's terrific, and went down and started to ride my bike again.'

Four-year-old Lorenzo in his mother Maria's arms in Sama de Langreo, Spain.

I have a close association with Spain. My wife and I own a little house in a small village there. Two hundred metres from the front door of that house is a plaza. When we lived there, at the end of a day's work, I would collect my daughter from kindergarten, walk with her and her bicycle to the plaza, and sit with a coffee or a beer and read the paper or chat to friends while she played in the traffic free area.

Like Jose, Lorenzo's father, I could safely have left her there alone, knowing that the people from the bar and others seated in the square would look after her and out for her. The plaza is an institution that I see fitting very comfortably and usefully into Australian urban—and suburban—life. And, thanks to the arrival of people like Lorenzo Garcia Villada, we are slowly moving towards such sane additions to our civic architecture.

The Garcia Villada family arrived in Australia on board the *Amelia*, an Italian boat once owned, curiously enough, by Adolf Hitler. Manuel learnt how to walk on board, and, when the family first left the ship, had the rollicking gait of a sailor. They travelled from Fremantle to Melbourne and then to Bonegilla migrant camp. Like most graduates from this institution, this was not a good memory. 'I remember my mother crying over the food there because she couldn't eat it, and the smell of food in the bungalows with people improvising over gas burners.'

Not for the first time, I wonder at their courage—to travel half way around the world with two small children to a country where you know no-one, about which you know nothing, and where you don't even speak the language—and the motivation for such a move. It's not as if the family were starving. It was not politically motivated. Lorenzo is as baffled by this as I am, except to recall that, 'They didn't intend to stay here as long as they did, it was my father's intention to stay five years, but then another son, Julio, was born, we started school and that was it.'

The family was given work picking grapes (near Bonegilla), then they were relocated to Adelaide, and finally to Whyalla on Spencer Gulf. There was a move to send migrants there to work in BHP's steelmilling and shipbuilding industries.

Lorenzo is quite sanguine on the subject of Whyalla, but from all accounts, it was as far from the warm, bustling and food-smelling atmosphere of Sama de Langreo as Nome, Alaska is from Papeete, Tahiti. One of the so-called iron triangle of towns on the gulf, the others being Ports Augusta and Pirie, I was told by another ex-South Australian that 'it makes our east coast steel towns look like Paris'. Is it unfair to suggest that the immigration authorities of the day sent Yugoslavs, Italians and (about 300) Spaniards there because no native-born Australians would want to live and work there in those days of full employment? Probably not. It did seem to be the official attitude to migrants at the time.

For young Lorenzo, 'It was all a bit strange. My first years at school were fairly difficult. I'd been to school in Spain, and while I wasn't at the top of the class, I was fairly bright. Now I found myself in a classroom full of people I couldn't understand. My first teacher was a Sister Josephine, and the first thing she did was to wave a rubber crocodile in front of my face to try and scare me in front of the whole class. That was my introduction to Australian schools.'

But Lorenzo Garcia Villada is not easily scared. 'They called me a wog, but I didn't know what it meant—a good defence. In secondary school I got Gus— Gus Garcia.'

Because his parents attempted to keep up a parallel Spanish education for the first couple of years, it was three years before young Lorenzo learnt enough English to start communicating. Then he became a sportsman, a champion swimmer elected to the Olympic youth squad, and captain of the state grass hockey team.

His father worked for BHP for three or four years, and then set up a photography shop in Whyalla. 'He did the weddings, and in those days people went to dances and they liked having their photographs taken.'

It was in the isolation of this grey town that Lorenzo and his mother grew close, and it was this closeness—this, and Maria's singular way of bringing him up—that encouraged his interest in food.

'I remember going shopping when we first arrived, and my mother pretending to be a chicken to buy some eggs. And walking, walking, forever walking, trying to find stuff to cook. We'd go into delicatessens and stare at all these cans—they didn't have photographs of what was inside them. My mother was suffering a lot. There was no food she could buy.'

Maria used young Lorenzo as her anchor. Jose was working in the steelmill, exhausted when he came home. Manuel was too young, but Lorenzo could speak to her in Spanish and help her come to grips with her new country. He shared with her memories of where they had come from. 'With me, Mum could relate to Spain. She didn't feel comfortable in this country and so our bond grew stronger, and one result of that was that I always watched her cook. I used to help her cook and I was always the first to get up and wash the dishes.'

'Then when I was about eleven, my mother went with two other women to Berri to work at the fruit cannery. It was partly financial difficulties, and partly because the three women wanted a break from their husbands. That was my first real test. I remember my mother saying, "Don't worry, Lorenzo will look after the family."'

A tall order for an eleven-year-old boy. But already he knew the basics of the Spanish kitchen. 'I'd cooked for Mum when she was sick. I cooked a *tortilla* (omelette) and *croquetas* (croquettes). And soup. She couldn't believe what I'd learnt.'

It was also around this time that he cooked his first dinner party. 'One night when my mother was away my father said so and so is coming over for dinner. The idea was that they'd cook. I said, I can cook, you just go and buy what you want. Are you sure? he said. My father has never bothered with the kitchen, he didn't know whether to believe me or not. But once he saw me in action, he just went away.'

There was no question that this was a vocation. It was survival. But Maria had taught Lorenzo to look after himself—to iron, to cook, so that he would never be dependent.

After finishing his schooling in Adelaide, he went to university. He did one year of Civil Engineering, and deferred. 'It was what my mother always wanted me to do and I hated it.'

And now he began to drift towards food as a living. 'My first job, on Sunday nights, was at the old Lion (a pub). It was Tina Turner/Southern Comfort and Coke days. I did the kitchen. T-bone steak or schnitzel with coleslaw. Twenty bucks a Sunday. I was staying at Aquinas College and not getting any government assistance.'

Towards the end of that first year, he got a job as a barman in a restaurant called Los Amigos. When he deferred his course, they offered him a full-time job. 'I never went back to uni. Three-and-a-half years later I was the manager. Then I tried to open my own restaurant. I was 21. It would have been called Cervantes.'

Lorenzo and his family fell under the spell of a Spanish conman. 'He was one of those charismatic guys who could fool anyone. I introduced him to my family, and then we went to Spain together. We bought a lot of gear there and brought it back to Australia. My mother's eldest brother, Lorenzo, helped a lot. At the end of the day, when it was up to this guy to come up with something, he had nothing. I went through my money, my uncle's, a few friends'. I was in all sorts of trouble. I managed to get out of the lease—I passed it on to someone else, and left Adelaide. The rest of the family stayed.'

First he went to Melbourne—his girlfriend at the time was with the Australian Ballet company based in Melbourne—but 'couldn't relate to Melbourne'. The two of them came to Sydney and lived in Victoria Street, McMahons Point on Sydney's lower north shore. On the corner of Victoria Street and Blues Point Road was a restaurant called La Potiniere, owned by Georges Polatidis, a Frenchman of Greek extraction. Lorenzo introduced himself, asked for a job, but was told there was nothing just yet but to keep in touch. Then he found a job as a captain at Wolfie Pizem's Waterfront Restaurant at Circular Quay West, got involved in industrial action (he organised a walkout of all the captains), and finally went to work for Polatidis at La Potiniere, where he stayed, first as waiter then as second chef, for almost five years.

Towards the end of this period, Polatidis expressed his disappointment with the restaurant business to Lorenzo—he was sick of the hours, the work and the struggle for custom. Lorenzo was again living in the area, and put to him the idea of a cafe, serving coffee and simple food, as a focal point for the residents. 'There was nothing open for a coffee at night. George said he wasn't interested in renting, but if I could find somewhere to buy, he'd have a look at the idea. One of our customers wanted to sell the terrace where the Blues Point Cafe is now, and that was it.'

Well, not quite. I remember the Blues Point Cafe well. When it first opened, in 1981, I rented an office in Blues Point Road. This new place was a godsend. Before it, there was nothing but a pretty rundown pub—I'd given up pubs many years before. Having already spent time in Spain, I was a cafe lounger. And here was a cafe to lounge in with—and this was quite extraordinary— outdoor seating. It was here that I first met Lorenzo and and his mother Maria.

The first time I walked in the door and looked at the food on offer, laid out *tapas* style in stainless steel trays behind glass, I knew there was a Spanish hand in the kitchen. Two of the dishes I remember were slices of *tortilla* and *sardinas escabechadas* (sardines marinated in vinegar and oil). It was the first time that Maria Garcia Villada had cooked professionally.

It soon became the local haunt of my office, and of everyone who lived and worked in the neighbourhood. It gave a focus to the street. It transformed a strip of small offices and a couple of retail shops into a community. But it didn't happen without a fight.

North Sydney Council and a handful of residents didn't really give up fight-ing against the Blues Point Cafe—and the others that followed—until 1994. Lorenzo told me, when first they applied to have tables and chairs on the pavement, the council officers came down to inspect the site and went through their list of objections. 'Finally, when I'd answered all their questions, one of them said—but what about the blind people?'

There were angry council meetings, outraged residents, fulminating letters to the *North Shore Times*. As late as August 1994, Councillor Jim Henderson described the burgeoning cafes of Blues Point Road as 'an outrageous use of public space', and had moved in council for a report into the problems of tables and chairs on the footpath. But sanity prevailed. Council director of design and technical services, Warwick Hatton, said that it was 'council's policy to encourage footpath use', and all that they were concerned with was that some cafe owners were overusing the pavement: there had to be some space left for pedestrians—blind or sighted.

Having ever so casually caused a social revolution, Lorenzo and Maria moved on. When next I heard of them, they had opened Casa Asturiana. Now it was a Garcia Villada family enterprise. Father Jose behind the cash register; Lorenzo and Maria in the kitchen; brothers Manuel and Julio and Lorenzo's German-Australian wife Monika on the floor. It is here that Lorenzo's ideas on food, on restaurants, have found expression. He recalls his earliest restaurant experience in Australia, in Whyalla.

'It was a Chinese restaurant in the heart of town. I'll never forget it because at every place there was a full setting: six knives, six forks and about three spoons, all silver. My father was trying to do the right thing by taking us out to the swankiest joint in town. None of us knew anything about Chinese food so my father just pointed. It was inedible. We went home and Mum cooked us dinner.'

That meal—like so many other events in this inhospitable new country—triggered off another discussion of what they had left behind, a pattern about which Lorenzo had mixed feelings. 'It got to the point of almost being annoying listening to my parents go on about the food in Spain. At the beginning, I'd listen with my mouth open. But after years of the same bloody thing—they talked about the variety, the seafood, the habits of the people—I just couldn't relate to it in a small town like Whyalla.' It was only when he was living in Adelaide and going to university that be began to get some inkling of what they had been talking about. Lorenzo discovered eating out: 'I went to Moo's restaurant. It was owned by Jill Evans and it was one of the most beautiful dining rooms I've seen. It was my first experience of French cuisine. The service was impeccable.'

Then, when he went to Spain for the first time as an adult, on that 1976 trip with his 'partner', he understood what his parents had left behind. 'I was taken to a restaurant in Madrid that was 400 years old. You had to bend down to get in the door. It rejuvenated that memory of being a young kid and going to the bar. I knew straight away what it was—and where I was.'

It was the rekindling of that feeling for Spain (more specifically, the province of Asturias) that Lorenzo and his family have used to inform the food and the feeling at Casa Asturiana. Spanish cuisine is elusive. You can re-create Italian, French or Greek food close in 'spirit' to the country of origin with ingredients and recipes, but with Spanish food, there is a third element—Spain—which it is hard to find elsewhere. Lorenzo explains it like this, 'In Australia, it's fashionable to invest in a restaurant. In Spain, people don't go into the restaurant business unless it's in their blood. You find restaurants that have been following the same recipe, putting out the same product for years. You can't emulate that.'

And, it must be said, that before Casa Asturiana there was a certain sameness and predictability to both food and decor in Little Spain. Lorenzo is a little more direct. 'They'd hang a few bulls on the wall, turn on a bit of Spanish music, throw a fish on the barbie, add a few chips and call it a Spanish restaurant.'

To be fair, I have to recall my first experience of garlic used as a weapon rather than in the manner of *The Australian Women's Weekly* recipes of the time ('rub a clove around the edge of the salad bowl and discard') was at the Costa Brava, at the corner of Liverpool and Sussex Streets. But it was the Spain of Benny Hill and Monty Python jokes about pommy tourists on the Costa Lot rather than any real attempt at reflecting the aromas and flavours of the Iberian peninsula.

Those of you still under the misapprehension that Spanish food isn't very good, firstly haven't eaten it in Spain, and secondly, have probably had your attitudes formed by a series of misunderstandings regarding the correct time to eat the evening meal.

What happened was the original English tourists in Spain wanted to eat at the ungodly (for the Spanish) hour of 7PM—or even earlier—when the average Spaniard is just sipping on their first glass of cold dry sherry, and nibbling at a little plate of mushrooms or prawn and ham—tapas, the fast food of the gods. The Spanish don't begin a main meal until, at the earliest, 9PM.

If they want to eat at that hour, said the restaurateurs, give them whatever they want—which was usually chicken and chips, served by waiters still surly from post-siesta torpor. And so the hordes of English tourists returned, decrying the quality of Spanish food.

But the question must be asked how faithfully can you re-create Asturian food in Liverpool Street? 'It's hard,' admits Lorenzo, 'because you don't have the produce. Just to get a good *jamon serrano* [cured ham] or a good *chorizo* [spicy pork sausage] is a problem. You deal in 50 kilogram batches, and one in every ten might be good. The seafood is different too. What we've tried to do is to re-create as closely as possible and practicable.'

And that means adapting the cuisine to the ingredients. The most important dish in the Asturian repertoire is *Fabada Asturiana*—a bean and sausage stew. Now that sounds quite simple, but there are beans—and there are sausages. The beans in *Fabada* are dried *fabas* (or *favas*, in Spanish *habas*, in Catalan *faves*, *faba* is an Asturian dialect word), and, according to Lorenzo, they are unavailable outside Asturias. On paper, they're merely broad beans, but that's on paper. In Asturias, apparently, the *faba* market is a little like the truffle market in France.

'They're a precious commodity. When they have a good season, the price goes up. There are different grades—it's a tight little circle and you have to be good friends with so and so to get the special ones. You can pay up to $30 a kilogram for them. The best ones you don't see in the shops.' And that's just the beans. Then there's the *morcilla*—a type of blood sausage. 'We're lucky to get them from an elderly Asturian couple who make them at home.' My own memory of *fabas* in Spain is of a much larger bean than that which we call the broad bean in Australia.

It is by this process of adaptation that Australian cuisine is emerging, although little has (as yet) emerged from the Casa Asturiana kitchen. Lorenzo tells me, 'We've done yabbies in a *salsa picante*, and we've played a little with the sardines from Western Australia but,' he adds ruefully, 'you can't compare them to *boquerones* [Spanish anchovies].'

There, in that statement, you probably have one of the keys to the problem of re-creating Spanish food outside Spain. It is, perhaps, of all the Mediterranean cuisines, the most place-specific in terms of ingredients—and cooks.

But to illustrate the success of Casa Asturiana in its mission to 're-create as closely as practicable'—and the difficulty of the task—let me quote from the review that I wrote of the restaurant for *The Sydney Morning Herald* in December 1992 (the restaurant opened in June the same year). I took with me, because I have no first-hand knowledge of Asturian cuisine (I've eaten it outside Asturias but have never been to the source), a Spanish friend who spent the summers of his youth in a house in a seaside village near Luarca in the province. During the course of the meal, he complained that it was making him homesick—a comment, I remarked in the review, 'at once accolade and analysis: for Spanish food is not haute cuisine, nor even the flamboyant inventiveness of the Italians—it's home cooking.' Perhaps, on reflection, another reason why it doesn't travel as well. To adapt is one thing. But to re-create the atmosphere of home—quite another.

(The following recipes are from Lorenzo and Maria Garcia Villada.)

# *Arroz con Pollo*　　　　　　　　Chicken with Rice

SERVES 4

I like this dish with its natural colour. If you would prefer it to be a little yellow, add powdered saffron with the boiling water. Arborio rice works well in such Spanish rice recipes.

1 No. 8 chicken
2 garlic cloves
salt
¾ cup (185 mL) olive oil
½ red capsicum
½ green capsicum
1 medium onion
1⅔ cups (150 g) champignons
1 fresh ripe tomato
1½ cups (375 mL) large grain rice
freshly ground black pepper
1 tablespoon finely chopped parsley
juice of 1 lemon

Cut the chicken into pieces and place the flesh, bones and skin in a bowl.

Pound the garlic to a paste in a mortar and pestle and add salt. Rub this paste over the pieces of chicken and leave aside for 10 minutes.

Pour the oil into a frying pan and fry the pieces of chicken over a medium heat until golden brown. Transfer the chicken to a casserole, preferably earthenware, or a *paellera*. Retain the oil left in the pan.

Cut the capsicums and onion into pieces and fry in the oil in which the chicken was fried. When the onion has turned transparent, add the champignons which have been cut in half, and fry together for a few more minutes.

Peel the tomato, cut it into pieces and add to the pan.

When all is sufficiently fried (when the tomato has been reduced to a pulp), spoon the mixture over the chicken, and add ½ cup of cold water.

Place the casserole over a medium heat and cook the mixture for 10 minutes. Then add the rice, black pepper and the parsley and stir through. Add 4½ cups boiling water, season with salt and stir the rice through the contents. Bring to the boil, allow to boil for 10 minutes, then add the lemon juice.

When the rice has absorbed the water (about 25 minutes) remove the casserole from the heat and serve immediately.

## Tortilla Española

SERVES 4

750 g potatoes
1 large onion
salt
1½ cups (375 mL) olive
  oil
5 eggs

Peel the potatoes and cut them into small, regular-shaped pieces. Cut the onion into slightly larger pieces. Season the potatoes and the onion with salt, and mix them together.

Heat the oil in a frying pan, and then add the potato and onion mixture. Cook over a medium heat, stirring frequently, and when the potato begins to brown, turn the mixture into a colander to drain off the excess oil.

Pour almost all the oil out of the frying pan and place the pan back over a medium heat.

Beat the eggs. Add the potato and onion mixture to the beaten eggs and mix them together.

When the oil is hot, add the potato, onion and egg mixture to the pan and flatten it around the pan. When the part of the mixture in contact with the pan is cooked (a matter of judgement), remove the pan from the heat, cover it with a plate and tip the pan upside down, leaving the tortilla on the plate.

Pour a little more oil into the pan, replace it over the heat and when the oil is hot, slide the tortilla back into the pan to cook the other side. When the rest of the tortilla is cooked, remove it from the pan, and turn onto a plate.

To serve: a tortilla can be eaten hot or cold. Serve it with salad or serve slices placed in a crusty bread roll.

# *Mejillones Escabechadas*  Mussels in Oil and Vinegar

SERVES 4

1 kg mussels, cleaned and bearded
5–6 garlic cloves
¾ cup (185 mL) olive oil
4 bay leaves
2 tablespoons sweet pimenton (or substitute paprika)
1 teaspoon salt
1½ cups (375 mL) white vinegar

Steam the mussels until they open. When they have opened, remove the top shell, leaving the mussel attached to the bottom shell, and put the mussel with shell aside.

Cut the garlic into slivers. Place the oil, garlic and bay leaves in a frying pan, and fry together over a medium heat until the garlic begins to brown.

Take the frying pan from the heat and immediately add the pimenton, stirring it through the mixture. Add the salt. Then add the vinegar and stir it through.

To serve: cover the mussels with the sauce and serve immediately. Alternatively, the mussels can be kept for up to 3 days, refrigerated, before use.

Dina Grilli at the winery, Virginia, South Australia.

'Wine and food were separated
in Joe's family. But in my
family, we always associated
wine with food.'

# CHAPTER FOUR

# Dina Grilli

O F THE trinity of foods that I've suggested form the acronym from which we've inherited the word 'wog', Joseph and Dina Grilli produce two: wine and olive oil. Wine a food? Well, at best—the way the Grillis make it—an indispensable accompaniment to food.

Primo Estate is in Virginia, on the outer edges of Adelaide, in a landscape of market gardens and market gardeners, another of the sites favoured by early Italian migrants, especially those who, like Dina's and Joseph's parents, came from and wanted to remain on the land.

I spoke to Dina in front of their Primo Estate winery, in the shade of an acacia tree and in full view of the grape-drying racks (of which more later), and the new and experimental olive grove. Joe was in Italy, at an olive oil conference in Florence. I was glad of the opportunity to speak to the more reticent half of the team. I had met Dina at a cooking demonstration and sensed that while Joe gets the media attention, this quiet woman exerts considerable influence in the company. With us while we spoke was Matteo, their youngest son, then three.

Both Dina's parents are from the Veneto, although they met in Australia. Dina's grandfather, Guiseppe Griguol, came out to Australia in 1937 from the village of Meduna. Initially interned during the war, he was released on the request of the farmer for whom he had worked before the war. His wife Rosa and their children, including Dina's future mother Silvana, came out after the war, and lived in primitive conditions in New Residence, out of Loxton. This was especially difficult for Rosa.

In Italy, although not wealthy, they had been landowners, and part of a strong community. Dina's mother's memories of her own mother are 'of her being sad. From being part of the community in a small village where she was liked and respected, she came to what was, to her, a desert. She actually died here eighteen months after coming out. Then my Mum, with the other five children and their father, moved to Croydon, near Adelaide, where he started glasshouse market gardening, mainly tomatoes. The older children moved out and my mother left school at fourteen to help my *nonno* [grandfather] grow tomatoes.'

Dina's father, Rinaldo Zamberlan, is from Treviso, where his own father died when he was one year old. In Italy he'd worked from a very early age making tiles, and when he came to Australia, he found work in a cement factory. 'He was one of the first to do *terrazzo* here in Adelaide.'

They met in a dance hall 'where all the Veneti hung out' and married. 'By that time my mother was working in a deli in Findon owned by a Veneto, only stopping work after the birth of Lidia, my elder sister. They lived in a shed when they got married, then moved to Kilburn and eventually to Waterloo Corner, a few minutes from here.'

In 1963, Dina was born and grew up 'in a market gardening area with uncles and aunts on two sides. One of my aunties married a Calabrese and he had olive trees. We used to have virgin olive oil all the time. He would have taken his olives to a press. It was very hard to get olive oil then, you had to know someone with a press.'

When Dina was eleven, the family went to Italy. 'I think that trip was fundamental to our education. We went to see my father's relatives, my eldest sister was fourteen, the youngest three. We had no concept of Italy.' From that trip, she remembers that 'everywhere you look there's art, paintings, statues. I thought they were so lucky to grow up with a sense of history. We have many things but we don't have that.'

Food memories were also powerful. 'Everything was so different, from the milk to the sugar—the milk is creamier. I remember tomatoes and strawberries being so sweet, here they're acid—and the bread! In 1974 we had no good bakeries here. And the *grissini* and the cheeses—they make beautiful cheeses in the Veneto. We learnt about food and cheeses and wines because they're so proud of it all. We came back with that enthusiasm. My father would have liked to stay there, but Mum wanted us to come back.'

And so did Dina. Unlike many of the second generation migrants I spoke to, she has never had any identity crisis, and is quite happy being of Italian origin in Australia. 'I always felt Italian,' she told me, a cultural certainty that even spread to the school lunch: 'I was never embarrassed by what I brought for lunch. I remember bringing salami sandwiches with tomato, and they used to get nice and smelly. I thought it was fantastic.'

But there was one problem. 'I don't look Italian. I really feel Italian, I feel my parents' heritage, but because I'm not from a known part of Italy and I don't look Italian, it's always been, oh, you don't look Italian, you're not really Italian.'

I remember my own mother (Australian-born of Russian-German ancestry) saying that so and so was 'not really like an Italian, he's tall and fair'. This was, I suppose, indicative of the fact that a large proportion of Italians who came to Australia did so from the south.

But Dina's strong Italian identification is not surprising, considering the circumstances under which she grew up. 'My parents were so proud of being Italian, and Italian customs. Every year we killed the pig and made the salami and *muset*—that's Veneto dialect—it's something like a *cotechino* [large pork sausage] only better. They're not doing it as much any more, but there is a butcher from the Veneto who'll do it for you. When the grapes have come in and the autumn has really hit, that's when you kill the pig.'

'My father and my uncle would make wine too, and we had radicchio in the garden, although you can't grow the real Trevisan radicchio because it's not cold enough. Winter and summer we'd always have a type of lettuce, hardly ever iceberg.'

The muset forms the basis of the most typical Veneto winter dish. 'You'd put it on to boil for a couple of hours in enough water to cover it, leave it overnight, take out the sausage, skim the fat off and with that stock make a *fagioli*, a minestrone with lots of beans—borlotti or red beans, then take the beans out and put them through the Mouli. Then we'd have the *cotechino* with radicchio and the beans on top and the soup. We always had the *cotechino* with horseradish.'

After school, Dina was studying to be a primary school teacher and saving money to go overseas when she met Joe, and married him in 1986. 'I finished teaching, then came to work at Primo Estate because Joe's brother Peter left.'

Joe's father Primo is from the Marche region in central Italy on the Adriatic coast, and came out in the mid-fifties. 'Primo also came out on his own and came to Virginia. His family were landowners, quite wealthy, they had vineyards, olive groves—but Primo chose to come here. Australia offered a new beginning to a lot of Italians like him; he was the eldest son, with a lot of responsibility to fulfil. He wanted to get away from that and make his own way. He came to Virginia, initially working for Australian farmers.'

He met Santina, Joe's mother, also from Marche, in Virginia. He worked hard enough so that he could buy some land, and planted the vineyard which is the basis of Primo Estate today. Joe was born in 1959, eighteen months before his brother Peter.

'After Virginia Primary and Gawler High, Joe went to Roseworthy Agricultural College. Joe chose to make wine while Peter preferred to work in the vineyard. But Peter left before we were married. Now he's driving a taxi. You see, the family thing is great, and it worked out well for our parents, but it doesn't always work that well these days. Primo had this big vision of the boys having the winery and the daughter selling the wine—it didn't work—Peter wanted to do his own thing. Santina used to bring them breakfast and lunch every day. It was very sad for him [Primo] but he understands that things must change.'

Joe produced his first vintage when he was 21, was in his third year in Roseworthy, and was working at Seppelts. He had none of the identity problems of Peter and is married, not only to Dina, but to his work. In fact, as Dina put it, 'Joe thought he was onto a good thing having a wife who really enjoyed red wine.'

Joe's father, although a winemaker, like Bill Calabria in Griffith, doesn't drink. 'Joe came from a non-wine-drinking family. All my family drank wine. We Veneti are renowned for drinking wine. My father used to buy wine from Joe.' So Dina Grilli fitted into both the wine business and the Italian family perfectly. And she added her own dimension to the business.

'I think before we got together, wine and food were separated. But in my family, we always associated wine with food. Now we never like to have a tasting without some type of food there, and in making wine, we're always thinking what will this wine go with? This has changed our wine style too. It has to be non-obtrusive while you're eating. That's the way Italian wine is, it doesn't assault your palate.'

It's probably fair to say that the wines from Primo Estate are Australian, but with an Italian accent. None more so than the Joseph Moda Amarone (Joseph being the label for Primo's better wines). 'We went to Valpolicella in 1987, and they made an amarone. [The wine of] Valpolicella is usually a light wine, but the amarone is an intensely flavoured wine, which they make by drying the grapes over the winter—they pick them at the end of autumn. We thought it would be a great idea for here because fruit tends to get overripe and you lose the delicate flavours. So that's where the idea came from. By picking early and drying we get the flavour.'

In Valpolicella they use local grape varieties: corvina, rondinella, molinara and rossignola. At Primo they use cabernet sauvignon and merlot. But the result is sensational—a richly flavoured, dark and velvety wine, which, as Dina says, 'we knew straight off would go with gamy food like pigeon and duck.' She points out that whenever they make a wine 'they taste it in the lab, then bring it home and taste it with food. And we always make decisions based on the way we taste it at home.'

In a telling reversal of cultural influences, in 1991 to 1992, Joe was employed by an Australian company to work in a co-operative in Umbria, making wine to sell to England, using trebbiano and san giovese grapes. 'We were teaching the Italians to smarten up their act. It was a time when Australian winemakers were being recognised and Italian things were *di moda*. Unfortunately, we had two very bad years, but the wines were good considering the vintage.'

It was in 1989 that they began making olive oil, using contracted olives. 'We started bottling it as a promotional thing—we were just getting the Joseph label up, and we gave the oil to people sq they'd think about the wine.' But it took off with a life of its own, and now there are two Joseph oils—the blended Joseph and Joseph Foothills in a most elegant bottle imported from Italy, made from olives grown in the Adelaide hills, and pressed at nearby presses. The latter oil is generally conceded to be one of the finest olive oils in Australia. Now the Grillis have planted a few olive trees, experimentally only at this stage, looking mainly at varieties and picking methods.

Like everything, the olive industry is changing. The modern olive tree is, for a romantic like me, disappointingly small, no more than two metres high, trained in a conical shape like a Christmas tree. It has a strong central trunk to enable a mechanical harvester to shake the fruit out of the tree—although the latest equipment for harvesting, at the time of writing, was what one grower in Spain described to me as like a 'vibrator for an elephant', with which the branches are pushed. The time-honoured way of harvesting olives was to beat the trees with a long stick.

The Grillis have planted one variety, a Californian hybrid with a number rather than a name. Eventually, they'll plant more trees, and do their own pressing, but for the moment, pressing is done by four separate contract pressers in the area.

One of these is Guiseppe (Joe) Bagnato, whose press is at Waterloo Corner. Joe Bagnato is from Varipodio in Reggio Calabria. 'I came when I was twelve—41 years ago. I went back three times. It was good. A good life.

We made a mistake coming out here.' Joe was of a poor family, and has vivid memories of the olive-oil making when he was a child in Italy, even then working as a farm labourer. 'For each 20 litres of olives, [we received] about 25 cents in today's money.'

For their own use, Joe's family would gather olives from the ground, because, as he put it, 'the trees were that big they'd need to get the birds to help you pick.' The olive trees in the Reggio 40 years ago were not like the olive trees the Grillis are growing in 1996. 'Just one tree where I come from is thirteen metres around the trunk. If you see one of those trees when it's loaded . . . when it snows and they're full of fruit, the branches break off. They lay nets below the trees and wait for the olives to fall off in a storm. Very little picking was done because of the cost of the labour.' The olives in Varipodio were crushed by a water-powered mill until 1951 when there was a flood, and the aqueducts were destroyed. 'Then they modernised. We only got electricity in the village in 1949.'

And as the olives they took to the crusher would have been lying around on the ground for a while before they got to them (contract picking came first) 'they came off the dirt, and when you had them crushed the oil had that special aroma of the soil—when it was fresh anyway. That's the oil I grew up with. It was beautiful.'

If I've learnt one thing about olive oil, it's that there's only one best when you speak to people who've grown up with it: the one they grew up with. In Tunisia, I was taken to the Berber village of Chenini in the dusty foothills on the edge of the Sahara, and shown the olive oil crushing and pressing plant. They use a camel to turn the wheel. But the thing that surprised me most was that they crushed olives which had been sun-dried on the roofs of their houses which were partly built into the sides of the hills. I'd never heard of that, and, more interestingly, neither had another member of our party, Claudia Roden, who knows that part of the world as well as anyone alive. The oil itself, to my taste, was unpleasant: musty and slightly rancid. Later, I asked one of the officials from the Tunisian government concerned with olive oil production about this use of sun-dried olives. He looked exasperated and told me, 'They've been doing it that way for hundreds of years, and we can't talk them out of it.' And neither should he. It's their oil, they make it their way.

Joe Bagnato has one of the very few traditional press machines I've seen in Australia. Most of the crushers currently in use are of the more modern centrifugal variety, they whirl the oil out of the crushed olives. Joe's machine

Joe Bagnato in his olive crushing room at Waterloo Corner, South Australia.

crushes the oil out, in much the same way as was done in ancient times with a hand or animal operated press.

The olives are first crushed using a hammer crusher, then packed on flat mats—today made of nylon, in times past made of a wild grass called *esparta*, and put under a press. The juice runs out of the crushed fruit into large containers beneath the machine, and the resulting oil is then filtered of the cloudy residue of olive bits in a centrifugal filtering machine. 'If you leave the cloudiness in,' said Joe, 'you get wonderful flavour, but the oil goes off quickly.' It's best to crush olives within twelve hours of picking them, otherwise the fruit will begin to oxidise. The EC regulation that stipulates an 'extra virgin' olive oil has to have less than one per cent acidity refers to free oleic acid— that is, acid that can begin the oxidisation process.

Joe Bagnato has also begun to plant olive trees. As we Anglos eat more olive oil, it becomes a lucrative business, much to the bemusement of the Greeks and Italians. But even today, he told me, most of his crushing work comes from 'people doing it for themselves. They go around picking the olives up in the hills, some have a few trees growing, like my neighbour, my cousin. As long as the olives are good, it doesn't worry me who comes.'

And now that Joseph and Dina Grilli are planting olives up the road at Virginia, it'd be fair to say the olives will not only be good, but continue to get better.

(Joseph and Dina have suggested a wine to accompany each dish. Comments on the recipes are from Dina.)

## Muset (Cotechino) con Radicchio e Fagioli

Pork Sausage with Radicchio and Beans

SERVES 6

This is very much a peasant dish from in and around Treviso. It was a good way to obtain protein when meat was very scarce. It will always remind me of 'salami season' and winter.

2 cups (500 g) dried borlotti beans
1 muset/cotechino (or a large pork hock)
1 cup each diced vegetables, like carrots, onions (sautéed first), potatoes or peas
1 tablespoon tomato paste
1 bay leaf
salt and pepper
grated Parmigiano
few drops of vinegar
1 head of radicchio
1 bunch rocket
1 salad onion
olive oil and vinegar

Place the borlotti beans in a large bowl, cover with water and leave to soak overnight.

Place the muset in a large saucepan over a medium heat. Add enough water to cover and boil until ready (1–2 hours). It must be cooked well. To test, pierce with a fork; if the fork is easily removed, the muset is ready. Remove the muset from the water and skin.

Skim the fat off the water. This is best done if left overnight to settle out. Place the saucepan over a medium heat and add the borlotti beans, vegetables, tomato paste and bay leaf. Boil until the vegetables are cooked. Season to taste.

Remove the cooked beans which by now have settled mainly on the bottom of the saucepan, and mash them to a thick custard consistency.

Remove the vegetables, purée them and stir them gently into the soup.

To serve: first serve the soup, very hot. To each bowl, add grated Parmigiano and a drop of vinegar. Serve the warm muset, sliced thickly, with horseradish and a radicchio, rocket and onion salad. The mashed beans at room temperature are placed on top of the salad on individual plates. Make a vinaigrette of three parts olive oil to one part vinegar. Sprinkle the vinaigrette on top of the beans.

Serve the dish with Primo Estate shiraz.

# Bigoli in Salsa
Spaghetti in Sauce

SERVES 4–6

This is a traditional Veneto dish. It is usually served, in my family, at lunch on Good Friday. It is one of my favourite dishes. Bigoli is actually the name of a large type of spaghetti.

olive oil
4 large onions, sliced thinly
20 anchovy fillets (small Italian variety)
freshly ground pepper
½ cup (125 mL) white wine
500 g spaghetti (or bigoli)

Heat some olive oil in a large frying pan, add the onions and cook gently until soft. Add the anchovy fillets and stir until they break up. Season with pepper to taste. Add some white wine if the mixture becomes too dry.

Cook the pasta in plenty of salted water until al dente. Drain well. Return the spaghetti to the pan and mix with the sauce. Add more olive oil if the mixture is too dry.

To serve: sprinkle the spaghetti with grated Parmigiano and serve with fresh, crusty bread.

Serve with Primo Estate Colombard.

# Quaglie in Umido
Stewed Quail

SERVES 6

A traditional method of cooking game birds, my mother often cooked this dish on Easter Sunday. She'd also cook her home-grown pigeons this way.

6 quail
6 slices pancetta or bacon
4 sage sprigs
8 rosemary sprigs
1 garlic clove
2 tablespoons olive oil
salt and pepper
½ cup (125 mL) white wine

Clean the quail and pat dry to remove excess moisture. Into each quail place a slice of pancetta or bacon, a few sage leaves, a small sprig of rosemary and a tiny sliver of garlic.

Heat the olive oil in a large saucepan. Add the quail and quickly brown them all over. Season with salt and pepper to taste. Sprinkle over some extra sage and rosemary and add the white wine to the pan. Place the lid on and turn the heat down to low to cook slowly until tender, about 30 minutes. Add extra white wine or water as needed.

To serve: serve quail and sauce with a radicchio salad and grilled polenta.

Joseph Cabernet Sauvignon Moda Amarone is an excellent wine to accompany this dish.

George Haddad at home in Hobart.

*'I re-constructed my [school sandwiches]—and now the silly bastards were happy to pay $5 each for them!'*

# CHAPTER FIVE

# *George Haddad*

I **FIRST HEARD** the name George Haddad on the island of Djerba in Tunisia. Stephanie Alexander served an adaptation of a *hindbeh* (caramelised onions, leaf chicory, coriander, paprika and olive oil) from his Hobart restaurant Ali Akbar, as an accompaniment to smoked kangaroo prosciutto during a seminar on Tunisian food as her contribution from the Australian cuisine. Haddad's reputation had preceded him home to the Arabic roots of his family.

George Haddad is an elegant man, with an acute mind and a highly developed sense of social justice. Since first meeting him, I have always seen him as the Grand Vizier to a Caliph of Baghdad. The photograph that accompanies this story captures that persona beautifully.

And then, curiously enough, browsing through his extensive library of food books, I came across this excerpt from *In a Caliph's Kitchen* by David Waines, a collection of anecdotes and recipes from the cookbook of Abu Ishaq Ibrahim ibn al-Mahdi, just such a personage in the court of al-Rusafa, from the Baghdad of the ninth century:

'Food and drink were no mere adornment of these assemblies at which poetry, music, story telling and debate on literary topics were of common and consuming interest. Food itself was a topic of conversation in both a literary and edible fashion. Ibrahim composed a number of poems on food such as one on the delights of salt, and certain recipes he even cast in poetic forms.'

This Abu Ishaq, although of a different tribe, was writing during a period when the Haddad tribe were in power in that part of the world, and, when you meet George, you can't help but feel that he would have been very much at home in such an environment. But let him take up the story of his—and his family's—beginnings, and eventual arrival in Melbourne in 1967.

'My mother, Rafia, came from a famous town not far from Beirut called Zahlé. It featured on the news throughout the civil war, but it's famous for other things too. Lebanese people would know.' What? I asked. 'Substances that are not all that legitimate. It's said that they produce the best hashish in the world. My mother's father was filthy rich. He owned olive groves in Palestine, commercial properties and a bus and taxi company in Haifa. They did no business in Zahlé, although my mother insisted they marry there.'

'My father, Elias, was a public servant. His last job in Beirut was as secretary for the Minister of Public Works. He had also worked for the United Nations, and before that for the British Army in Palestine. Prior to 1948, Palestine was the business centre and Beirut was the holiday centre, very generally speaking. My father's father had a distillery brewing arak in Haifa. [Arak is a distilled white wine flavoured with aniseed.] His family came from the south of Lebanon.'

'According to my father's research, the family can be traced back to Mesopotamia. Haddad means blacksmith or ironworker. The clan was called Ghassan, and were given the name Haddad after a battle they were involved in. They were outnumbered, so they set traps in the battlefield to cull their enemy, and were the first people in the region to use iron in battle. Although they were to a certain extent nomadic, they must have been a powerful tribe, because they ruled for 90-odd years, between the ninth and tenth centuries. When their days as the leading tribe were over they retreated to a mountain in Syria, Mount Horan, where they distinguished themselves by being one of the few Christian tribes. They remained neutral (during the Crusades) until Saladin approached them to help him in the fight against the forces of Richard the Lionheart. They were talked into it and were a significant part in turning around an important battle in the desert.'

'When I left Lebanon [in 1967] there were about 80,000 Haddads in Lebanon alone. I have some great uncles who live in the highlands of Jordan who, by all accounts, have always lived as an autonomous community. They take no notice of the king, they pay no taxes—the king was very much a Johnny-come-lately as far as they are concerned.'

For a time, the modern day Haddad family lived in Damascus in an 800-year-old house, but on returning to Beirut, they moved into an apartment. These Haddads included Elias and Rafia, eldest son William, then Samir, Therese, Violette, Susanne, Samira, George, Kamal and John. It was—and is—a close family. One family ritual explains, in part, that closeness.

'I'm not suggesting this is a ritual in Lebanon, but in our household, there was a rule, it didn't matter where you were, you had to be home before midnight on New Year's Eve to see the new year in as a united family. The table would be laid. We'd all sit down to have a meal, the cooked version of *kibbeh* (cracked wheat and lamb) was a must. And red wine. The tradition was, Mum and Dad sat at the end of the table. You know that it's bad luck to take off the wedding band, but on this night they would take them off, put them in one wine glass, and pass them around the table in that glass. It was a reaffirmation of the family bond.'

George also remembers Sundays in Beirut as important days. 'Sunday was dedicated to eating. Dad also liked to drink. He was six foot two, a trim fifteen stone, bolt upright and extremely fit. He liked to drink arak. Sunday his quota would have been one or two litres between midday and 9PM. He wasn't a drunk—I don't recall ever seeing him drunk. The meal would start with *mezza* (little dishes served ahead of or as a meal), and the hot meal would be on the table by 3PM. Mum was a finicky person who didn't like help— she had a couple of servants before I was born but not in my life. Some of the preparations for this meal would start the previous Tuesday or Wednesday: the preparation of food was a continuous project.'

'The hot meal was big on meat. Chicken was special in those days. From time to time there was pigeon, which is revered in the Middle East, roasted and massaged with spices. If we cooked red meat, it was more often than not a pot roast for two reasons. First, beef and veal are inferior in the Middle East, and second it was never part of the kitchen to have an oven. Everything you wanted roasted, you took to the bakery. It might only be a hole in the ground, but it was always there. When you had a pot roast, it was often studded with garlic and cooked in some stock, which I now see was the French influence.'

'I would still say of all the Middle Eastern and Arab cuisines, the Lebanese put on the best *mezza*. Anything else is an excuse for a *mezza* table. I remember the excitement of going to any restaurant in the hills behind Beirut. You'd order a bottle of arak with 20, 40 or 80 dishes—and there was no repetition. I can't remember exact dishes, I was too young to remember detail, but offal was important.'

'One big thing is raw lamb's liver from specialist butchers—the lamb has to be in 100 per cent health and condition. The liver is sliced like sashimi and you eat it with fresh mint, salt and pepper, a little oil, a piece of bread and an onion. The other must on every *mezza* table is *kibbeh nayé*. *Kibbeh* is the dish that's made from lamb virtually pulverised and blended with onion and cracked wheat. *Kibbeh nayé* means raw *kibbeh*. If you were going to cook it you'd have a filling of *hashweh*, which would add spices and pine nuts to the lamb. You eat the *kibbeh nayé* with similar condiments to the raw liver. There'd be piles of roast sparrows, little fish like sardines or small whiting with a sauce made from tahini, as well as brains, lamb's tongue and heart. Then vegetables, such as zucchini and tomato, dips made from various pulses, and so on. These are the things you think of in preparing a *mezza* table.'

'There was also a version of couscous here in the Lebanon, called *Maghrebia* [referring to the Maghreb, the Arabic name for North Africa]. I remember my mother and grandmother making it from some form of grain, but the finished version was the size of a chickpea. That led my Mum to make a cheap version with chickpeas.'

'Breakfast was mostly cold things—sometimes boiled or fried eggs, otherwise white cheeses like *fromage blanc* with olive oil. This always appeared on the breakfast table.' George showed me a saucer full of coarsely ground spices and herbs: 'it's a mixture of oregano and sumac [the dried leaves and berries of a plant originating in Turkey] with a filler of roasted ground chickpeas. It's called *zahtar*. You'd have that with fresh tomato and cucumber, mostly with flat bread, but we'd often have French bread.'

*Zahtar* is one of those words that seems to have several meanings. In *Good Food From Morocco*, Paula Wolfert says that it is '*Origanum cyriacum*, a sort of hybrid thyme-marjoram-oregano' and tells us to 'use any of these three commonly available herbs or mix them and substitute for *zahtar* in a recipe.' She warns us not to 'confuse it with the mixture of thyme and sumac sold as *zahtar* in some Middle Eastern markets.' Greg Malouf (see Chapter 8) told me that it has a double meaning, either a 'collection of spices—thyme, salt, sesame seeds and sumac—mixed with olive oil, generally two-thirds oil and one third *zahtar* and painted onto raw dough and baked.' He tells us 'he lived on it as a kid, turning up my nose at Vegemite.' Another meaning is, again according to Greg Malouf, 'the herb wild thyme or possibly wild marjoram. Mum has some growing. To me it has the smell of thyme and the leaves of marjoram.' I tried some of George's version by dipping a piece of bread in oil then into the mixture and, whatever it is, it's delicious.

Lunch is the main meal in the Middle East, and school lunches were an important ritual. 'We'd take a pack of pots that stack on top of one another. The canteen was a large room with burners around the edges. We'd all congregate there and one of my older sisters would serve us and we'd sit down and eat a hot meal, usually a one-pot dish with rice. We'd sit around the table as a family group.'

The Haddads left Beirut for Melbourne just before the six-day war. George was fourteen. Elias Haddad had been working quietly but feverishly to get the family out of the country. 'Dad had hurriedly put in applications to three countries. In his heart of hearts, he had a preference for Australia, because he recalled fondly his contacts with Australians in Palestine during and after the war. Coincidentally, it was the first one to come through.'

'We were the last out of the Suez Canal. When we pulled into Port Said we were mobbed by kids saying there was going to be a war. I had heard nothing, but I suspect my father knew. He was sort of politically involved. It was probable he wanted to get out because his involvement might have complicated things for the family.'

They landed in Melbourne in June 1967. Samir, an elder brother, had come ahead to secure a house for the family in Clifton Hill. George remembers 'driving through Port Melbourne and looking at the houses. It took me years to realise that they were actually permanent residences. I thought they must have been temporary wooden boxes for people working on the wharfs. We'd just come from the Middle East where buildings are made of stone and look as old as Jesus. But the distances looked fantastic. You don't get a long-range view of anything in the Lebanon unless you're on a mountain looking out to sea.'

George spoke Arabic, French and reasonable English. His father found a job working for the Motor Registry Branch. For one whose admiration of Australia—and Australians—is notable, George's early experiences of us were not good. 'The first few months, I would have gone back at the drop of a hat. I was dislocated socially. Age fourteen is a very important age where you fit in with your peers. Back in Lebanon, I was king shit, top of the school. You come here and no-one knows you, and they laugh at you because you don't speak as clearly as they do or as fluently. Suddenly you're being seen as a dumbo. We make that subconscious assessment that because someone doesn't speak as well, they're of a lower intellect. My reaction was to clam up. I was concentrating on how the language sounds, so I listened.'

He first went to a Christian Brothers college, but didn't last long. 'I didn't adjust well to their system of justice. It came as a surprise to the head brother that when he hit me I hit him back. He took me down to his office and said this will never happen again. I said I guarantee it will never happen again as long as you never hit me again. He said I think you should leave us at the end of the year.' George went to a state high school, and was again confronted with insensitive teachers. 'I remember the geography teacher, such an unkind person. For a start you're trying to concentrate on a continent instead of 10,000 sq km (Lebanon), which is smaller than a cattle station in Northern Queensland. Everything is arse about face—north is hot and south is cold. He suggested to me at fifteen I might as well go and get a job because I must be that bloody thick because I didn't take to his subject as quickly as he'd have liked.'

School lunches were, as usual, a source of discomfort. 'We adjusted very quickly, although we still looked ridiculous. I took sandwiches, but when I unpacked my lunch to eat, they all fell off the bench laughing because it was about six or eight sandwiches made of thick slices of Vienna bread—lunch was the main meal—and I'd be laboriously making my way through my food long after they'd finished! Curiously enough you change—there's no way in the world that I could eat that much lunch now. But even when we adjusted down, they'd still make fun of the woggy food we brought.'

'I did try. I remember one funny incident just after we arrived. There was always a long queue outside the tuckshop. I stood in the queue and thought I'd ask for the most popular item. I heard what sounded to me like a single word—pinesauce—so when my turn came I asked for a pinesauce. Because I saw pastry, I expected it to be sweet. I took one bite and it was the most awful thing that had ever passed between my lips! I went behind the shed and dumped it.'

'There was a Lebanese community in Melbourne and you could get some food but it wasn't as easy as it is now. I remember the first Lebanese bakery was in Clifton Hill in the backyard of someone's house, the Telstar Bakery (now called Kaddami), the biggest in Melbourne. We used to buy Vienna loaves, we liked them very much because of the French influence in Lebanon. In those days bakers used to deliver to your house—the baker used to swear that he dropped more Vienna loaves at our house than he did at the milk bar—you need a lot of bread for a family of ten [one remained behind in Lebanon]. We used to go to the Victoria Market during the wholesale hours and buy by the crate.'

In 1970, basically because of Rafia's unhappiness here, the family decided to go back to Lebanon. 'By this stage, in spite of all the problems I was having, I was determined to stay. So when Mum and Dad said we were going back it was another thought of instability.'

Then tragedy struck. Rafia went ahead to pave the way. 'Dad got a letter from her. He'd been working out in the back garden and he came in and said, Good, she's in Beirut. Which she wasn't. It became evident he wasn't well. He said, I can't focus on this, I'd better lie down, which was unusual for him.' Elias Haddad died that day of a heart attack. He'd had one fourteen years earlier.

Elias' death created enormous practical problems for the family. When Rafia had left, she had done so without a re-entry visa. The Australian Government gave her two choices. She could come back, or they'd send her three under-age children to her, in Beirut, at their expense. 'She weighed it up and decided to come back. Living in Lebanon as a widow is not as easy as living in Australia as a widow. Also—this is two or three years before the outbreak of the civil war—she knew only too well if we'd stayed in Lebanon, we'd more than likely be carrying arms. One room in the house in Damascus we had lived in was an arsenal. If you heard a disturbance in the night, you didn't walk out in your dressing gown, you walked out with a submachine gun or a rifle. If it weren't for his death, you and I wouldn't be talking. I'd probably have been somewhere in one of those factions in Lebanon.'

When Rafia returned, George had to make 'a lot of adjustment'. Even before his mother came home he felt a sense of responsibility. 'I took it on myself to leave school and start work. I was sixteen, going on seventeen. But then Mum came back and told me to go back to school.' But that wasn't smooth sailing either. The Haddad family history of political involvement was passed from father to son. 'At University High School, a small group of us led the first secondary school strike in Australia. We went out and closed the school down. It culminated in a march of a few thousand students up to Parliament House. That was 1972. At the end of that year, we saw the Labor Government.'

Because of this disruption, George didn't finish his matriculation, but in 1973 he did a year of a Hotel Management course at William Angliss College, a formalisation of his part-time work in restaurants as a student. He went to work for Joe Powell, the restaurateur at Dimples in West Melbourne, as a waiter, and was offered a full-time job. 'I was good at it. But I certainly wasn't thinking I'd be in restaurants, it was an interim thing.' He still had a desire to continue his education, in fact, 'it's only recently, at age 42, that I've come to terms with the fact that I'm not going back to full-time education'.

Dimples was a good experience, and especially useful for an apprenticeship in wines and spirits. 'Joe Powell used to hold the best structured tastings I've ever attended. Single malt whiskies, fifteen in one afternoon. Cognac, either from one house or a range of VSOPs. I learnt, through the experience of the passage of fluid from one end to the other, rather than just reading about a huge range of wines and spirits. Except for Australian wines—he wasn't big on them.' It was 'a small restaurant, maximum 39, very classical French menu.'

By now George had become, if not a member of the party, 'Labor aligned, I gave my first vote to Labor, to Frank Crean.' He would have huge arguments with Joe who was a 'blue ribbon Liberal'.

Dimples closed down—there were council problems—after George had been there for two-and-a-half years. He did a variety of odd jobs, working for hotels, driving cabs, he went to Adelaide for a while, and on his return met Anne Ripper, now his wife. He went to Royal Melbourne Institute of Technology and matriculated, then enrolled at Melbourne University in a part-time BSc course. 'A few months after that Anne told me she was pregnant with Eloise.' He'd been working nights at Glo Glo's, then he was offered a full-time job at Fanny's. He deferred his course and took the job. 'I needed the money. I was 24 and didn't even have a savings account until Anne told me she was pregnant.'

It was 1977. Fanny's was in the vanguard of Melbourne's restaurants. 'It was an establishment restaurant, one of the leading such in Australia. We may look back at some of the food and have a laugh, but you could do that with any period and any restaurant. The Staleys [Blyth and Gloria who owned both Fanny's and Glo Glo's] made a great contribution to the restaurant scene in Melbourne. At any lunch there you had a few squillion dollars sitting around the table—stockbrokers, barristers, company heads. Some of the conversations you overheard were disturbing,' not least to the young Labor stalwart George Haddad. 'Sometimes legislation was taking place at the tables of Fanny's rather than the chambers of Parliament. I remember Malcolm Fraser was brought there by Tony Staley [then Minister for Communications and Blyth's cousin] towards the end of his campaign in 1983. On the way out he looked at me and shook hands and said, thank you very much [by now George was the Maitre'd]. I was tempted to say, it's great to shake hands with a loser for a change.'

George tells another story of diplomatic discretion—if not his—about the night Melbourne food critic Stephen Downes visited Fanny's. Downes was not a Fanny's fan. 'He sat with his companion at a table at the top of the stairs. The Staleys saw him and went white. Of course the whole place goes into a flap. The other 48 customers can go to buggery. We're only serving two people. So I went up to Mr Staley and I said, look, we've never had a chance of getting any positive comment let alone an endorsement from Stephen Downes. Why not throw him out? I'll do it. Let me say we don't want to serve you, go away. He said you can't do that. I said why not? There's one thing for certain he's going to write about you anyway. You're either going to feed him and he's going to shitbag you as usual, or you can throw him out and gain some sort of vindication from other restaurateurs saying, yeah, good on you Blyth. You'll get notoriety which is not as bad as a bad write-up. Sure as the sun rises, there was a bad write-up of Fanny's. I would have thrown him out.'

George was with the Staleys for seven years, moving between Glo Glo's and Fanny's. 'Fanny's was a chic, conservative restaurant. Downstairs was the bistro, upstairs the Garibaldi room. Staley bought it as Cafe Drosso in the early 1960s. Drosso was one of those original wog cafes, if you like, which brought something different to Melbourne. Glo Glo's was the fashionable night restaurant. It was a cavern lined with mirrors, hot pink, low slung lights—a fashionable tart if you like, where Fanny's was a chic lady.'

'The food at Fanny's had Gloria Staley's signature all over it. We went through nouvelle cuisine but she did a better job than most. Just as I was leaving we were going back into what she called gutsy food. She came under various influences. She used to subscribe to any magazine that had anything to do with food from anywhere in the world. When they went overseas I had to clear the mail and I'd get a back injury lifting magazines. She also used to be impressed by other people in Melbourne, particularly Stephanie [Alexander]. If anyone's going to write the treatise on Australian cuisine—it'll be Stephanie. Gloria eventually became a little more Mediterranean, which I suspect was Stephanie's influence.'

By 1985 George was seriously considering opening his own place. 'I looked at a place that was offered for peanuts in Brunswick Street Fitzroy, a warehouse for $150 a week. Because I'm a cautious operator, I consulted with the Victorian Small Business Advisory Service. They said forget it—not in Brunswick Street. You'll get your fingers burnt.' Brunswick Street is now one of Melbourne's major eating streets, home to places like Akari 177 and Cyrano's.

On a family visit to his sister Samira, he was, as he puts it, 'seduced by Hobart', and a good and under-utilised site there. It was then called Don Quixote, and was in a city arcade. This eventually became Capers, a cafe bistro planned on paper to be sold within five years.

'It coincided with the end of the free lunch. Top-end dining rooms were losing trade, and people were looking for a cheap lunch. The smart thing to do was produce good food without the trimmings—and do it at half the price. And because it was the centre of the city, we couldn't ignore the sandwich. Anne said—you're going to make sandwiches? I said if we're going to make sandwiches, we'll make sure they talk about them. We shocked Hobart by putting on sandwiches at $5 to 6.50—in 1985 $1.80 was tops. But this was a meal between two slices of bread. I re-constructed my lunch from the sandwiches I took to the Christian Brothers college—and now the silly bastards were happy to pay $5 each for them!

'What made them popular were the flavours I was putting in there which was what I used to do for myself at home. I used the things I did when I was a kid—a bit of *baba ghanoush* [eggplant and garlic purée], some olives, whole spring onions, and rolled it up in flat bread. At Capers I did it between two slices of rye. We sold it three and a half years later. Eighteen months into it we were already talking about the next place.'

But the man who invented Lebanese-Australian food didn't want to know about a Lebanese restaurant—and certainly had no intention of inventing a new cuisine. 'I was virtually coerced by the locals. When they found out my background, there were a few people hanging out for something different. They said, go on, open a Lebanese restaurant. I said don't be ridiculous. I know what we in Australia have come to expect to pay for Lebanese food—and I don't want to work like that. I know how my compatriots in Sydney and Melbourne make money out of it by being lethargic and cheating a lot, not using the right ingredients. But the unsuspecting punter says, oh, isn't that lovely, because there's a bit of top flavour. I'm not interested in working on that level.'

But he was talked into it, found a location, and thought that he would set it up, get it running, and get out in six months. 'It didn't work out like that. Before it even opened we were saying, laminex top tables, keep it nice and kitsch, that's what people expect of a Lebanese restaurant. We ended up with table cloths. We just didn't feel comfortable with the format.'

'A restaurant becomes a person. You build them, they look cold. But the minute the tradesmen get out, you get rid of the glue smells, and you fire up the equipment, the burnishment is worn off and you start to smell food, that's when it starts to assume a life force. It has a heart beat. It has various temperature zones, it's got different noises. The bank manager picked up on it. I'd say, well, Ali hasn't been that great the last few months. He said you talk about them as if they're people. I said, well, they are.'

The food began with many hours on the telephone to Rafia in Melbourne.

'In the beginning it was very important, laboriously taking down instructions. Mum wasn't one of those disciplined cooks who wrote things down. It was, oh well, I'd probably use two, two and a half kilos of meat, oh dear, how much nutmeg, just a good amount. Then I'd have to remind her—Mum, I seem to remember . . . oh yes, naturally you put that in. It was laborious but it was also very important. Because that's where I got what people in the Middle East call spirit—the spirit of cooking. I remember my maternal grandfather, a very quiet man who loved his food. Sometimes when he was eating and didn't finish he would say this is cooked without spirit. The usual thing was if you were eating in someone's home and the food was without spirit, the logical step is that that person is mean, it was done with reluctance, no spirit was put into it. It was important to absorb that and apply it even though you were at an experimental stage. You couldn't have done it without that vital ingredient, and that was definitely downloaded, thanks to Telecom, from Mum.'

Speaking of the evolution of the food at Ali Akbar, George remembers, 'It was intended to run on banquets—which meant I cooked what I cooked and it went out as a series of courses. There were compromises—I wasn't going to send out 80 little dishes. So I reduced the number. Still people didn't like it. Too bitsy they said. So instead we put out a large platter dotted with the same things. It presented better visually, people related to it better and it made it easier in the kitchen. Then they wanted à la carte—entree, main and dessert. I said, all right. So I just hand-wrote a few things on the menu. That was the seed of developing the cuisine that Ali ended up with. I never thought of developing it, never had any desire to do that. It happened by circumstance.'

What was the turning point? 'The first one they talked about was when we started using Tasmanian salmon. 'We fashioned a dish called *samké harra* (hot fish)—basically made with a walnut and chilli sauce, and I like the flavour of tarragon with salmon so we fashioned the dish to suit the whole salmon, and that dish was always cooked as a whole large fish. It was probably the first dish that you could say used local produce fashioned along traditional Lebanese lines. That was the start.'

On critics of this style of merging of produce and techniques, George has this to say. 'The finger of authenticity is quick to be raised. The cuisine itself—any cuisine—came under different influences in different periods. If they like it they adopt that change, whether it's art, literature or food. Middle-Eastern cuisine never stood ossified in any one period, it always evolved—except when you took it out of its home. The immigrant's view of everything to do with their homeland freezes the year they leave it.'

Then along came the second major influence in the formation of Australian Lebanese food—appropriately enough (for Australia) in the form of a young Dutch-Australian by the name of Kathy Witbreuk. She started as a kitchen hand, became an apprentice, and then began working with George on dish development. 'As soon as she had completely absorbed the use of spices she started to see things in a way that would not have occurred to me because of the structured and rigid way I was brought up in the Middle East. For example, it's not an exclusively Jewish thing that you don't mix meat and dairy, especially fish. To cook a fish dish with chilli and yoghurt would just not occur to a Middle-Eastern mind like mine. She added another dimension.'

Ali Akbar opened in 1987, and was sold while I was in Hobart speaking to George (I witnessed the signature of the final document) in March 1995, to a Turkish baker Ismet Aydin and his wife Fiona. In between times, George and Anne had opened the Atlas Cafe with a young chef of whom they are particularly proud, Chris Jackman—'I don't think you meet two like Chris in one lifetime—if you do you're bloody lucky'—who is, as a Tasmanian Aboriginal, uniquely qualified to cook modern Australian food. Chris first worked for George at Capers, turning up as a schoolboy, and later worked for Stephanie Alexander, and as a pastry chef at Paul Bocuse in Melbourne before returning to Hobart as head chef at Atlas.

George has followed the evolution of Australian cuisine for some time. 'The period we were playing around with nouvelle cuisine, you might remember, also incorporated a bit of Asian, in concept and flavour. Later, young chefs experimented with various dishes from different ethnic backgrounds—it was more of a collage—you'd have a Thai dish, an Italian dish, a Lebanese dish—we didn't do any of them particularly well, but it looked good on the menu—like a plate of flags from an atlas. But in the last five or ten years, we've seen the emergence of some young chefs who've shaken off the pretences and opulences of—a loosely used term—French cuisine, and are on about substance. Some of the dishes that are coming through are an amalgam of the dishes from the various ethnic groups who have had a profound influence on the way we eat—the more profound ones have actually crept into domestic kitchens.'

'Have a look at the things you do in your kitchen now, and have a look at what people of your age were doing in their kitchens in Sydney and

Melbourne ten, twenty years ago—you'll see the vast difference in ingredients you have in the pantry, the techniques used, the approach to food. Those cuisines are starting to give the foundation colour of what is now emerging as Australian cuisine—or modern Australian cuisine, which is a term I used about five years ago that is being flogged a lot now. That's where Atlas is.' (Or rather was. Before this book went to print Atlas closed due to a dispute between George and Anne and George's brother-in-law and partner in Atlas. Chris Jackman opened a restaurant in northern Hobart called Mit Zitrone. In 1996, George Haddad left the restaurant business. He is now working as adviser to Duncan Kerr, shadow Minister for Immigration, and is advising the Leader of the Opposition on multicultural affairs.)

I asked George to comment on Beppi Polese's observation that it's not the ingredients that make the cuisine, but the cuisine that makes the ingredients. 'It's an old mathematical rule. The whole is not merely the sum of the components. It comes back to the same thing—the spirit of cooking. He's absolutely right.'

## Kibbeh Nayé

Cracked Wheat and Raw Lamb

MAKES ABOUT 10 KIBBEH

In my childhood the task of pounding the kibbeh meat to a paste was always assigned to the men of the house using a large granite mortar and a large wooden pestle.

500 g trimmed topside of
 lamb
1 onion
200 g burghul
2 teaspoons salt
1 teaspoon ground black
 pepper
1 teaspoon ground paprika
pinch of chilli flakes

Trim the meat perfectly of any fat or silver skin. Cut it into cubes and grind in a food processor until it is the consistency of a very smooth paste. Remove the pulverised meat from the processor and place it in a large bowl. Grind the onion in a similar manner and add it to the meat.

Soak the burghul in plenty of cold water until it softens to a degree as tested on the tooth: chew a few grains, they should feel slightly hard—for comparison chew some soon after soaking. This should take about 15–30 minutes.

Once the burghul is ready, drain it into a strainer and then take a cupped handful and squeeze as much of the water out of it as possible with your other hand and add it to the meat/onion mixture. Repeat until all the burghul is used.

Add the salt, pepper, paprika and chilli flakes and mix with your hands as if kneading dough.

Shape the mixture into a ball and run a small knife through the mix, making a cut right through which will collect some sinew onto the blade of the knife. Remove with your fingers and discard. Repeat this action across the whole mix, say cuts 1–2 cm apart, then turn 90° and continue the same action. Reshape and repeat until satisfied you have removed all the sinew from the meat. Reshape and refrigerate for at least 1 hour before serving.

To serve: serve kibbeh nayé with the following condiments: white onion wedges, olive oil, sea salt, cracked black pepper, chilli flakes, fresh mint and/or fresh basil leaves, and bread.

# Tawook

SERVES 6

This is one of Ali's early signature dishes. It was frighteningly popular. It is a marinated barbecued chicken dish. In the late 1980s we had the idea of rivalling Kentucky Fried Chicken by seeking the consent of Colonel Qathaffi (mispronounced in the West as Gaddafi which irritates the Libyan leader) and start a chain named Colonel Qathaffi Barbecued Chicken.

1 kg chicken thighs, skin removed
1 large onion
1 large lemon
1 green capsicum
1 bunch parsley
2 teaspoons salt
1 teaspoon black pepper
1 head chopped/crushed garlic
½ bunch spring onions, roughly chopped
½ cup (125 mL) lemon juice
1 cup whole crushed peeled tomato
1 teaspoon dried tarragon leaves or 2 fresh tarragon sprigs
½ cup (125 mL) vegetable oil
½ cup (125 mL) olive oil

Roughly chop the onion, lemon and capsicum. Place all of the ingredients (except for the vegetable and olive oils) in a bowl and mix well. Cover with the vegetable and olive oils. Marinate for at least 24 hours, before barbecuing the chicken as desired.

# The Sandwich

I must have had worms when I was a kid. I was scrawny and lanky but my sandwiches were of a large diameter. Yes, diameter, because in Lebanon sandwiches were made with Lebanese bread ordinarily using one flap of the splittable round of bread. However, I used to lift and peel back the top flap far enough to open the round of bread almost fully, leaving the two attached by about a quarter of the circumference. There was no given recipe for a sandwich of that magnitude, although there was some discipline and good taste in what went into it.

For example, if looking in the larder and seeing *baba ghanoush*, then I made a point of including peppers. If *labna* [salted drained yoghurt] was to be the base paste, then green pickled olives were a must and, of course, a sprinkle of *zahtar*.

What followed was along similar rules of association. There would sometimes be left-over baked lamb, so that would compel a small sprinkle of cumin, or if lambs' tongues were in the offing, then tahini and lemon juice and chopped tomatoes. Ham or mortadella necessitated the inclusion of fresh cucumber and black olives. Spring onion and sprigs of parsley almost always had a place.

The result was a large mound that presented a challenge to roll neatly and a further challenge to get one's mouth around. Never had it occurred to me that it would one day be the delight of so many other people—thousands it must have been—in its new found form as the Super Sandwich at Capers.

# Orange Brandy and Mascarpone Zuccotto

SERVES 6–8

From the Atlas chapter. Chris is exceptional in that there is no area in a restaurant kitchen where he has any weakness. If he has a greater strength in one area it's in the pastry cooking and desserts in general. Therefore, it's appropriate that a single entry from Chris ought to be a dessert. This is one he created entirely. It needs to be prepared a day before it is required.

**ORANGE MARMALADE**
1½ oranges (250 g)
1 lemon
1 cup (250 g) sugar
1½ cups (375 mL) water
2½ tablespoons brandy

**SPONGE**
⅓ cup (60 g) currants
⅓ cup (60 g) sultanas
6 eggs
⅘ cup (225 g) sugar
2½ cups (310 g) plain flour
3 teaspoons baking powder
½ teaspoon salt
2 cups (500 mL) cream, whipped
⅓ quantity orange marmalade (see recipe)
80 mL brandy

**FILLING**
500 g mascarpone
100 g caster sugar
1¼ cups (300 mL) cream, whipped
⅔ quantity orange marmalade (see recipe)
50 mL brandy

To make marmalade, cut the oranges and lemon in half and slice thinly. Place them in a pot, add the sugar and water, bring to the boil and simmer until thick. Allow to cool and add the brandy. (Makes a great breakfast marmalade.)

To make sponge, soak the currants and sultanas in hot water for 30 minutes and then drain.

Beat the eggs and sugar until thick and creamy, fold in the sifted flour, baking powder and salt, and the cream. Add fruit, marmalade and brandy.

Bake in a 38 cm × 28 cm pan at 180°C (355°F) for 20–25 minutes.

To make filling, whip the mascarpone with the caster sugar and then fold in the other ingredients.

To assemble the zuccotto, slice the sponge into three layers. Cut the bottom layer in half across the width, cut each rectangle of this bottom slice into seven wedges and arrange around a stainless steel 23-cm diameter bowl, alternating baked side and cut side.

Place a round side of sponge to fit in the bottom of the bowl. Spoon in the filling to half way up the sides and place another round slice of sponge to fit. Spoon in more filling. Repeat the process until the bowl is filled.

Refrigerate for one day before serving.

Lew Kathreptis driving home a point at Zeffie's in Rundle Street, Adelaide.

'*Whether it's Arab or Greek*
*or whatever—who cares?*
*There's Greece right in*
*the middle.*'

# CHAPTER SIX

# Lew & Zeffie Kathreptis

WHAT IS it about Adelaide and cooking? Lately, it's become more like the city of chefs than the city of churches. Run the roster. Phillip Searle. Cheong Liew. Chris Manfield (originally from Queensland but she learnt her licks there). Mary Jane Hayward. Genevieve Harris. And Lew Kathreptis. The thing about that list, you may have noticed, is that all bar one of those princes and princesses of the pots and pans—Cheong Liew being the exception—have left the city of their birth for Sydney, Lew being the latest, at the time of writing.

Like George Haddad in Hobart, stories of the glories of the Kathreptis' table had travelled the country before Lew had. I had spoken to Lew, by telephone, a few times when he announced the closure of his (and Zeffie's) first restaurant, Mezes, and he was, even then, planning a move to Sydney. But his country called first.

The first time I met Lew he was, tenuously, still in Adelaide, having just returned from working as chef-in-residence for the Australian High Commissioner, Doctor Neal Blewett in London, which he had followed by a sniff and taste tour through Spain and Morocco. A month or so later he was ensconced in Sydney, cooking in the Botanic Gardens Restaurant, as he is at the time of writing.

We met in his mother Zeffie's new place, Zeffie's, in Rundle Street across the road from their original restaurant, Mezes, which, we could see through the plate glass windows, had now been transformed into a flower shop.

Zeffie's—also since sold—was a big, clean, white-walled bistro dedicated to the simple Greek/Turkish food that Zeffie does so well, and from which base Lew has built his own multi-Mediterranean style.

The interview began without Zeffie, which proved interesting, because I was given two versions of family history. As these stories are usually embroidered and embellished through the years anyway (a very similar process to the fictive one), I'll give both versions.

'My [maternal] great grandfather, Christopher Pouleas, was a tobacco planter in Turkey,' begins Lew's version, 'doing very well for himself, with a palatial home in Izmir, then called Smyrna.' When the Turks began expelling the Greeks in 1922 (the enmity between the two peoples simmers on), established Greek families, like the Pouleas, would have been torn apart by dual loyalties to their Greek nationality and the land they had adopted—and prospered in. Lew continues, 'Because he had so much investment in the country and didn't want to leave, he joined the Turkish army. He couldn't cope, he deserted, and went back to his house to hide.'

'In the house was a huge tapestry. During the day he hid behind this, and at night he and his wife would get together and talk. One particular day, he needed some water, and there was a well in the courtyard. There was a staircase on the outside of the house and as he was coming down the stairs, the doctor's wife saw him. She told the doctor, the doctor told the officials and he was executed in front of his family. The women of the family had to flee. They went to Athens, where my grandmother's marriage to my grandfather, who was already there, was arranged.'

In Zeffie's version, Christopher Pouleas simply resisted the Turks taking over his property, and was killed. The rest of the story remains the same, with Zeffie adding that her mother had told her 'they had to dress the girls as boys so they wouldn't be raped by the Turkish soldiers.'

Lew's maternal grandfather, Apostolis (Paul) Taliangis, also born in Turkey on the island of Livissi (in spite of checking this name with Zeffie, I still can't find it in any atlas), came to Australia when he was fifteen. He worked cutting cane in Queensland, and on the Afghan camel train in Central Australia before settling in Adelaide. Zeffie's mother Demetra married him in 1927. Zeffie was born in 1929, and eventually had two brothers and four sisters.

Before the Second World War there were few Greeks in Adelaide. Zeffie remembers as a teenager 'most of us Greeks could fit in the one church', and that 'to get together before the cars came in, we used to hire two or three buses every first Sunday of the month and go up to the hills to have picnics.' Because they were so few, there was not a high level of intolerance displayed. 'We used to get wogs and dagos, my father once talked to my young brother in the bus and some people turned around and told him to speak in English— but nothing really serious.'

The Greek community congregated around the Hindley Street area, known as the West End. 'I'll tell you who used to live there,' Zeffie recalled, 'Senator Nick Bolkus and his parents. Robert Stigwood. A lot of the Greeks from the West End became millionaires.'

Initially, finding suitable food was difficult. 'My mother told me when she came to Australia she used to fry a lot of things in dripping and lard. We used to eat a lot of parsnips and potatoes and mince and things like that.'

But it wasn't long before Zeffie's parents opened a fish and chip shop, Don's (her father's nickname), which prospered, and things improved for the family. 'In those days the only thing to take away in Adelaide was fish and chips. So during the war, when the ladies worked in the munitions factories, they used to have big queues of people wanting to take hot food home.'

'He was very fastidious, my father. He used to go to the fishmonger every morning—he didn't believe in fridges, he used to think that fridges dried the fish out, so he'd buy fresh every day. He didn't believe in potato chipping machines either, everything was hand-cut. My parents used to line us children up to peel potatoes for them.'

When they began to make money, Zeffie's mother brought out her mother and her sister from Greece. 'My grandmother when she came to Australia used to go and pick the olives and make her own table olives.'

Olives have been grown in and around Adelaide parklands for nearly 150 years. The first olives, planted by one Sir Samuel Davenport (an aggressively unwoggy name for an olive pioneer), were imported from all over the Mediterranean as rootlings and planted in 1844, in the very sensible belief that they would prosper in Adelaide's Mediterranean climate. The then sheriff of Adelaide used the prisoners from Adelaide Gaol to tend the trees. Later, these trees 'escaped' and propagated throughout the hills, especially around Burnside. Today, the descendants of these trees are harvested to make Joseph Grilli's Foothills Oil (see Chapter 4). In 1851, oil made from these olives was shown in the Great Exhibition in London, and compared favourably with oil from Lucca, Italy.

Originally, many varieties were planted, and it can only be assumed that those that have survived and prospered are, by now, a new hybrid, adapted to local conditions—and, almost certainly, have developed a local flavour. The post-war Mediterranean migrants have cared for and cultivated the trees for the last 50 years. One early olive oil pioneer was Emmanuel Giakoumis, who made oil in Edwardstown in the late 1950s, and who, at the time of writing, is working at McLaren Vale Winery for Coriole as a consultant for their olive oil business.

I asked Zeffie about olive oil in pre-war Adelaide. 'I tell you who we used to buy it from. Mr Kratsis of Star Grocery on the corner of Hindley Street near where Hog's Breath Cafe is now. He was an importer of olive oil. He also used to make his own tomato sauce . . . My parents didn't make oil, but I think Mr Kratsis also used to make oil.'

When Zeffie's parents started doing well, they moved to North Terrace, 'But even then,' Zeffie remembers, 'they used to make us kids go down to the police barracks and pick up the olives and take them home.'

In 1954, Zeffie married George Kathreptis. Although from a Greek family, he was born and raised in Port Said in Egypt. His father worked for the company that built the Suez Canal, but with the uprising when King Farouk was exiled in 1952, the family had to leave, and did so with minimal money and possessions. We often forget how much the Greeks have been pushed around by forces beyond their control.

In 1959, Lew was born. He was Zeffie and George's second child; first came Irene, and, after Lew, Anthony. Lew's earliest memory is of being taken to his grandparent's house. 'On the bathroom door there was a dart-board. I went into the bathroom and there were ducks in the bath—real ducks.'

Zeffie recalls that, 'In those years you used to have to go to the fowl market and buy your chickens and ducks live.' Young Lew didn't mind. 'My brother and I took off our clothes and played with the ducks in the bath.'

He also remembers that there was 'always a lot of food around, especially on name days [for most Mediterranean people, the name day, the birthday of the saint for whom they are named, takes the place of a birthday] we'd go to someone's house to celebrate and there would be huge tables of food.'

'When the Greeks entertain you,' Zeffie explains, 'there won't be an entree, a main course and a dessert—there'll be a table of food and you'll help yourself. There'll be the *moussaka*—still in the baking pans as they came out of the oven, and there'll be *pastitsio* [pies], vine leaves, figs, things like that.'

Because the family heritage on Zeffie's side is Turkish, there would also be Greek/Turkish specialities on that table, and Lew reminded her of the *soudzoukákia*. 'The Australians seem to love them,' she told me. 'You put in minced lamb [or beef], garlic, cumin, cinnamon then you roll them up like sausages with no skin, fry them in oil, then make a tomato sauce with a bit of cumin and a bit of wine in the sauce.'

One of the Kathreptis' neighbours, an Australian woman, (a 'country woman' according to Zeffie) baked, and Lew would help her. At the age of ten, he baked a cake for his mother's birthday. 'It was a pineapple sponge,' he remembers.

His schooldays were not happy. 'I went to Goodwood Primary school. The Greeks hung out with the Greeks, the Italians with the Italians, and the Australians with the Australians. There was a lot of infighting and carrying on and kids throwing their school lunches around. I didn't particularly like that. Then, when we moved up to Bellevue Heights, I was one of two or three ethnics in the school. It was worse, really hideous, I hated that.'

Young Lew Kathreptis found refuge in art. 'I used to spend a lot of time painting and drawing. That's what I wanted to do, to become an artist. This was not encouraged from home, not at all.' Zeffie, who'd been listening to this in silence, added, 'his father wanted him to become a dentist.' But Lew persevered.

'I did what I had to do. I went to art school. Stanley Street School of Art. Then I became an art teacher and I absolutely hated it. I enjoyed the students, it was just the staff—all the politics. It was overstaffed during that period, and a lot of people were losing their jobs.'

Although not his original choice of career, food played a part even then. 'My final assignment for art school did include a meal—it was a performance at a table, including goblets and wine. I made the plates, the tablecloth, the food, the whole thing. It was based on an ancient Greek custom where, after you dined at a symposium, one of the customs was to throw a libation onto the floor to honour the gods. Guests would write the name of the person they loved in the wine. The performance was a contemporary re-enactment of that ritual. During that period I was reading a lot about classical Greece.'

And he was cooking. 'I always cooked. I remember one party I had when all I made was a really huge bowl of tomatoes in vinegar and oil, and huge bowls of zucchini cakes and pilaf.'

In 1985, unhappy with teaching, and none too sure what to do with the rest of his life, Lew took off for Greece for the first time, and spent six months there, a lot of that time in a flat that the family had inherited from one of his aunts. At first, he didn't like it—especially Athens, and especially the food. 'I recognised it, but it was nothing like my Mum's—it was disgusting. Everything was poorly made, for the tourists. The olive oil was poor, the produce was poor.'

He did find one or two exceptions to this general rule.

'There were little taverns that specialised in one or two dishes. In a place called Sica (figs), all they sold was *kolokythia* [zucchini salad] and *melitzánosalata* [eggplant salad]—really simple but delicious.' Mostly he and his sister Irene, who joined him there, went to the markets, and cooked at home.

Later, they toured Turkey together. And this was a far more pleasurable experience. 'I had a wonderful time in Turkey.' This was despite the difficulties still encountered by Greeks in Turkey—on one occasion Lew's Greek name caused trouble with the Turkish authorities, which his Turkish friends had to sort out. Lew then went back to Greece, to the Greek Islands, and had a completely different experience. 'I went to the family island, Kassos, between Crete and Rhodes, where my father's family had come from before they went to Egypt. I went with my father, my sister and my brother-in-law. When we arrived we had to pick the lock of the family home.' Here, he discovered Greek food at its best. 'As soon as we got in there, three or four women came into the house and did a whirlwind clean-up, set up a table in the courtyard and made us a meal. Delicious. Wild greens, tiny *dolmades*, you'd grab a handful—well, I did anyway—goat's cheese, bread, fish, octopus, tomatoes. Simple, wonderful food.'

After Greece, Lew went on an art pilgrimage to Italy, France, London and New York—which was also an opportunity to sample the food—before heading back home in 1986. 'I've always been aware of food—not haute cuisine, but simple, fresh food. I loved the food of Italy. I spent a lot of time in San Gimignano, ate wonderfully well there. France? I spent most of my time in Paris, not really interesting food that time. Same in London and New York, in New York especially it was art and parties.'

After the irresponsibility of the extended holiday, he had to face up to one question: what was he going to do next? 'Well, I thought, I'm not going back to teaching. Mum had set up Mezes, so I thought I'd try my hand at cooking.'

'When he came back,' Zeffie added, 'he said to me do you mind if I come and work in the kitchen with you, Mum? I said, why ask, you're a son too (brother Tony was already working there). Then he gradually took over, and the food changed from my Greek to his Mediterranean.'

Mezes was set up by Zeffie in 1980. She had divorced George and they had sold the family house. Zeffie opened Mezes as 'a Greek snack bar. A lot of people loved it. A lot thought my way was better than Lew's because it was more homely. But then his food is what made Mezes.'

Initially, Lew helped Zeffie with the food. 'All the Greek/Turkish things ... making the *moussaka*, char-grilling the fish, making *rabbit stifatho* [stew] and putting all the *mezes* together. I got bored with it. The same thing day in, day out. That was when I started going out to restaurants and seeing what was around and reading a lot. In that reading, I learnt how all the countries of the Mediterranean influenced each other, and I thought, well, I'd like to expand the food at Mezes.'

'At first I was still using Greek

Lew and his mother Zeffie at Zeffie's.

ingredients, still cooking Greek food. That was when I started playing around in the way that Peter Conistis is doing now. Then I broadened out.'

He began to experiment—in his own time. 'I didn't want to put on any dishes until I was satisfied, so I'd stay behind after service and cook, sometimes until four or five in the morning.'

A transition in his cooking began to take place. 'Some of the ingredients I had tried when I was away [overseas] stuck in my head. Especially mastic. A great flavour, I remembered the mastic ice creams.' Mastic is the hard resin extracted from an acacia tree that grows mainly on the island of Chios. It is made into chewing gum, and the dried form is used in desserts and ice creams, and also to make a liqueur called Mastic. According to Claudia Roden, it was formerly used in stews.

'Mum made a dessert called *crema kataifi* (thin strands of vermicelli-like dough)—kataifi pastry, then custard, then cream on top of that. I changed it almost straight away to kataifi pastry with syrup and nuts and a mastic bavarois on top. Then I changed it again. I put pressed figs in the kataifi, then mastic on top, using the mastic resin. There's no other taste like mastic. It's a taste all of its own—earth, resin.'

'Then I did things with mussels and clams, just cooking them and putting them in a simple vinaigrette with lots of herbs and garlic. I still do it today, it's a very successful dish. And oxtail boned and wrapped in crepinette in a fava-type sauce served with a celeriac purée. Then I thought about putting lots of garlic in that and calling it a celeriac *skordalia*—lots of raw garlic and celeriac and vinegar. I'd serve that with grilled tuna and a salsa of tomato and capsicum.'

'Then I went a bit haywire and thought what if I do this and that and I started working with French and Moroccan recipes, and putting all those flavours and techniques into the one dish. Admittedly some of them were not very good, but I didn't put them on.'

'During this period I was reading history and cookbooks. Homer, Plato, Elizabeth David. I read Claudia Roden's Middle-Eastern book, *A Book of Middle-Eastern Food*, from cover to cover. I started reading Escoffier and all the other French cooks, then about the history of food and ingredients. I was teaching myself.'

'During this period in Adelaide, everyone was doing Asian food. There was the Cheong (Liew) group—he influenced all that East meets West food. And I thought, no, I'll stick to what I know best, to the ingredients I know best, and be honest to myself. I think it's one reason I've achieved what I've achieved.'

Mezes ran with Lew creating sparks in the kitchen from 1981 to 1994. 'The place was becoming shabby and tired looking, the lease was running out, the rent was going up and I thought, no way I'm paying that much rent for a small building. So we closed.'

Next stop was London, as the first chef in a plan to use the High Commissioner's office to promote Australian produce—and Australian chefs—in Europe. He was to help Doctor Blewett 'create a scholarship so that every year there'd be a young Australian chef cooking at the High Commission. It didn't work out. It was a very brave idea, but there wasn't enough money.'

But it was very good experience for Lew. 'I organised cocktail parties for the Australian Choir, cooked private dinner parties and business lunches for Doctor Blewett. I had two chef's tables and they worked extremely well. For the first one, John Susman (then with Martin Groen, seafood suppliers, The

Flying Squid Brothers) flew over the seafood, Simon (Johnson, Sydney food wholesaler and retailer) flew over Australian cheeses and olive oils.'

'In the second chef's table I used the ingredients that were around me. But the seafood in Europe—with the exception of Spain—is shocking, even in France I was disappointed. Going to Billingsgate, I was devastated, I couldn't believe it. It was tired, it smelt ammonic, in comparison to the Sydney Fish Markets where everything is firm and smells of the sea.'

'We invited writers, food journalists, wine writers. But by the second one, nothing had been printed in the London papers. I understand it takes more than two chef's tables to get a story.'

On the way back to Australia, Lew went to Morocco and Spain. 'Jerez and Granada, mainly for the Arab influence in the food. Then I went to Valencia in search of the perfect *paella*. I think I found it in a restaurant called (I think) El Rek, in the little village of El Palmar, outside Valencia, amongst the rice fields. It has to have the biscuit coloured crust [in the Valencian language, a variant of Catalan, *socarrat*] and the rice has to be *al dente*. You can't do a *paella* during restaurant service, but at dinner parties one of my apprentices and I would make a wicked *paella*. The *tapas* bars in San Sebastian were mind-boggling—you could make a meal out of the *tapas*, or *meze* or *mezza*, whatever you want to call them.'

Of particular interest to Lew was Moroccan food. He'd been trying to cook it himself, but had never been to Morocco. 'I cooked Moroccan-style food—I say style because techniques and ingredients were not necessarily traditional. But then going to Fez and Marrakesh, tasting the food and putting a spoonful in my mouth and thinking—yeah, boy was I close. That made me feel pretty good. I was surprised by how peppery the couscous was in Fez—they use a lot of pepper. One dish I tasted in Marrakesh was snails in a broth and the broth was one of the most delicious things I've ever had in my life.'

I was interested to ask Lew whether his experiences as a painter had influenced his cooking. 'Often when I was painting I would think, keep the colours clean, keep them pure, make sure you don't make them muddy. And it's the same with ingredients—I always think, don't put too many flavours in or you'll make the taste muddy. In other words, I like to keep the palette— the palette of flavour being the tongue—clean. And I don't care what anyone says, it's important to just take another minute to make sure it looks OK, because initially food is a visual treat.'

His thoughts on the Australian food explosion are interesting. 'We [second generation migrants] were lucky enough to have the multicultural influ-ences—we could go out and try the tastes, the produce was available, we had first-hand knowledge of the techniques. And as these ethnic groups became assimilated into society, more Australians became aware of what we had to offer.' Lew speaks of a generational process he calls the re-grouping of the ethnics. 'The first generation assimilated, the second and third gen-erations began to re-group, re-think their status and explore their origins. They were more comfortable about being Australian, so they could have a closer look at being Italian-Australians, or Greek-Australians or Lebanese-Australians. They'd noticed that Anglo Australians had allegiance to this potty little ex-empire headed by a fairy tale queen, which of course had nothing whatsoever to do with them.' And this began the process of exploring.

But there was another factor. 'People like Peter Conistis, Steve Manfredi and I basically got a bit bored with what we were doing, and we wanted to improve on it—which depends on the individual.'

Lew's roots are very important to him. 'Cheong Liew and I were talking about the soul of food and the cooks who are just following trends—there's no soul, no spirit in that food.' Does that mean you have to have roots in a country to understand its food? 'It depends on the individual. I'm not Mor-occan, but I'm pretty sure I understand what Moroccan food is all about. Mainly because it's Mediterranean food. OK, the ingredients are different from Italy and Greece and the south of France, but the idea of eating is pretty much the same, and the treatment of the ingredients is again quite simple.'

He illustrated this by talking about a Greek salad. 'A lot of Mediterranean food does rely on the ingredients. In a Greek salad tomatoes have to be perfect and the fetta has to be perfect to capture the essence of that simple salad.'

'And because of that basic Mediterranean spirit, I've been able to expand my repertoire and use other foods from the region, because of that thread. Whether it's Arab or Greek or whatever—who cares? There's Greece right in the middle.'

# *Soudzoukakia*  Spicy Sausages in Tomato and Cumin Sauce

SERVES 6–8

From the first day it opened, Mezes' popularity just snowballed. It won instant appeal in Adelaide. The menu was simply mezes—from *tatziki* to *skordalia* to *dolmades* to *moussaka* and *kapamas* [aromatic beef in red wine]. The concept was that people abandon the idea of first, second and third courses, and, instead, order a variety of dishes to sample different flavours and textures. One of the most popular *meze* of that period was *soudzoukákia*, little ground beef sausages in tomato and cumin sauce.

SAUSAGE
¾ cup (90 g) dried
 breadcrumbs
¼ cup (60 mL) white wine
½ cup (125 mL) water
1 kg finely minced beef
2 teaspoons toasted and
 crushed cumin seeds
2 teaspoons ground
 cinnamon
5 garlic cloves, minced
salt and pepper to taste
olive oil

SAUCE
2 cups fresh tomato pulp
¼ cup (60mL) white wine
5 garlic cloves, minced
2 teaspoons cumin seed,
 toasted and crushed
pinch of white sugar
salt and pepper to taste
handful of finely chopped
 flat-leaf parsley

To make sausages, soak the breadcrumbs in the wine and water. Combine the meat, soaked breadcrumbs, the spices and garlic, and season with salt and pepper. Knead well to make sure the ingredients are mixed together thoroughly. Allow the mixture to stand for at least 1 hour for the flavours to develop. Shape the mixture into small sausage shapes and fry in hot olive oil until just cooked.

To make sauce, while the mince mixture is standing for the flavours to develop, combine all the sauce ingredients, except for the parsley, in a medium saucepan. Cook over a low heat, stirring, until you have a thick sauce.

Place the sausages into the sauce and cook for a further 3 minutes. Transfer to a serving dish, sprinkle over the parsley and serve.

# Duck and Quince Pie

SERVES 4

(The duck confit recipe adapted with permission from Paula Wolfert's *The Cooking of South West France*.) Make the confit a week before use.

**PASTRY**
200 g chilled unsalted butter, cut into small pieces
3 cups (375 g) sifted bakers flour
1 teaspoon salt
1 teaspoon white sugar
1 small egg, lightly beaten
1 tablespoon strained lemon juice
3 tablespoons soda water

**DUCK CONFIT**
2 kg duck fat
1 tablespoon coarse sea salt
¼ cup coarsely chopped shallots
¼ cup chopped fresh parsley
½ tablespoon black peppercorns, crushed
2 bay leaves, crumbled
½ teaspoon crushed garlic
½ thyme sprig, chopped
4 duck legs

**DUCK AND QUINCE PIE**
One lot of pie pastry (see recipe)
4 confit duck legs (see recipe)
3 onions, finely chopped
2 cinnamon sticks
3 cloves
½ teaspoon ground allspice
1 teaspoon salt and pepper
2 tablespoons pomegranate syrup
4 cups (1 litre) duck stock
2 quinces, peeled and cored
beaten egg for glazing

Make the pastry the day before baking. Place the butter, flour, salt, sugar, egg, lemon juice and soda water into the food processor. Process until the pastry just begins to form a ball. Turn out onto a work surface covered with greaseproof paper. Pat the pastry into an even rectangle.

Cover with another sheet of greaseproof paper and roll into a larger rectangle. Remove the top sheet of paper. Fold the pastry into thirds. Replace the top sheet of greaseproof paper, and roll into a larger rectangle. Refrigerator overnight.

To make duck confit, in a large, heavy saucepan combine the duck fat with 2 litres of water and simmer, uncovered, over a low heat for a couple of hours until the fat turns clear. Strain the rendered fat into a large container and allow to cool. Cover tightly and refrigerate overnight.

Combine the salt with the shallots, parsley, peppercorns, bay leaves, crushed garlic and thyme in a large bowl. Toss the duck legs in the mixture. Cover with plastic wrap and refrigerate overnight. The following day:

Remove the duck fat from the container, leaving behind the jellied meat juices. Slowly melt the fat in a saucepan over a low heat.

Rinse the duck legs well. Drain and then pat dry. Place the duck legs in a single layer in a large baking pan and pour over the melted fat to cover the legs. Place a sheet of baking paper over the surface of the fat and weight it down with small, ovenproof plates.

Bake the legs at 90°C (195°F) for 5 hours, or until a wooden skewer easily pierces the thickest part of the leg. Remove the pan from the oven and allow the legs to cool in the fat for 2 hours.

Place a stainless steel rack in the bottom of a large, deep, stainless steel tray. Remove the legs from the fat and place them on the rack in a single layer.

Strain the fat into a transparent vessel and allow it to settle for 1 hour. Pour the fat into a large saucepan, leaving behind all the meat juices. Heat the fat to near boiling point, skimming off the foam that rises to the surface. Let it bubble for 5 minutes, or until the spattering stops and the surface of the fat is left undisturbed. Watch carefully and adjust the heat if necessary to avoid smoking and burning. Remove from the heat and cool for a few minutes. Ladle the warm fat over the duck legs, covering them completely. Allow the fat to congeal. Cover with foil and refrigerate for at least 1 week before using.

To make pie, remove the confit of duck from the duck fat. Place a little of the fat in a pan over a medium heat. Cook the onions in the fat until transparent. Add the cinnamon sticks, cloves, allspice, salt and pepper, pomegranate syrup and the duck stock. Simmer and reduce to a thick syrup. Remove the cinnamon sticks. Cook the quinces in a sugar syrup (1 part sugar boiled in 2 parts water for 1 minute) over a low heat for 4–5 hours or until they are a dark, ruby red.

Take the duck flesh from the bones, making sure to remove all cartilage and fine bones. Combine the duck meat with the quince. Pour over the syrup, and allow to cool completely.

Divide the pastry in two and roll each half to 4 mm thick. Line a 23-cm pie tin with one sheet of pastry, and place the duck and quince on it. Cover the pie with the remaining sheet of pastry, making sure to pinch the edges securely. Glaze the pie with beaten egg and trim the edges of the pie. Cook the pie in a moderate oven at 180°C (355°F) for approximately 35 minutes or until golden brown. Serve immediately.

# Kataifi with Mastic Bavarois

MAKES ABOUT 24 PIECES

The prime function of mastic, as described in ancient Greek manuscripts, was to mix it with a little bees' wax and use it as a chewing gum—to masticate. Even today, throughout the Middle East, it is still used as chewing gum.

Mastic is also used, when ground into a powder form, to flavour liqueurs, milk puddings, ice creams, sweet breads and biscuits. Just recently, during my travels through Morocco, it was used to flavour a spicy broth in which snails were cooked.

However, the perfect use of mastic is to add another dimension to green fig preserve. Small granules of mastic are inserted into the base of green figs and then they are slowly cooked in a sugar syrup. My grandmother used to make jars of the preserve, *glyko*, and my family devoured them in no time. Greek delicatessens stock kataifi pastry.

**PASTRY**
3 cups (750 mL) water
1 cup (250 g) sugar
1 cup (375 g) honey
zest of 1 orange
2 tablespoons orange
 blossom water
⅓ cup (90 g) clarified
 butter
400 g kataifi pastry
2 cups (250 g) pistachios,
 ground
2 teaspoons ground
 cinnamon
1 teaspoon ground nutmeg
1 teaspoon allspice

**MASTIC BAVAROIS**
22 ripe fresh figs
4½ teaspoons unflavoured
 gelatin
2 cups (500 mL) milk
3 teaspoons ground mastic
2 split vanilla beans
8 large egg yolks
½ cup (125 g) white sugar
2½ cups (625 mL) whipping
 cream
1 cup pistachios, ground

To make pastry, in a small saucepan, combine the water, sugar, honey and orange zest. Over a low heat, stir until the honey and sugar have dissolved. Bring the syrup to the boil and simmer for 15 minutes. Allow to cool, remove the orange zest and stir in the orange blossom water.

Meanwhile prepare the pastry base.

Preheat the oven to 180°C (355°F).

Grease a 30 × 40 × 6 cm baking tin with some of the clarified butter. Line the base of the tin with half the kataifi pastry. Sprinkle the pistachio nuts over the pastry. Sift the spices over the pistachios. Cover with the remaining pastry. Dab the remaining clarified butter evenly over the surface of the pastry. Bake for approximately 20 minutes or until golden.

Remove from the oven and allow to cool for 3 minutes. Pour the cold syrup over the warm pastry. Allow to cool completely.

To make bavarois, cut the figs in half and evenly distribute them, cut side down, onto the pastry.

Soften the gelatin in 2 tablespoons water. Place the milk, mastic and vanilla in a saucepan and bring to a simmer. Remove from the heat.

Beat together the yolks and sugar until pale and fluffy. Slowly pour in the milk mixture, beating constantly. Transfer the mixture to a clean saucepan and cook over a low heat, stirring continuously, until the custard coats the back of a wooden spoon and the froth has disappeared. Remove the custard from the heat and stir in the softened gelatin. Strain the custard into a stainless steel bowl.

Whip the cream until it is light, thick and just holding peaks.

Set the bowl containing the custard in another bowl containing crushed ice. Cool the custard until it begins to thicken and holds the same consistency as the cream. Immediately remove the bowl from the ice and fold in the whipped cream. Pour the bavarois over the figs and pastry.

Refrigerate until the bavarois has set. Sprinkle with ground pistachios.

To serve: divide into desired portions and serve.

Clockwise from top left: Rosalinda Tasca, Maria La Spina, Joe La Spina, Raimond La Spina, Sam La Spina and Julian Tasca at the family home at Whorouly in north-eastern Victoria.

*'Rosalinda came home from school one day and demanded of the family, "Do you know what Italians eat? They eat worms in blood!"'*

# CHAPTER SEVEN

# Maria La Spina & Rosalinda Tasca

O F ALL the people I spoke to for this book, Rosalinda Tasca and her mother, Maria La Spina, best illustrate the profound changes that Australia has made on these now not-so-new Australians and, conversely, the changes they've made on us, its slightly longer-term occupants.

We spoke in the kitchen of the family house on their property at Whorouly in the Ovens Valley. It is a big house surrounded by a beautiful garden with the usual array of farm outhouses behind it. The large kitchen is obviously the nerve centre of an extended family home, with a long dining room table behind a practical (it has to be—it's professional) work space. Behind the dining room table there's a shelf of family photos of the entire La Spina and Tasca families, including one, especially treasured, of Maria's father, Raimondo Troia, taken just three days before his death in November 1992.

Maria la Spina, then Maria Troia, arrived in Australia at the age of ten with her sister Caterina aged seven. Raimondo had left before them, leaving the girls and their mother behind for a little over a year in the small country town of Ramacca in Sicily.

Hardship had driven Raimondo out. A small farmer living on the edge, he had a couple of bad years, and that was it. An early memory of Maria's says it all. 'I must have been very little when my grandfather came to call on my father, and I remember going to the stables with him and there was this horse lying down and they had to kill it and my father breaking down and saying I'll never be able to get back on my feet now.' After that, he took a job building roads to pay for his trip to Australia.

The women of the family moved in with the grandparents. Maria's mother, Tina, with no man in the family went into a period of—'not mourning,' Maria said, 'that sounds awful, but it was like that. Grandmother used to cook for us, because once Dad left to come here, Mum couldn't see cooking as necessary—cooking was done for the man. She didn't go out much any more, she didn't do the *passeggiata* [afternoon walk around the square]. She stayed home most of the time.'

And because the children were leaving, they were indulged by their grandparents. '*Nonna* [grandmother] used to cook a stew of snails, a *spezzatino* with tomatoes and onions, it was just yummy. We'd sit on my grandfather's knee, my sister and I, and he'd pull the snails out with his little pocket knife and we'd eat them and Grandma would yell, take them off your knee and have a good meal yourself, and he'd say no, leave them alone, I'm not going to have them for very long, they'll go. And we didn't see him—or her—ever again. We'd sit on his knee and drink his wine, we could do anything to my grandfather.'

The more Maria thinks about this period, the more she remembers. 'They [the grandparents] would make bread twice a week, and they had a big wooden bowl—a *maida* [in Sicilian dialect] they called it—we've got one here, and they used to put the flour in and then they'd knead it, they'd put the plate low and stand above it and put their arms into it up to the elbow. They used to make focaccia, that's what they'd make waiting for the loaves to rise. *Nonna* would come home [from the fields], she'd grab one of those loaves, and cut it in half, she'd put olives, anchovies and salt on top and put it in the oven, it would come out fairly quickly, and that was lunch.'

Meanwhile, Raimondo had landed in Melbourne on New Year's Day 1954 and stayed with his wife's family in Coburg. Later, he told Maria, 'he went to the city, walked into a pub and got a job washing glasses. He had no English. Not a word.' He landed a second job, and began putting money aside to pay the passage for the rest of the family. 'We arrived thirteen months later in February 1955, on my tenth birthday. I was sick all the way because I'm a guts and I kept eating—Mum and Dad never let me forget that either. The ship was the *Oceania*, it was Italian, and the food was very good.'

'Dad was working in a pie factory by that stage—an Italian cooking the meat in pies! He wasn't allowed to use garlic. The factory was in Armadale and he got two rooms for us near it.'

'He still had a night job, another pie and cake factory near the Victoria Markets. When his boss knew we'd arrived, he'd send home treats for us, little custard tarts. We didn't like them. The food tasted different.'

And, once more, food—the problematic school lunch—was a cause of grief and unhappiness for little Maria and her sister. It's hard to convey the way a story is told in a transcription. But Maria La Spina is a natural actor and a brilliant mimic, and the way she told these stories had me in such fits of laughter it was sometimes difficult to hear her on the tape recorder.

'Although we lived in an Italian house—they were Calabrese—there weren't many Italians around where we lived. So when we went to school we were the only Italian kids, my sister and I. We couldn't make ourselves understood at all. And we wanted to have our lunch at school. Sliced bread just wasn't heard of where we came from so we used to buy the *pane* and Mum would slice it and we'd take these two bricks with a bit of salami between them. All the kids would come around, and kids can be so cruel, they used to point and laugh at us and we'd cringe and hide, and nobody could understand us. It was awful. Mum had a job as a machinist by this time so we had to have our lunch at school, so we said we'll have to have sliced bread. There were no Italian grocers around but there was a guy who had a milk bar. He was born here but his parents spoke Italian.'

'So my father took us in one day, and he said I don't know what kind of bread these kids want to take to school. And the guy said this is the one, he pointed out the white sliced bread, like marshmallow—so we had to have it. Dad asked what did they have in their bread and the guy said Vegemite and peanut butter—yuk, no way! We weren't going to eat that, and Dad said, look, you'll just have salami sandwiches and we said all right.'

'The first day back with our lunch, we were wrapped! We had the same bread as everybody else. We get to school and we sit in the lunch shed and we pull out our lunch box and the kids are looking in our sandwiches to see what we've got and it was Friday. Oooooh, they said, look, salami, you can't have that, and they went to the nun and said look, meat on Friday—and we had to throw them in the bin! So they got us anyway. After that—no more—we never took our lunch to school.'

After five years in Melbourne, and with Raimondo doing two jobs, they decided to move to where they are now, the Ovens Valley in north-east Victoria.

Italians have been farming in the King, Ovens and Buffalo valleys since the 1930s, having escaped from the pre-war turbulence associated with the rise of Fascism. These early settlers were mainly from Piedmont and the Veneto. They planted their foods—corn, eggplant, garlic, tomato, herbs and various lettuces and kept the local table wine industry—then mainly consisting of the Brown family (now Brown Brothers)—alive. Most other makers in the area concentrated on fortified wines.

These Northerners felt at home in the cool valleys of the north-east: they fished the rivers for trout, Murray cod and yabbies and gathered wild mushrooms. They grew grapes and made wine—professionally and for home consumption—and later, the post-war wave (more often from the South by now) became heavily involved in the cash crop of the time, tobacco.

'My mother's family was large, nine brothers and sisters. Some were up here growing tobacco, so my family decided to come and join them. We didn't buy land up here—we had bought a little house in Alfred Street, North Melbourne by then—but we did buy a house eighteen months after we arrived. And a little car. We were sharefarming at my uncle's, we never did buy land. Dad wanted to, but Mum discouraged him. There was no son to take it over.'

I asked Maria whether she had been happy about the move. 'No! I was fourteen and I was wild. I was waiting to go to work. You see, once we got a few words of English, we were OK. We were Australian kids—we even mastered the sandwiches. But you take a 14-year-old girl away from the city into the bush—how could you live here?'

They may have felt Australian, but their parents were still very Sicilian. 'I didn't go to school when we moved up here, didn't go to work, it was so boring, so awful. I did nothing, just sat around the house all day. I just wanted to get out because they were so strict—I wasn't allowed to do anything. I lasted about three and a half years. Then I got married [to Sam La Spina]. But in their eyes I was still a child, so they didn't approve of him. So we did it the traditional Sicilian way. We eloped.'

The atmosphere in the kitchen changed. Rosalinda, Maria's daughter, was fascinated that Maria was going to let this skeleton out of the family closet. Maria herself was a little shocked at her own boldness. But once she started, there was no stopping her.

'I used to drive my youngest sister (Lucia, born in Australia) to school although I didn't have a licence. We used to meet there. Sam and I talked to each other, half an hour at the school gate, no more than three times a week. Then he proposed to me and I said yeah, but you know what the story is, and he said yeah, and he sent word to my father who said no. I was too young. We kept meeting like that for two years. Finally we decided to elope.

'We set a date. That night I did the chores, and I was waiting around— 9 o'clock was the time set. I walked outside and the next door neighbour put the light on. She'd heard the car slow down and stop, so she poked her head out, and I thought, oh no, I can't go out now, so I waited a bit and the car took off again and I thought, oh God! I walked back inside and I looked out and he did a U-turn up the road, so I crept out again in the shadows and we took off. I had absolutely nothing with me. I thought if he wants me he can have me with nothing.'

'We went to Albury and from there he took me to Surfer's Paradise for three weeks. We were too scared to come home. Thirty-two, 33 years ago Surfer's was just nothing and we were walking around hand in hand thinking—what if they don't want us back there, what if they send us away? And he said, it's all right, we'll buy a property up here and live and work.'

By the time they returned, the two sets of parents had talked, and everything was fine. 'What could my parents say in the end? The deed was done.' Later, Maria Troia and Sam La Spina had a big wedding and then four children, Rosalinda, Joe, Tina and Raimond. The two sons live at home and work on the farm.

In 1984 Rosalinda married John Tasca (mother Calabrese, father Veneto) a psychiatric nurse, and they live in Markwood, five minutes away from the La Spinas. They have two children, Anthony and Julian. In October 1994, Tina married an Australian, Darren, who Maria reports is 'becoming a wog' so successfully that he loves Italian food more than his wife does.

Rosalinda remembers very little prejudice growing up, with the exception of one incident. 'There was one girl who came along, half way through primary school and she was from another area and she'd say things like (here she puts on a Kylie Mole voice, mimicry is obviously a family trait) what are you having, salami sandwiches? and what time does your father get up in the morning? does he work on a farm? and all the other Australian kids would rally around her.' Maria also has vivid memories of this family. 'They came, they ripped the town apart and they left.'

'After that,' Rosalinda went on 'I went to school in Myrtleford, and every second kid was Italian so it was nothing.'

Rosalinda went through a period of rebelliousness against all things Italian when all she would eat was Vegemite sandwiches. She came home from school one day and demanded of the family, 'Do you know what Italians eat? They eat worms in blood!'

'Mum always had sun-dried tomatoes and I remember sitting on the bench here and having lunch and her saying, go on, try these tomatoes, they're beautiful, and I'm going, eergh, get out, I don't want to eat that, that's really woggy.'

But she grew up and out of that, and in 1985, after she married, opened Rosemary's Coffee Shop in nearby Beechworth with her mother. 'It was a run-down coffee shop,' recalls Maria, 'and we put our own stuff in—including pastas—and we did our own cooking.'

'But we did have devonshire teas and Dad did a mean scone,' Rosalinda reminds her.

'We were there for five years,' said Maria. 'In April of 1985 we bought our first pasta machine. I think we were about five years too early for fresh pasta. At first no-one came in, they'd go, ooh, wogs, wogfood, but they were reading about it. And when they did come in they'd say oooh fettooseeny, I've never had fettooseeny. We did seven or eight sauces for the pastas. Ooooh, mu-mu-mu-marinara—what is that? But business picked up. We only sold because Rosalinda had Anthony, and he hated being in the shop. When we sold we kept the pasta-making machine, we sold it to hotels and restaurants. We still make it.'

Fresh pasta needs different treatment to dried. Maria explains. 'If you don't know how to cook it you can end up with a gluggy mess. I cook it fresh, but in most restaurants they pre-cook it. On a Friday night we'd cook two and a half kilos of pasta—the restaurant only seated 45 people.' The secret is 'very, very quick cooking and lots and lots of water. The diner has to sit there fork in hand and wait for it to come. Never let fresh pasta wait for the person to eat it. I'd put it in the pot, walk around the island bench, get the bowl and take it out—never drain it in a colander, scoop it out with the spaghetti scooper so it always has a little bit of liquid sticking to it.'

The La Spinas no longer grow tobacco. 'About twelve years ago we put our kiwi fruit in. We saw the writing on the wall for tobacco. Forty years ago, it was a big thing, but now, you talk about growing tobacco, you're a drug dealer!' The old tobacco kiln is now the office for their substantial market gardening operations.

I went with Sam La Spina, Maria's husband, for a tour of the property. Sam, and before him his father, have been farming this land for 46 years. In all he and his brother (who still has a bit of tobacco in, but is gradually pulling it out) have around 80 hectares of rich river flats. 'I don't know whether it's the best country in the valley,' Sam said, standing in a field of corn as high as an elephant's eye, 'but it's not bad.' He stripped young ears of corn off the stalks and handed them to me to eat. They were unbelievably delicious. A short distance from the corn fields, Sam has 8 hectares of tomato and capsicum. They also grow egg-plants and kiwi fruit, as he explained, 'like normal Sicilian farmers, a bit of everything.' You can't help thinking, as you stand in a field of capsicum that stretches almost as far as you can see, that it wasn't that long ago it was hard to find capsicum or eggplant in a fruit and veg shop.

Sam La Spina in the capsicum patch on the banks of the Ovens River in north-eastern Victoria.

But the La Spinas at Whorouly live on their land, whereas in Sicily as in most of southern Europe, Maria's family, the Troias, although farmers, didn't live on the farm, but in Ramacca, the nearest small town to their land, going out to work the fields by day. This had its origins in security against marauding gangs of bandits, but has had an important social effect on rural people from these regions.

Although there is not a provincial centre and subsequent grouping together here in the Ovens Valley—the town of Myrtleford and its Italian club, the Savoy, is something of a centre—there is a strong sense of community amongst the Italians here (and elsewhere amongst ethnic pockets used to the same ways of living, like Griffith), and this community—at least until recently—rallied together, especially around the various food rituals, the most important of which was the killing of the pig.

The La Spinas, although they still kill a pig every June—the long weekend in June is the traditional time—feel the tradition in the community is dying out. 'My husband's family [the Tascas] do the lot,' reports Rosalinda, 'they're still very traditional. They make the *cotechino*, they even clean the insides [intestines] of the pig and use them as casing [for the sausages]. It's a real man's thing, so John'll trot off and I'll stay home with all the kids and go over at lunchtime.'

Maria tells me that the men in her family make 'salamis and sausages and the *pancetta* and *coppa* [preserved meat]. They get together with their homemade wine and they go erblerblerble [she mimics drinking from a bottle] and they get sozzled and by the end who knows what they put in it? They chop up a bit of meat and say here you are, so we make a sauce with it, cook it, and take it over there. In between the red wine we make endless cups of coffee. We don't have much input into it.'

Maria's obvious distaste for the 'maleness' of the process reminds me of a tradition that I came across in a village in Spain. The first pig to be killed is led up to the square in front of the church, where it's beaten and yelled at by the village women. This kind of treatment would do nothing for the flavour of the meat, but it may well be a cleansing experience for the downtrodden women (in this village, until quite recently, they had to enter the church by a back door), and could just be the original male chauvinist pig.

A pig being killed by Italians on a property just outside Sydney. The identity of the family must be hidden because home slaughter is illegal.

Maria and Rosalinda are out of their restaurant, but not out of the food business. In addition to pasta, using locally grown produce and their own from the farm, they produce a whole range of products like *peperonata*, sun-dried tomatoes, quince jelly, olive pâté and marinated eggplant.

Much of which I tried at a family lunch—spaghetti with a sauce of crushed tomato from the garden marinated in olive oil and balsamic vinegar overnight topped with torn basil leaves just picked by Rosalinda; cold grilled zucchini with slivers of fried garlic; *peperonata*, dried tomatoes, crusty bread, homemade wine and a few slices of *pecorino pepato* (peppered sheep's milk cheese).

And it's quite obvious to me, after observing this family for some time, that were history to repeat itself, and the La Spina family were forced to leave Australia, and Sam, like Maria's father, had to go on ahead as a scout for a new life, Maria wouldn't remain behind, like her mother, in semi-mourning. This family operates as a partnership of equals. Influence cuts both ways.

Wherever I went on this trip, Italians spoke to me about the pig killing, but I was too early in the year. So when I got back to Sydney, with the help of some Italian friends, I located a family near Sydney who carry on the tradition. Let's call this family the Campesinos: what they did that Saturday morning just west of Sydney is, strictly speaking, illegal.

At 7AM, Luigi, the father, went into the field with a bucket of kitchen scraps for the pig they'd been fattening for the past fifteen months. This pig ate better than most of us. Unsuspecting, he tucked into the broccoli, corn and leftover meat scraps. Luigi took from behind his back a .22 rifle and shot him, point blank, between the eyes. The pig died instantly. He cut the neck to bleed it as it lay in the field, saving some of the blood for use in making salami.

At 7.30AM, the carcass was carried by two of Luigi's sons into an outbuilding by the house and laid out on a table top. A fire on a base of bricks crackled nearby. Other sons (he has many) carried in pails of boiling water, and poured it over the fresh, still steaming carcass. The boys and their father scraped the bristles from the skin, then hung the animal up on butcher's hooks by its Achilles tendons, and singed off the remaining hairs.

Luigi and his brother Gino, helped by the older boys, then butchered the animal. They cut off its head and washed it. Luigi made a cut along the belly from rectum to sternum and slid out the liver and wrapped it in the cawl. All the intestines were removed, cleaned and prepared for use. Nothing was wasted—those few bits the family didn't want were fed to the dogs.

Luigi gave me a tour of the small (7 hectare) property. At the back of the shed where the pig was being butchered was a bread oven—they make all their own bread. They grow broccoli, parsley, tomatoes, basil, chillies, corn, eggplant, artichokes and cos lettuce. There are oranges and lemons, chickens for eggs, and Gino has a few head of cattle on his nearby farm.

In a larder behind the kitchen were three barrels of homemade wine, bottles of artichokes in oil, oven-dried black olives, marinated green olives and eggplants. Everywhere there were jars of food preserved in some manner for storage.

Back in the butchery shed, squares of belly pork were salted and sprinkled with black pepper and crushed chillies to make *pancetta*. By 12.30 PM, the carcass had been completely processed. Maria, Luigi's wife, sliced thin fillets and barbecued them, and we ate them by hand with hunks of bread, olives and homemade wine. By the end of the day the shed would be hung with three kinds of salami. This would last the family some months.

Writing in the English magazine *The Spectator*, dour realist Theodore Dalrymple reminds us that multiculturalism means the stoning of adulterers as well as eating couscous. I was reminded, by watching this ritual, that Italian food is as much about the killing of the pig as it is about eating the salami.

Down in the Ovens Valley with Sam La Spina, while he was showing me around the property, I'd questioned him about the killing of the pig. I was puzzled that there did not seem to be a name for this ritual, so important amongst rural Italians. Finally, sick of my insistent questions, he blurted out, 'Whaddaya mean, what's it called—you kill the pig, you make the salami, that's what it's called.'

## Maria's Roasted Artichokes

SERVES 6

a large handful of mint
a large handful of parsley
1 head garlic, cloves
  peeled
½ teaspoon ground chilli
½ cup grated pecorino
  cheese
salt
6 fresh artichokes
6 tablespoons olive oil

Finely chop all the ingredients (except the artichokes) and combine with salt to taste. This is the filling.

Wash the artichokes and peel off the tough outer leaves. Turn each artichoke upside down and hit it against the chopping board to open the leaves.

Divide the filling between the six artichokes, spreading it evenly through the leaves. Place in a baking dish and drizzle 1 tablespoon olive oil over each artichoke. Pour 1 cup water into the baking dish and cover with foil.

Bake in a hot oven at 200°C (390°F), covered, until cooked, about 1½–2 hours. If the leaves pull off easily, they are cooked.

## Rosalinda's Fresh Tomato Sauce

Scald, peel and chop 2 kg ripe fresh Roma tomatoes.

Fry a small chopped onion in about ½ cup olive oil with about 4 cloves of crushed garlic.

Add the tomatoes and stir until pulpy, usually about 45 minutes over a medium heat.

Halfway through the cooking, season with salt, freshly ground black pepper and add chopped fresh oregano and basil and 1 tablespoon sugar.

# Melanzane Maria

SERVES 4–6

3 medium eggplants,
 sliced 1 cm thick
salt
olive oil
1 quantity of Rosalinda's
 fresh tomato sauce (see
 recipe)
grated Parmesan cheese
4 eggs
salt and pepper

Layer the eggplant slices in a colander and sprinkle salt through the layers. Leave for ½ hour. Wash and pat dry.

Fry the slices in a little olive oil until golden.

In a pie dish, layer eggplant slices, fresh tomato sauce, and Parmesan until the eggplant slices are used up.

Break the eggs into a bowl, add salt and pepper, beat with a fork, then, using the fork, drizzle the beaten egg over the pie dish mixture. Sprinkle over extra Parmesan and bake in a moderate oven at 180°C (355°F) until set.

To serve: cut into wedges and serve with a cos lettuce salad.

# Maria's Wild Fennel Salad

In the springtime in Sicily my grandmother and I would go for a walk in the fields carrying a large wicker basket to gather wild grasses, in this instance wild fennel.

Take fresh shoots of fennel—one large bunch—washed thoroughly, blanched in a large pot of salted boiling water. When tender, drain, and toss through with virgin olive oil and a sprinkle of lemon juice.

To serve: serve with a bowl of fresh, crusty, homemade bread to sop up the juices. To have a bowl of this is like going back to my childhood.

Greg Malouf at Carlton Place Restaurant in Carlton.

*'Do you know what* harissa *is? Or* chermoula? *What's more terrifying is I've got it on my menu.'*

# CHAPTER EIGHT

# Greg Malouf

**B**Y THE age of 35, Greg Malouf had survived a triple bypass, a heart transplant, and was running his own kitchen at O'Connell's Hotel in South Melbourne. That's when I met him. We shared a meal and a bottle or so of Victorian wine.

Speaking of his medical history, he tells me, 'I get called back every now and then to talk to people who've just been transplanted. I'm the success story. I work fourteen, sixteen hours a day. The quacks come into the restaurant—we've got an open kitchen—and they look at me—when you're cooking for 60 to 70 people all at once, it's hard work—and these guys are really proud of what they've done.'

I learnt about Greg's new heart (from a 26-year-old male donor) only halfway through our meal together. I looked at him in a new light. Should he be taking things easy? Should he slow down? After the transplant, the doctors told him he was not to go back to cooking. 'I thought, if I can't go back into the kitchen, you guys have lost me.' When you realise the depth of this third generation Lebanese-Australian's dedication to his work, you know he has no choice but to live the way he does.

Greg is another of those offspring of immigrants who owes his nationality to a hazy notion on the part of his forebears as to exactly where this place called Australia was. 'The story goes my great grandfather got on the wrong ship and ended up in New Zealand in the 1890s. My grandfather had a grocery shop in Brunswick.'

Greg's mother, May, is from the Lebanon. She and his father, Kevin, corresponded for ten years, then he flew over to Beirut in 1956 and married her. Her father was a newspaper editor, May had been an air hostess. She came from Beirut—then the 'Paris of the Middle East' to North Balwyn—the heart of Melbourne suburbia in the mid-1950s. 'A scary time and a scary area,' says

Greg of her move, 'she hated the country for a number of years. Things improved around the mid-70s for her when my parents moved close to town.'

I asked what she hated. 'It was based on hospitality. There's no welcome. There's a term in the Lebanon '*ahla wa sahla*', which roughly translates as: you're welcome. The host sets the table and everything is laid out for the guest. You don't have to ask for anything. When you walk into someone's home they say '*ahla wa sahla fekum?*' which has the meaning of 'welcome, are you hungry?' The Chinese have a similar thing, they don't ask how you are, they ask are you hungry? That's what I've always thought hospitality was.'

There was a small Lebanese community in Melbourne when Greg was growing up, and there were close links between the Maloufs and the Bacashs—Michael Bacash, the same age as Greg, is also a cook, and also experimenting with Middle Eastern/Mediterranean influenced food at his own restaurant in Carlton called Toofey's.

The young Greg Malouf never, for a moment, entertained any other profession. Was it in the blood—or the water? 'I always wanted to cook. When I was a kid I used to sit in the bathtub—you may laugh—and I'd grab all the shampoos and conditioners and I'd line them up along the rails of the bath and I'd mix them in a little tray and to me this was cooking. I'd tell my parents I want to cook, I want to cook, and Mum would say no, no, you're going to be a barrister, a solicitor.'

In spite of later travel and the assimilation of food cultures from all over Europe and Asia, his passion has always been for Middle Eastern and mainly Lebanese food. 'When I was a kid, I'd come home from school and gobble up Arabic and Lebanese things, *zahtar* with olive oil brushed on bread, while my peers were having Vegemite sandwiches. Later, it was really annoying going to friends' places in the suburbs for dinner and having corned beef and cabbage and three veg. I'd wake up in the middle of the night and raid the fridge for pickled okra.'

As a group, the Lebanese have assimilated well into Australian culture. And Greg is, after all, third generation Australian. But still he had to put up with the racist taunts of children, especially to do with food. 'I'd stink of garlic and get ridiculed. Wogfood, they'd say.' What did Greg say? 'I'm hungry! I looked at what they were eating and I thought—you eat yours. I'm happy with what I've got. But when you're a little kid and you get called a wog you try to compromise. I ate the Vegemite and the corned beef. But I couldn't stand it.' We discussed a parallel phenomenon. In the gay world, what he did would have been called 'straight acting'. 'Same thing,' agreed Greg, but

went on to add 'if anyone approached me now and said you're a wog, I'd
say, thanks very much, would you like some watercress tabbouleh?'

At fifteen he ran away, leaving a note with his best friend to pass on to
his father—his mother was in Africa at the time with her sister. The note
said, simply, I WANT TO COOK.

He came to Sydney and washed dishes in a Mexican restaurant in North
Sydney. 'My family were devastated. I came back three months later, grabbed
the papers, and found a job.' He'd proved his point. There was no more
resistance to his career choice—and eventually he ended up with an apprenticeship at Hagger's.

It was the late 1970s. Melbourne food was, on the whole, classical. But
just over the horizon was the nouvelle cuisine revolution. 'Clichy was the
place,' Greg remembers, 'the first nouvelle cuisine restaurant, run by Iain
Hewitson, brilliant.' Hagger's, owned by Dennis Hagger, was a forty-seater
bistro. 'I was seventeen at the time. I was scared, I wanted to learn as much
as I could, I shut my mouth and kept my head down.' After Hagger's, he
went to Two Faces run by the very influential Hermann Schneider, described
by Greg as 'the godfather of 60s and 70s food.'

Then Dennis Hagger organised a job for him in France in a place called
Meaux, north of Paris, home of the famed cheese Brie de Meaux. 'I was
working at Hotel de la Sirène. I loved it. I learnt pastry. Brilliant, that's all
I did. They had lots of weddings, so I used to get up very early—I was a
*commis*, making *petits fours*, *amuse gueules* [tiny appetisers], *canapés*, *croquembouche*.
But it was hard. I had a little conversational French from my mother, but I
had to learn the language quickly. Being Middle Eastern in Europe, when
you open your mouth and speak fluent English, they love it.'

It was here, in 1981, at the age of 21, that he had his first heart problem.
His mother had a sister, quite wealthy, living in Paris and she came to his
rescue. 'I had to have an ambulance from Meaux to Paris, about 60 kilometres,
800 francs, and the ambulance wouldn't release me to the hospital until I paid
them. My aunt appeared out of nowhere. She paid the money. I had angi-
ograms, all the tests. Then I had a triple bypass.'

The irony of this medical problem is that it more than likely had nothing
to do with the pastries. As explained by cardiologist Doctor Ross Walker, if
you have coronary disease at that age you have to have a genetic disorder.
'Life is a balance,' Doctor Walker reminds us, 'between genetics and
environment.'

Wisely or not, Greg Malouf wasn't about to let his triple bypass interfere with his favoured environment: the kitchen. On returning to Australia, he landed a job as second chef at Mietta's (Chapter 12) under Fred Chalupa. 'I was in a really fantastic position. From being a 21-year-old shitkicker from nowhere to being second to Fred. He was a nightmare to start with, but he was European, and because I'd worked in Europe he took a liking to me.' Greg stayed for eighteen months, and then it was back to Europe, this time, after a quick trip to Italy, to Austria, where Fred had organised a job for him in Salzburg and Vienna, again working mainly with pastry. But Austria was tough, especially for a boy with Middle Eastern appearance. 'I was called an Auslander—foreigner is fine, but Auslander means you're from out of the country. I looked Turkish to them, so I was already convicted.'

After two years he got homesick, went to Ireland, then back to Melbourne in 1984. This time to Glo Glo's, one of two restaurants at the time (Fanny's the other) owned by Gloria and Blyth Staley. Here he met the other prominent Lebanese–Australian restaurateur, then a head waiter, George Haddad (Chapter 5). Then it was off to Hong Kong for three years, firstly as chef at 97 in Hong Kong Central, and then a year's catering. Here, he worked with a brigade of Chinese chefs and learnt Chinese techniques and dishes—*char siu*, barbecued duck—again, first-hand.

The year he spent catering, working with expat Australian Michelle Garnaut (her restaurant M at the Fringe is one of Hong Kong's most highly regarded) was a lucrative one. 'Extraordinary. Money, money, money. If the chefs were at the table cooking for [the customers] in the hat and the clobber, they loved it.' He took some time off to go to Italy, got a job in Mantova, and learnt how to make risotto properly. 'Every day for eight months cooking pasta and risotto, there's no secrets any more.' Then back to Hong Kong and disaster. His heart again.

'The arteries got clogged up. I had to come back to Australia. This was in 1988. I went to Sydney for a transplant assessment. They said, sorry Greg, your heart's stuffed—you need a transplant. So I had one on the first of July 1989—my seventh anniversary [of the new heart] is coming up. The heart works well. My friends ask how I feel. I feel lucky.'

Now he was back in Australia again. And with the prospect of a lifetime as an invalid. Not Greg Malouf. 'It was a hard period. Dealing with my future, my health. All I wanted to do was get back to my profession. Once I convinced everyone of that—quacks and family—it was better. I was young for a transplant patient—a lot of them are in their forties, they retire—I just wanted to get back to work.

By now it was 1990. What did he want to do? 'What I wanted to do was the Middle East meets West thing. I decided to do that a long time ago, in my second year of apprenticeship. We had assignments to write menus, and I'd always incorporate what I was eating at the time. The teachers really loved it. Back then [early 1980s] Middle Eastern cuisine was left to Middle Eastern restaurants.'

In 1985, George Haddad had begun exactly that process in Hobart at Ali Akbar. I asked Greg was he aware of it. This was a difficult question for him, he'd been beaten to that particular goal by his heart. Sickness had pushed his career around. At first he was evasive, telling me only that he was aware of what George had been doing, and reminding me that he had met George at Glo Glo's in 1984. Then, after a long pause, he spat out the truth. 'I was jealous. Let's be honest. I was pissed off because I wanted to beat him but I wasn't healthy enough.' An understandable reaction. But bitterness isn't in Greg Malouf's nature. Like the eggplant—an important ingredient in his culinary culture—a little salt, a little water, and it soaks out.

His first job back in Australia was at Stephanie's. 'Maybe because I was a bit ethnic. Stephanie's is a great kitchen. You've got to remember I'd just had a heart transplant and I was trying to get back into the industry. She hired me as a middle man, not even a second. If I hadn't had a transplant, I wouldn't have accepted the job. She took me in because I annoyed her. She said, Greg, you've had a transplant, why am I employing you? I said because I want to work here and I know I can do better than anyone else you could hire. The only reason I took the job was to eventually get the senior position.'

'But then O'Connell's came along. After a couple of months at Stephanie's, I was offered the job to run the kitchen. That was through Terry Durack and Jill Dupleix.' The owners were renovating and upgrading the hotel, and asked Durack and Dupleix if they knew of a good chef. 'I think it was Jill who said Greg Malouf.'

Stephanie gave him her blessing. Later, with her partner Dur-é Dara, she came into the kitchen at O'Connell's, and wrote about it in her book *Stephanie's Seasons*:

'Dur-é and I lunched at O'Connell's where one-time employee Greg Malouf is the chef. Greg's family is Lebanese and his food is a delicious reminder that it is possible to blend cuisines other than Asian and Western. His exciting mix of Middle Eastern and European ingredients results in a very personal cuisine.

'How I long for the day when Australian cuisine will be rich with examples of such personal "food-ways".'

Now he had his own kitchen, and was creating his own food. The dreams of the little boy in the bath have come true, against all odds. Having waited so long, he had very well-developed ideas about what he wanted to do.

The first of the tenets of the Greg Malouf school of cooking is to have a wide repertoire: if you're going to cook in a certain style, go there and learn how to do it first-hand. 'I've been lucky working in certain areas, experiencing certain things. I was brought up with Middle Eastern food, but I've cooked in France, Austria, Italy, Hong Kong, so I know a little about these cuisines.'

One example. While in Austria, he learnt how to make sauerkraut. 'There are not many cooks in Australia who can make sauerkraut from scratch. It takes up to two months to ferment fully. A couple of years ago we had sauerkraut on at O'Connell's with pickled veal tongue. It's a traditional dish called *bauernschmouss*—there's a dumpling, smoked tongue, rib of pork. I learnt it and I understood it because I lived it.'

The second tenet, very much in line with the first, is to cook what you know. 'Writing menus is a little like re-inventing the wheel. I looked at what I ate as a kid, and I worked from that. Take *kibbeh nayé*. I'd look at it and I'd think—why can't we make it simpler and do it with salmon?' He sums up the idea behind his style very simply. 'The flavours you remember as a child, the flavours of your mother's kitchen, recreated with what's around town.'

And then, in 1994, he went back to the source. In April 1994 he married Lucinda, an English woman, and they went to Lebanon for their honeymoon. 'I'd never been. I'd heard all the stories, and my father had 8 mm movies. Over the years, I'd heard all the talk and read about the bombing and the wars. But the first time I'd set foot there was last year. It was fantastic.'

Did this experience have any influence on the food that he was developing? 'I think it was more a personal reaffirmation. People used to say—you're a wog. But I'd never been there! Now I feel a bit more Lebanese or Arabic than I did before.'

What did he learn about food? 'There were some ingredients that I'd heard of but hadn't seen. But overall, eating a *baba ghanoush* or a *felafel* over there reinforced what I was doing here.' Is the food you cook here better than Lebanese food in Lebanon? 'As good.' But what he is doing is not being done in Lebanon. 'My brother's wife Amal who was brought up in Syria is a brilliant cook. She thinks that what we're doing at O'Connell's is quite revolutionary and if ever I went to Lebanon and cooked what I did I'd be a superstar.' He laughs delightedly at this.

At the end of our meal and discussion, when Mr Malouf and I had eaten and drunk rather well, we began to discuss the history of Middle Eastern food in Australia. It was then that he raised *chermoula.*

'There was a time in the late 1970s and early 1980s when Middle Eastern food was really hot,' he recalled, 'and all of a sudden it died and Asian food went bang! Now it's back, but it's not Lebanese, it's North African. It's really weird that North Africa has eclipsed the rest of the Middle East. What's the North African community here [in Sydney or Melbourne]?' I replied I wasn't sure, but that I knew of only three North African chefs in Sydney at the time (at Cafe Tunis, the Algiers and Casablanca). He went on.

'Do you know what *harissa* is? Or *chermoula*? [Both North African, harissa is a chilli sauce and chermoula is a herb and spice marinating paste.] Ask a Lebanese person what *chermoula* is and they wouldn't understand what the word means. What's more terrifying is that until a few years ago, I didn't know either. But I read up on it, messed around with it, liked the idea and added it to the menu.' And there it was: "O'Connell's Niçoise salad with chermoula roasted tiger prawns," a true Australian dish of the late twentieth century. 'Where does this craze originate?' he asks. Hesitantly, and somewhat shamefacedly, I offer an answer.

A tin of Tunisian harissa.

In 1993, along with over 100 chefs, food writers and academics from around the developed world, I went to Tunisia as the guest of the International Olive Oil Council (IOOC) and the Oldways Preservation and Exchange Trust. While the function of the IOOC is both transparent and laudable, that of Oldways needs some explanation. A non-profit organisation based in Massachusetts, it is the brain-child of Kennedy era (and one-time Kennedy aide) lawyer and businessman K. Dun Gifford. His research into diet and his own observations had convinced him that the Mediterranean diet, based on grains, vegetables, legumes, pulses and olive oil is the holy grail of diets for optimum world health. It's Dun Gifford's mission to stop the Americanisation of world food in its tracks. He sounds like an American crackpot, a Kellogg figure, but he's an intelligent, shrewd and passionate man: a one-man Mac-attacker—an

American version of Carlo Petrini, the founder of the Slow Food Movement in Italy.

What we were doing in Tunisia was studying—and eating—Tunisian cuisine, and discovering that it is one of the unknown wonders of the world. On our return, we proselytised: we raved about couscous, we ranted about *harissa*, and we went on about *chermoula*. And we did so in the influential newspapers and magazines that we write for.

'So you see,' I told Greg, 'for the first time in the history of the development of Australian cuisine, in addition to the contribution of the post-war immigrants—the Greeks, Italians, Lebanese—there's a new group influencing the mix: the tribe of food writers. That craze for Tunisian food is where fashion takes over from authenticity—whatever that is.' He shook his head in bewilderment—by this time there was a bottle of very good Armagnac on the table—and told me a story.

'My mother said to me these eggplants are really tricky. She told me there's the bum and the head of the eggplant, and if you understand *baba ghanoush*, you understand the eggplant. It's a funny thing with chefs and mothers. Because mothers don't like chefs, Mum thinks I've taken a part of her history. My kitchen is different from her kitchen. I've got to go to her kitchen for ideas. To me it's an exciting profession and I love it, but to her it's a different thing— perhaps a way of life.'

This attitude, this spirit, will, of course, prevail over the tales of the food writer tribe.

# Baba Ghanoush

To me, this is the best dip salad the Middle East has to offer. The lush, smoky, creamy, peppery tastes washed down with a tall glass of arak could possibly match foie gras and Sauternes. My sister-in-law, Amal Malouf, taught me the Syrian style of making Baba Ghanoush which includes yoghurt.

A Middle Eastern tale of choosing an eggplant is to look for green leafy tops that cover at least a quarter of the vegetable. The rounder side should have an oval belly button rather than circular. All this indicates an eggplant with fewer seeds resulting in reduced bitterness.

3 eggplants
¾ cup (155 g) plain yoghurt
2 tablespoons tahini
1 garlic clove
1 teaspoon salt
juice of 2 lemons

Prick the eggplants all over with a fork and hold them over a gas flame. Rotate until the whole eggplant is quite soft, blistered and well charred. The flame will give the characteristic smoky flavour that an electric grill or oven can't give. It must be a flame or nothing else.

Allow the eggplants to cool and gently peel off the charred skins. Do not scrape any flesh left from the skin or you will end up with a burnt rather than a smoky taste.

Lightly mash the pulp with the back of a fork. Crush the garlic with the salt, mix in the lemon juice, and add to the pulp. Add the yoghurt and tahini to the eggplant mixture and stir.

# Watercress Tabbouleh

SERVES 8

This makes for great conversation, especially around Lebanese housewives who generally scoff at the idea but are surprised at the peppery refreshing taste. Mum still has a laugh at the thought.

large bunch watercress (about 2 cups picked)
2 tomatoes, diced very small
4 spring onions, finely diced
¼ cup chopped mint
⅓ cup cracked wheat, soaked and squeezed
juice of 1 lemon
pinch of allspice
pinch of cinnamon
⅓ cup (90 mL) olive oil
salt and pepper to taste

Mix all the ingredients together. Adjust the seasoning as necessary.

# Sauerkraut

*Bauernschmouss* is a classic Austrian dish usually found in Salzburg. It generally consists of a mound of sauerkraut surrounded by roast pork belly, Kassler (smoked pork loin) which is lightly boiled, speck (smoked pork belly), a few small potatoes lightly boiled, a boiled frankfurter and a bread dumpling (*semmel knodel*) made with diced bread, onions, bacon, eggs, parsley and seasoning. The whole dish is drizzled with juice from the roast pork belly pan. The French have a version called *choucroute garnie.*

1 firm white cabbage
plenty of fine salt
juniper berries
carraway seeds
bay leaves
crushed garlic

A wooden barrel or vat is generally used with a wooden lid that is at least 3 cm too small for the top.

Remove the core and slice or shred the cabbage to 1-mm thick, long, thin, thread-like pieces.

The cabbage is spread on the bottom of the barrel in a layer about 5-cm thick. About ⅓ cup (90 g) fine salt is sprinkled on top together with a few juniper berries, carraway seeds and a bay leaf or two. Alternate layers of cabbage, salt and spices are built up to within about 5-cm of the top of the barrel. Add a few cloves of crushed garlic then cover with the wooden lid and weight the lid with a clean brick. Place the barrel in a cool, dark room with an even temperature of about 12°C (54°F).

The cabbage will take around 6–8 weeks to fully ferment. It will also stink! The cabbage should yield about a third its weight in liquid. Remove the brick and the lid, gently pour off some of the liquid and remove about 2–3 cm of the rotted brown cabbage. Beneath it you will find beautiful white sauerkraut.

When making sauerkraut for any dish you must briefly rinse it under cold water, drain it slowly and cook it with finely chopped onions, garlic, bacon, juniper berries, carraway, a little salt and pepper and white wine. Some Omahs (grandmothers) bind it with a white wash mixture of flour and water.

Cook it only for 15–20 minutes.

# Turkish Coffee Ice Cream

MAKES ABOUT 2 KILOS ICE CREAM

A rich, smoky, velvety ice cream which O'Connell's marries beautifully with fresh strawberries and hazelnut florentines.

½ cup (125 mL) water
200 g caster sugar
200 mL liquid glucose
60 g dark chocolate
¼ cup (60 mL) Turkish
  coffee
75 mL Tia Maria
3 cardamom pods, crushed
12 egg yolks
4 cups (1 litre) thickened
  cream

Place in a saucepan the water, sugar, liquid glucose, chocolate, Turkish coffee, Tia Maria and the cardamom pods and bring to the boil. After boiling for 1 minute, simmer for 5 minutes then strain.

Whip the egg yolks at high speed until they are light and fluffy (about 5 minutes). Beat the coffee syrup into the whipped egg yolks along with the cold thickened cream.

The ice cream mixture is ready to churn. This recipe does not work any other way than in an ice cream maker. Follow manufacturers's instructions to churn.

Bill Marchetti at home in Melbourne.

*'The chef is Italian, but the businessman is German. No two ways about it, but thank God it's that way!'*

# CHAPTER NINE

# Bill Marchetti

A RECURRING SOUND on my Bill Marchetti tape is laughter, mine and his. His is huge and rich and rolls off him in glorious waves. Bill Marchetti eats life smothered in gusto. He gobbles it up and it tastes as good to him as his *risotto al porcini* tastes to me.

It's no surprise then, that the list of recommendations for his restaurant, Marchetti's Latin, is the longest (at 37 mm) in either the (1995) Sydney or Melbourne editions of *The Good Food Guide*—and stars everyone from Dame Joan Hammond to Ronnie Burns. Bill—sometimes Willi—Marchetti is a man of great good humour and charm: important qualities in a restaurateur.

What is also surprising (until you observe him at close quarters for a while) is that Guigliemo Marchetti is half-Italian, half-German, born in Munich of a Bavarian mother, Lotte Siebzehnreubel, and an Italian father, Guiseppe (Pepe) Marchetti, originally from Ascoli Piceno in the province of Marche. His mother's family were farmers, his father's, members of the *carabinieri*, the Italian military police.

Bill grew up in Munich speaking German and going to a German school, although like a lot of migrants he was sent to Italian language school as well. It was, as Bill put it, 'another experience of being Italian growing up outside Italy', although as a child, 'I really wasn't so much of an Italian, more like an Italian kid growing up multicultural, a bit like the Italian kids growing up here. They're Aussies with an Italian heritage. I certainly didn't think of myself as Italian.' He didn't have much trouble because of being Italian, 'not at my size, I've always been the meanest and ugliest—perfect for a chef.'

Pepe worked in the central fruit markets in Munich, a large clearing house for the produce of Europe, and did most of the cooking for the family. 'You know what the Italians are like—they don't eat anything that's not Italian. Mum would cook Bavarian occasionally, just for her and me, but we could only eat it when Dad wasn't there. He wouldn't let her do any of the major cooking, except when he got older. There was only one way to make the sauce for his *pasta asciutta* [dried pasta], and she'd always do something wrong that she thought he'd never discover. All arguments in our house—and they were fierce and there were many—had to do with food.'

Bill is another who, very early in life, discovered 'an almost pathological desire to feed people. I was always a kitchen-hanger-arounder kind of kid. I think it's the comfort, the warmth.' He has fond memories of his mother's family in the Bavarian countryside. 'At my grandmother's place, [in] Passau, close to the three country borders—Czechoslovakia, Austria and Germany— on the Danube and surrounded by the forests, we'd go to the forest and pick mushrooms and pickle them. And blueberries, real blueberries, not the rubbish you get here, and make jams, and there were cherry trees so we'd preserve cherries. That was all just part of the upbringing, everyone stood around and stirred the pots.'

When Bill was thirteen, he and his father went to Italy, the intention being to eventually move there ('I think my parents are inherently Gypsies—more so my Dad'). Lotte stayed behind until everything was set up. His father got a job driving semi-trailers back and forth from Italy to Germany, and Bill was left in the Adriatic resort town of San Benedetto del Tronto with his father's family. After Germany, Italy was 'magic, bloody magic. Because my mother had married a foreigner, there was always tension with the rest of the family. In a way at school as well. I handled it fairly well, but with a fair degree of aggro, I guess. Going to Italy was just totally opposite. Such a friendly open society. From that day, from spending that summer in Italy, I always felt a damn sight more Italian than German.'

I asked whether he could differentiate between his German half and his Italian half. He told me that there were actually two Marchettis: Bill was the Italian, Willi the German. 'Anything that's to do with emotion is 100 per cent Italian. Anything to do with logic, German. I find that quite useful in my life. The chef is Italian, but the businessman German. No two ways about it: but thank God it's that way!'

It was during that Italian summer that he got his first job: in the kitchen of a small resort hotel. 'It was a family hotel, more a pensione. San Benedetto is a touristy place, but for Italian tourists—the food was superb.'

He was the apprentice, so was given 'all the shit jobs. But I still remember the *cannocchio* [praying mantis prawns]—we used them to make up a big seafood risotto for lunch. And fish stews and simple grilled fish—the boss' wife would go to the markets every morning. We used to give the customers roasted chestnuts towards autumn, that was the first time I got near the frying pans, including a big one with holes in it over the open fire.' He worked from April to October, at the end seven days a week, and, to his surprise was paid the equivalent of $25. 'I'd expected to pay for the privilege.'

At the end of that year, Lotte came down from Germany, and the Marchettis decided there was no future for them in Italy. In 1966 they went back to Germany, and then immediately applied for migration to Australia. In the early 1960s, they had applied for, and received, permits to go to America, but had never taken them up. Bill still sometimes dreams of what might have been: 'I still like the idea of having the best Italian restaurant in New York.' But Australia it was, and in 1968 the Marchetti family took off on an assisted passage, 'some of the last of the $25 wanderers' with a curiously and persistently sick Lotte. 'A couple of weeks into the trip we found out why. She was pregnant. Which was fine. Dad and I had a really good time. We were two of the very few who didn't get seasick. You used to get a carafe of wine for four people to share. Everybody else got seasick and left the wine on the table. Dad and I got pissed every lunch and dinner! Oh great, they're all sick again, you grab that one and I'll grab this one.' So much did young Bill and his Dad enjoy the trip that, when they got off at Sydney, which is where they originally had decided to go ('it sounded bigger and more exciting'), they succumbed to official encouragement to go to Melbourne because the trip was 'such a good time we thought, oh, all right, fine. At fourteen I'm sure I had a major stake in encouraging this, but I don't know why my mother put up with it—she still wasn't that well.'

Once off the boat, it was into the train and off to Bonegilla. 'It was the second year of a major drought, you're a fourteen-year-old kid and you haven't closed your mouth since you left Germany, it's all wonderful. But your parents are looking at all this with a slightly different view. They're thinking we're going to have to make our life in this country, let's have a look. Four hours, five hours on this train through countryside where you never saw a blade of green grass. And you could see the faces on the old people thinking, this is it, we're going to die here. We saw the bleached skeletons of animals from the train window. All that was missing were the huge cacti and the vultures.'

The arrival at Bonegilla wasn't a lot more encouraging. 'An army camp in a dustbowl. And this coming from Bavaria where everything is storybook green and lush. The food was disgusting, unbelievable, army mess food. I remember walking past the kitchen and all you could smell was mutton, everything was mutton fat.'

By the late sixties, the balance in the camp had shifted. 'Not a lot of Italians, the largest group were Turks, and a good amount of poms. The poms had probably never eaten so well in their lives. The Turks were in no hurry to leave, some had been there for six months. "This is a really good life," they said. We didn't think it was so great.'

The Marchettis stayed five days. 'The idea was you were supposed to stay until they allocated work for you at places like Mount Isa and Kalgoorlie. We got on the next train and left. It wasn't appreciated. You were made to feel a bit ungrateful.'

After renting a flat (at Noble Park in Melbourne) the family had $200. Pepe found a job with General Motors (the post-war Holden wouldn't have existed without migrant labour), but Lotte was by now very pregnant, and couldn't work. So it was up to young Bill to supplement the family income. 'I was fourteen-and-a-half. Going back to school never came up.' Bill and his mother went into Melbourne, and began doing the rounds of the big hotels—starting with the Southern Cross—without success. One joker even said, sure, he could start work tomorrow—the only problem being that was the day the hotel was being demolished.

Exhausted, they stopped for pizza, and asked the owner where they should go next. 'He said there's only one place in town. Florentino's. He'd been a waiter there. I walked up the back stairs and said (here Bill executes a very credible German accent) I would like to see the chef. The chef came over, Good afternoon, I would like to have a job here as a cook's apprentice. He looks at me and said how long have you been in Australia? I have been here one week. All right, he said, start on Monday. I did the whole interview as Willi.'

Florentino's is one of the last of the two surviving pre-war Italian restaurants (Marchetti's Latin is, interestingly enough, the other, but more of that later). Founded in 1928 by Rinaldo Massoni, by the time that young Bill Marchetti started there, it was owned by George Tsindos, who had himself begun there as a waiter in the 1930s, and, after various other jobs (including working for Mario Vigano at Mario's) had returned as co-owner with Rinaldo's son Leon. In 1962, he bought out his partner. For Bill Marchetti, it provided very good initial training—and the inspiration for his own cooking career.

'I stayed just over a year. The first Thursday I was there I saw the kitchen staff heading off somewhere and asked where they were going. To be paid, they said. Oh, see you later, I said. And where are you going, they said? On my break. Aren't you going to collect your wages? I didn't think they paid apprentices—I got $25 for 65 hours. I'd worked an entire summer in Italy for $25.

'The chef was Costa Tziotis (there was a solid 'Greco-Roman' connection in Melbourne, they frequented the same social clubs), a great big buffalo of a man. He'd worked in all the five-star hotels on the Cote d'Azur, he'd been King Farouk's chef, he was an ex-boxer. I really liked him.'

Bill was sent to work in the larder—the usual first stop for apprentices. It was a big, 'pumping' kitchen, which must have, at first, been daunting—even for Bill Marchetti. 'We did between 100 and 150 for lunch, and 250 a night plus stuff for the bistro downstairs. Thirteen or fourteen chefs, in those days we were open for six lunches and six dinners, and everybody worked six lunches and six dinners—the thirteen cooks worked every shift.'

He was a keen student, and, on finding out the chefs started at 7.45AM, began to do so himself, even though official starting time for apprentices wasn't until 9AM. He remembers one day missing the train, not getting in until 8.30, and being hauled in front of the sous chef and told this is not a good attitude. 'I didn't need to be told. I was mortified, sure I was going to be sacked.'

But he loved Australia, and has thought about the origins of that love. 'Australia represented freedom from all the baggage I was carrying around from being an *Auslander* in Germany. But we've lost a lot of what Australia was in those days. I admit there's a fair amount of romanticism in this view, I have no problem with that. When I came here, it was pretty much what I expected. There was a pioneering spirit. Nobody gave much of a shit about your predicament. Ultimately, it was your problem. I thought it bred a pretty robust society, and I really liked that feel about Australia. I don't think it changed until Whitlam came in. I almost told him, but I didn't, such a lovely old man.

'It [the Whitlam years] changed the self-reliance that Australians had from being in a harsh country. I got that feeling from the first day I was here, and I knew that most of the country wasn't like Sydney and Melbourne, it was parched and tough. It bred a people who were tough and good-humoured—I wouldn't necessarily call them good-natured—but good-humoured about their predicament and their life in a country like that. I fitted in with that. I grew up in the emotional equivalent of that. Then we started to become a country where someone else will look after us.'

This, then, was the young apprentice chef who, inside a year, decided he didn't really like the way the kitchen was being run in one of Melbourne's leading restaurants. 'I took a cold hard look at the food that we were producing there—for a little while they put me into the pass [where food is plated, and goes from the kitchen to the waiter]. It was not very impressive. I can recite the entire menu: prawncocktail-lobstercocktailseafoodcocktailoystersmornay-kilpatricktzarina—you remember *tzarina* with the lumpfish roe masquerading as caviar?—lobsternewburgmornayamericaine and lobster salad—where we opened a tin of Edgell's Russian salad and put it on the half cray—chickenmarylandkievchausseur . . . and I thought—this is going to take me a year to learn—and what am I going to do after that?

'Sure, everything was fresh. We'd cook a bag of crays every day, most of the fish was actually fresh—I didn't realise how rare that was in those days—there were fresh ducks and chickens, it was just so boring and basic. The sous chef in those days was Tony Adami [who today has a restaurant called Quadri in Armadale]. I think he's from the Veneto. One day he cooked spaghetti with squid in their own ink, and I'd never had that, because it's a dish from the north. I went, wow, this is fantastic! How come it's not on the menu? And Tony looks at the other chef who was there, and they're pissing themselves laughing. They said, you've got to be joking—Australians eating this?'

Finally Bill cornered the chef. 'There were just the two of us in the kitchen. Knowing his background, knowing where he'd come from I said, look—do you think I'll ever be a chef working in a restaurant like this? He took it in the way that I meant it. He said, this is Australia in 1968. And this is the standard. If you don't like it, change it. He was already in his mid-fifties then. He died about eight years after that. I always carried that with me.'

Next stop was a restaurant on the Brighton Beach Marina called Captain Cook's, where he was paid better, indented, and sent to do his formal training as a chef at William Angliss. 'It was unbelievable. After a year I thought—I'm going to have to give up what I really enjoy doing, which is cooking in a restaurant, to spend eight hours a week learning about the merits of essence of parsley and essence of garlic versus the natural versions for the sake of assured quality and consistency? I don't even think I lasted a year.'

It was now 1970, and Australia—and perhaps especially Melbourne—was on the cusp of a food revolution. All over the country, there were

**Bill, laughing.**

young chefs, like Bill Marchetti, saying—this just isn't good enough. We can do better. 'My big hero in this story is the Boeing 747. All of a sudden everybody could afford to get on a plane and fly to wherever they wanted and taste the food there. And they were coming back, and they weren't going to Florentino's any more—they were opening their own places and remembering the cafe they went to in Paris. It was all a bit haphazard in the beginning—but it was a beginning.'

The other change that fed this new industry was the change in the law that resulted in the BYO restaurant in 1972. Restaurateurs no longer had to have glasses off the table by 8PM, and no longer needed to apply for a full liquor licence. They could concentrate on the food. And their customers could buy wine at bottle shop prices—and experiment with their own food and wine combinations. Bill Marchetti's first important cooking job was in such an establishment, La Cuisine Bourgeoise in Commercial Road, Prahran, owned by a French couple, Michel and Claude Kerlero de Rosbo. 'They didn't have any money, they hired the furniture, the walls were covered with hessian, there was one huge electric stove, one domestic fridge—an old rattler—that was it. They'd started to make a name for themselves and they wanted someone to give them a hand. I took a major pay cut and a major step back in prestige, standard, whatever. And it was great. It was only open at night, and we'd cook all day. Intensive French bourgeois food. Superb pâtés and terrines and *rillettes* [pork spread] and *fromage de tête* [head cheese, brawn]—just magic, all done with that domestic care. They were cooking the food they'd been cooking forever. Nobody had ever seen it like that. Stephanie [Alexander] was a regular. Tony [Knox] and Mietta O'Donnell dined there regularly.' Michel, it seems, was something of an expert on the wines of the Bourgogne region, and 'all the money I earned and they made went into wine. So I got a really good education not only in food but in Burgundy wines—and met another fanatic like my Dad, fiercely regional, he could only drink Burgundy. I was hearing all these French things that I'd been hearing from my father in an Italian version.'

Bill stayed with Michel and Claude for over a year. 'That place re-launched my career. Before that I was starting to think about getting out of cooking. Thank God the revolution came. After that I went to work for Tony Rogalsky [currently the chef/co-proprietor, with his wife Adriana, of Rogalsky's in South Melbourne] which was then the Hot Pot Shop. I was the head chef, had a totally free run. I could cook all the stuff I'd learnt. Cooking with gas we were, cooking real food.'

During this period with Rogalsky, Bill also married his first wife, Cheryl Galpin, and went to live in Europe. One day he came to work and 'someone said something terrible to me like good afternoon. I got pissed off, went home and said to my wife we should go to Europe. My son Alex was just born, he was four months old. We sold everything. Dickhead here picked Germany and not Italy.'

'The logic wasn't so bad. I thought, Munich's nice and central, a good place to establish myself. But as soon as I went back I remembered why I'd been so happy to leave.' Within two weeks of arriving he was called up for the German national service, a prospect that he didn't relish, decided not to go, and spent the next six months in semi-hiding. With money running out, Italy was no longer an option, and the Marchettis returned to Australia, with Bill 'cured of Germany forever'.

Except his next job was with a German, Peter Schieron, in a restaurant called Loui's. But just before this, he found the other great influence in his life: the Swami Muktananda, and the practice of Siddha Yoga. He met Muktananda in 1978, and went to work in the ashram in Melbourne as chief vegetable chopper—an important post in a vegetarian kitchen. 'Muktananda was a really good monk cook. He embodied everything I admired about being a chef. He expected his kitchens to be run in a certain way. I remember once somebody had a tape recorder playing and he came in and threw it against the wall and smashed it into a thousand pieces. He said what are you focussing on? You should be focussing on your food. It took me two months to perfect the art of precision vegetable chopping.'

It was also around this time that Nouvelle Cuisine was finding its way into the kitchens and onto the tables of Australian restaurants. Michel Guerard's influential book, *La Grande Cuisine Minceur*, had been published in French in 1976, in English in 1977, and had found its way to Australia in a paperback as *Cuisine Minceur* in 1978. The position at Loui's cemented Bill's style: 'We were all eating at each other's restaurants and finding out how Stephanie had adapted a Michel Guerard recipe and Hermann Schneider didn't give a shit, he did his own thing. He was our guru at that stage. That was when the products available snowballed. You'd read crème fraîche—you couldn't buy it but sooner or later someone would make it. Someone would sooner or later start growing or making what you wanted. That's something I've always appreciated about Australia.'

'For me it [Loui's] was a fabulous time. It gave me time to establish myself as a chef. I stayed for five years (with a break in the middle to go to India). I was also then in the height of my yoga practice. No smoking, no drinking, leading a healthy fit life and working in a very focussed manner. And I was working for a German who was as tough as nails on quality. He brought out the Germanic side of me. I knew at one stage I'd tightened it a little too much. When Michael Bacash [now at Toofey's in Carlton, then with Bill in the kitchen] came up to me distraught, with a tomato in his hand and said—there's a spot on this tomato! I thought maybe it's time to relax the guys a little.'

Once again, acting the Gypsy like his parents, in 1981 the Marchettis sold up and moved—this time to India, to an ashram connected with Muktananda's outside Bombay called Ganesh Puri. 'It was absolute bloody paradise.' Bill ran the restaurant for the westerners in the ashram. 'Americans can't eat curry all the time. We set up a restaurant that cooked western food—pioneered a lot of processes replacing eggs. I was a cheesemaker for six months, we had buffalo on the property, we were making mozzarella—bea-uuu-tiful—in India! By the time we left the food was stunning. Forget the yoga, come for the food. Kitchen meditation is what it was.'

Back at Loui's in Melbourne, Bill and Peter Schieron were looking at going into partnership together—but, this didn't work out. Eventually Schieron sold

Loui's to 'a Greek ex-milk bar owner who then wisely sold it to the wife of a refrigeration engineer, who wanted to have a restaurant because she did really good dinner parties. She sat me down and asked me are you a very creative chef? I said I'll be leaving. She said but when I bought the restaurant I thought the chef came along with it. I left. The place folded.'

'But in spite of the fact that I needed my own place, there was this thing called money. I put my name down with a couple of agents to see if there were any restaurants for sale that didn't cost money. I looked at a whole bunch—the going price was $50,000 for a standard BYO. Finally someone rang and said I've got the place for you. It's $18,000, it seats 110 and it's licensed. It was the Latin. When I finally got it [in 1984] I realised I'd paid too much. It had been run into the ground.'

Bill and Cheryl Marchetti bought the Latin from David Triaca, son of Camillo, who, in partnership with Rinaldo Massoni, had bought the Cafe Latin from Phillip Navaretti in 1924. This was the restaurant with the oldest pedigree in Melbourne—even older than Florentino's. The original Cafe Latin in Exhibition Street had been opened by Navaretti in 1919. Navaretti, the son of an editor of the newspaper *Corriere della Sera* in Milan, had come to Australia in 1914 with the Italian Consulate in Melbourne, and married the soprano Elsie Davies before establishing himself as a restaurateur. The Cafe Latin—which later moved to Lonsdale Street, the current site—was the haunt of theatrical and artistic Melbourne, the inheritor of the mantle of Fasoli's. 'The best spaghetti I ever had, I had at the Cafe Latin,' announced one Signor Paoloantonio, a visiting conductor.

This distinguished history makes what the Marchettis found at the Latin even sadder. 'We had three pages of health orders. We had the health inspector in the week after we moved in [they lived in a flat above the restaurant at first]. The health inspector told Bill that they were writing a new manual for training health inspectors and he told him that if you let us take the photos for the manual here we won't have to go anywhere else. That's what we had to work with.'

But make it work they did. And the big decision was—what kind of a restaurant was this new place to be? 'The first year we were there we tried to please everybody. I wanted to attract the Loui's customers, so I put on some Loui's dishes. I also had to keep the 110 customers a week that were already coming—I couldn't afford to lose them—they told me the first day I was there—every Wednesday we have Irish stew. I couldn't quite get myself to make Irish stew so I did a sort of a lamb casserole. That passed.'

'But after a while, when it looked like we weren't going broke just yet, I realised it wasn't doing it for the Loui's customers, and it wasn't doing it for me. And I thought, what do I want to do now? Already at the later stages of Loui's I was heading back towards the Italian—making risotto and my own pasta. And I thought—I'm ready now. I thought—what epitomises to me this sort of freedom, the freedom that means I'm going to cook what I want to cook? It was the spaghetti with squid ink.'

'I remember when I first presented it to our archetypical table of regulars— who'd had the same table for 25 years. The only one I could sell it to was Stan Keon [a Victorian Labor politician]. The table was all Irish Catholic and DLP. Stan was quite an adventurous eater, I could give him all sorts of stuff and he'd eat it. Sooner or later the rest of the table would try some of the less revolutionary dishes. It gave me courage. These were Australian establishment types. If I could get even one of them to eat it there was hope.'

Gradually, Marchetti's Latin became 100 per cent Italian. 'This was in our second year. It wasn't a good commercial move. We put a sign out the front saying "Italian Restaurant". But it had actually been an Italian restaurant all along: an Italian restaurant that served Irish stew every Wednesday. It had the menu I remember from Florentino's in 1968, only badly done.'

It took until 1988 for Marchetti's Latin—now a real Italian restaurant—to turn the corner. Curiously, for a city with a long and distinguished history of Italian restaurants, Melbourne was not keen on Italian food. 'We were very popular in Sydney, but Melbourne couldn't have cared less. If it wasn't for the support of Sydney customers and the Sydney press, like Joan Campbell of *Vogue*, we would have died. By 1988 we were starting to become fashionable. Five years later we were an overnight success.'

'Then we became stricter and stricter trying to introduce Italian specialities, trying to do them the way they would have been done in the region. Also, I developed this idea of Australia being the twenty-first region of Italy. Think about it. If we'd been lucky enough to have been discovered by the Italians rather than the bloody poms, they would have used a lot more of the indigenous ingredients a long time ago. I'm not that far advanced—I'm not as advanced as Stefano [Manfredi], he's gone the next step. He's said, OK, I'll use bok choy, I'll use all these Asian ingredients. I'm still using more classic Italian ingredients.'

But why was it so difficult to establish an Italian restaurant in Melbourne? And why has it been easier for the Manfredis and the Poleses to serve real and regional Italian food in Sydney? Bill's answer is polemical, and will not win him many friends in Carlton. 'Probably because you've never had a Lygon Street.

It's not the same as Leichhardt [Sydney's Little Italy]. Lygon Street here has always been a major cultural and economic force in anything to do with Italy, and it was ruled by a cultural mafia—not the mafia mafia, but like you have the art mafia. These are the same people who cooked one thing at home and a totally different thing for the skips [Anglo-Australians] in their restaurants. And when they relented a little bit, it was still half-arsed.'

But why is this so? 'Maybe,' he offers, 'because they're so parochial, they expect everybody else to be.' This is an interesting theory. And one that crops up often in this book. The wogs won't eat any food but their own: it's the skips who've been culinarily adventurous. He tells a story to show it's not just Italians out of Italy who are like this.

'I went to a Ciao Italia Congress in Italy [Ciao Italia is an arm of the Italian Agriculture Department that fosters links with Italian restaurateurs worldwide to sell them Italian agricultural products]. The first address was by the Italian Under Secretary of Agriculture who was warning us about the Yellow Peril. He said five years ago we had only four Chinese restaurants in the whole of Italy. Now, there are over 100—and they're organising. We have to be vigilant, to keep our cultural integrity. And we're going—heil! Mind you, when you look at these Chinese restaurants [in Italy] they are pitiful. They're all serving a bit of pasta to survive.'

'Then I said to a group of Italian chefs that one of the places I want to try here is Marchese [Gualtiero Marchese's L'albereta outside Milan is one of Italy's leading *nuova cucina* restaurants]. There was stunned silence. I said, you know, Gualtiero Marchese. Is it my pronunciation? I thought, this is weird, so I really pushed the point. I said, you know the guy, he studied with Bocuse. They said, oh, you mean the Frenchman. You don't want to go there—it's French food.'

In 1992 Marchetti opened Marchetti's Tuscan Grill on Little Bourke Street. Designed as a lunch place, it's Bill's idea of a New York brasserie. It was to be run by Cheryl, but the marriage finally succumbed to the strain of the restaurant life. 'You struggle for years, and always take it out on the one that's close to you. But we're still friends.' He's since re-married—Fiona Snedden, the daughter of the late Bill Snedden, who was, curiously enough, Immigration Minister when the Marchettis arrived in Australia. 'On our papers there was the stamped signature of the Minister of Immigration. When I told my father who I was marrying, he said, oh, that's fantastic. My father was a communist from way back, but this was one right-wing politician he always held in high esteem.' While this book was being written, he launched his range of Marchetti pasta. 'Squid ink was the first—it had to be. Porcini, saffron, seaweed, all the flavours known to man and all the colours of the rainbow—I don't know about this one.' He showed me a brilliant blue pasta—I called it Adriatic Blue. He said 'Why not? It's a flower petal shock treated with some high PH level substance.' More recently he's opened The Latin on Crown—in the Crown Casino—and, always, he's struggling with his weight. 'I was having lunch the other day with another restaurateur—steamed fish, mineral water—I thought—this is not the way it's supposed to be.'

But nothing will stop Bill Marchetti. I ask him the standard question—why are Australians so open to all this new food? 'When there isn't a strong dominating culture, something will come in and fill the vacuum. How long can you eat Irish stew? And the Australian mentality is open. Australians have always been great inventors and adaptors. VCRs, the mobile phone, we grab them and chew them up. It's an open mentality that leads to innovation in all ways. We may have lost some pioneering spirit, but, Jeez, I hope we never lose that. This country can do and be anything it bloody well wants to be.'

## _Tripes a la Mode de Caen_    Tripe as cooked in Caen

The food at Cuisine Bourgeoise was a revelation to me. Here was tasty food from recipes centuries old. Everything they did was new and exciting. My particular favourite was this dish of tripe from Normandy. (The following quantities are for a restaurant full of people.)

15 kg 'honeycomb' ox tripe
1 kg pork skin
6 large carrots, sliced
4 onions, diced
200 mL Calvados
2 handfuls of rock salt
ground black pepper
4 whole hot chillies
3 garlic cloves
10 cloves
1 tablespoon dried thyme
2 bay leaves
2 tablespoons MSG
2 bay leaves
5 cups (1.25 litres) dry
 alcoholic apple cider

Wash and dry the tripe. Cut it into pieces about 5 cm square. Cut the pork skin into pieces. Place all the ingredients in a large pot. Bring to a boil, then turn down to simmer for a good 6 hours. Let the pot cool and refrigerate the mixture overnight. Cook for a further 2–3 hours the next day.

_Note:_ The addition of MSG (monosodium glutamate) probably has to do with Michel having spent his French National Service in Vietnam.

## Spaghettini Neri — Spaghettini with Squid in its Own Ink
SERVES 6

Spaghettini is a thin spaghetti.

500 g calamari, cleaned
  and sliced
ink sacs from the calamari
1 cup (250 mL) dry red
  wine
2½ tablespoons virgin
  olive oil
1 teaspoon chopped garlic
2 tablespoons chopped
  anchovies
2 tablespoons chopped
  parsley
2 red hot chillies, seeded
  and sliced
1½ onions, diced
2 medium tomatoes,
  peeled, seeded and diced
salt and pepper
500 g plain spaghettini

To clean the calamari, first detach the tentacles from the main body. Remove and retain the ink sacs. You'll find the ink sac on the upper part of the intestines that come out when you detach the tentacles. It has a shiny, silvery gloss. Remove the long, plastic-like backbone and discard. Remove the wings, then remove all the purple skin from the wings and body. Thoroughly wash the insides, then slice the body into rings and the wings into strips.

Place the squid ink sacs and the red wine together in a saucepan and bring to the boil. Let the ink infuse for a few minutes, then pass the mixture through a strainer. Discard the ink sacs.

Heat the oil in a large, heavy saucepan, add the garlic and sauté very lightly—the garlic should not brown. Add the anchovies and sauté until they are completely dissolved. Add the parsley and chilli and sauté about 5 minutes. Add the onion and sauté until glassy. Add the calamari and sauté for about 5 minutes or until the calamari has changed colour. Add the wine, ink and tomatoes and season. Simmer for about 40 minutes. Adjust seasoning when cooked.

Cook the spaghettini in ample salted water for about 6 minutes (the strands should still be firm).

Add the pasta to the sauce and continue cooking until the spaghettini are *al dente*.

## Risotto al Porcini — Italian Rice with Porcini Mushrooms
SERVES 8 AS AN ENTREE

Frozen porcini may still be a bit hard to find in retail shops. For me they have been one of the great new imports of the last few years. They lend themselves very well to freezing, and when cooked from frozen (which helps to retain their juices), they taste so close to the fresh version, you would have to eat them one after the other to taste the difference. As an alternative use some fresh shiitake mushrooms. The textural contrast between dry and fresh is a bonus.

45 g dried porcini
  mushrooms
150 g frozen porcini
  mushrooms
about 6 cups (1.5 litres)
  meat stock
75 g butter
a little olive oil
1 cup finely diced onion
2½ cups (500 g) Arborio
  rice
salt and freshly ground
  black pepper
⅓ cup (90 mL) white wine
100 g butter
2 tablespoons chopped
  parsley
½ cup (125 mL) thin
  cream
½ cup (60 g) freshly
  grated Parmesan cheese,
  plus extra

Soak the dried porcini mushrooms in a little warm water for several hours. Decant the soaking liquid and set aside.

Take each piece of soaked mushroom individually and rinse it under a tap, being careful to remove all sand and grit. Chop the porcini and set them aside.

Defrost the frozen porcini just enough to be able to cut them into thick slices, then return them to the freezer.

Bring the stock to the boil, then turn it down and keep it at a very low simmer.

In a heavy braising pan, melt the 75 g of butter and add the oil. Add the onions and sauté until they are translucent. Add the soaked and chopped porcini and the rice, season and sauté over a medium heat for a couple of minutes. Deglaze with the wine, simmer and stir until all the liquid has been absorbed.

Now begin adding the porcini soaking liquid and the stock, ladle by ladle, only adding more when the previous stock has been completely absorbed.

Meanwhile, melt the 100 g of butter in a frying pan. Add the frozen porcini mushrooms in a single layer. Fry them to a golden brown colour on both sides, sprinkle with the chopped parsley and set the pan aside.

As the rice gets close to being done (it should take 20–25 minutes in total), be very careful about adding more stock, as the rice should be cooked at the same time as your last addition of stock has been absorbed. Add the cream and Parmesan, stir well, check the seasoning and let it all absorb a few minutes before serving.

To serve: divide the risotto between eight plates and top each portion with the sautéed porcini—juice, butter and all. Provide extra grated Parmesan cheese for sprinkling over the dish.

Rosa Matto.

'Witness my mother—she even brought
her own rolling pin. She had no
intention of falling into whatever
the natives of the new land ate.'

# CHAPTER TEN

# *Rosa Matto*

S UNDAY, SOME time in the 1960s. The Adelaide suburb of Prospect. The back garden of a house whose windows and doors are, inexplicably, barred tight. Two dark-haired, brown-eyed children, about six years old, are eating something, almost furtively, in amongst the tomatoes, the eggplants and the herbs. What is it? It looks like—roast potatoes. It is. It's Armando Matto and his younger sister Rosa enjoying forbidden fruit. There must be a story to these illicit potatoes. There is.

I spoke to Rosa Matto in her cooking school at Goodwood in Adelaide. From the outside, it looks like a large, cream-brick garage with a glass brick wall. Inside, it is a most attractive room, painted in cream and pale Adriatic blue, dominated by a long, dark and light wood, inlaid table, a huge teaching kitchen at the far end, with a curved bench and high chrome and black leather Eames stools. While we spoke, a Spanish cook, Justo del Amo, was preparing the fish for a lesson on northern Spanish dishes.

Rosa is an Australian-born Italian, her parents Alberico and Elvira from the village of Altavilla Irpina in the province of Campana, not far from Naples. 'The Irpini,' Rosa told me, 'were a barbaric band driven out of the north by the Romans.' Altavilla was their last stronghold. 'It reminds me very much of our own Adelaide hills, even in terms of what they grow there—cherries, hazelnuts, chestnuts, pears, apples, olives—which is why I feel comfortable in both places.'

'My parents were *contadini*, they owned some property—at least my father's family owned property. My [paternal] grandfather was a very fair man, which was the downfall of the family. He divided each of his three plots of land into three equal parts [for each of his three sons]—this meant that none of them could make a decent living. After the war, all three brothers came out here. One sister remained, she took over the land, and managed to make quite a good living out of it.'

There was a large migration from Altavilla Irpina to South Australia in the 1950s, and Rosa's parents were among the first of that wave, the three brothers travelling together, leaving their wives and families behind. Armando, Rosa's brother, was one when he left. 'They went to the docks in Naples. There were two ships, one was going to Argentina, one to Australia. It might as well have been Mars. They got on the closest boat. It was as arbitrary as that.' They came to South Australia because 'that's where the boat was landing, and they already knew some people here.'

'My father worked at British Tube Mills, one brother went off to cut cane in Queensland, the third went to Riverland to pick fruit. But they worked together, and bought a house together. The elder brother, Pasquale, brought his family out first, then they saved money for the next brother's, Francesco's, family. My mother was the last, two years after Dad. When she arrived, there were far too many people in the house, so they went off to buy a small house in Thebarton. Just about every Italian family in South Australia started in Thebarton. My mother took in boarders from other families doing the same thing.'

'They all had productive backyards. There are a lot of—uncles I call them, friends of the family is what they are—who still have fabulous backyards, and that's what you talk about when you visit. You'll admire the tomatoes and all that sort of thing. My mother who now lives in a small unit on her own has a back garden the size of a pocket handkerchief, she grows tomatoes and basil and some beans. She doesn't have to, but she does have to.'

I mention that it's as if they had to literally put down roots in this country. 'They do,' agrees Rosa, 'I know that when my mother goes on picnics she'll go off and wander around and find some nettles or wild lettuce and she'll say this will be lovely in the salad. She feels she's made some connection. and the place isn't quite so foreign. I say, Mum, you were only twenty when you came from Italy and you're 63, and you're still trying to make connections with this land. and she'll say, yes, of course. Because she's a foreigner, and she always will be.'

'This was one of the tragedies of my father's life. After 25 years he went back and had a notion that he would sell up and live in Italy. When he got there they loved him, they accepted him, but he was a foreigner. He realised he didn't belong there either. He had to see with his own eyes that it had changed, and hadn't crystallised in the 1951 that he left. It was such a shock to him that he was a changed man when he came back.'

Thebarton is the first suburban migrant community I've heard of on this journey through Mediterranean Australia—most of the Italian and Greek enclaves I've come across—Marrickville, Leichhardt—have been inner city. But 'it's not that far from the city,' Rosa reminds me (nothing in Adelaide is), 'so they still used the Star Grocery [at the bottom of Hindley Street, the same Star used by the Kathreptis family, Chapter 6]. Up on Norwood Parade Mr Vari set up about 1958, and then one of my father's cousins, Pelegrino Matto, had a grocery store in Norwood as well. When we finally moved to Prospect there were other Italian fruit and veg shops and that's where you met everybody.'

They moved out of Thebarton because 'it was never a long-term project. Houses were cheap—you'd buy a small house or a flat and then you'd move on to a place where other Italians were making good. That was Prospect or Campbelltown or Norwood or Rose Park.'

I've mentioned elsewhere in this book my puzzlement over the fact that none of the post-war immigrants developed the piazza or plaza, the public space that is used so effectively around the Mediterranean. One use for this space in Italy and in Spain is the *passeggiata* (*paseo* in Spanish), the slow stroll around the square in a family group before and often after the evening meal. I spoke to Rosa about this, and wondered why, in these Italian dominated suburbs, the custom wasn't revived.

'I can understand why if my father is at all typical. We would go for a drive to the beach to have a *passeggiata*, or go to town and window shop, or walk along North Terrace or go down to Hindley Street and have a gelato from Flash (a well-known gelateria) and the adults would have a coffee. But we wouldn't walk up and down our neighbourhood, because they knew Australians wouldn't understand such a notion. For instance, if ever we said we were going to take a walk down to the park, he said you want everyone to know you have nothing better to do? We had the *passeggiata*, but elsewhere.'

Some years ago, a Roman friend came to Sydney, and we took a *passeggiata* along the boardwalk at Balmoral Beach. It was the first time I had done such a thing with a southern European in my own country, and I remember being shocked (and then delighted) at the pace of his walk. It was slow, deliciously slow, and I had to adjust my pace right down to suit his. I remember noticing how much more slowly we were walking than the other Australians around us on this balmy Sunday evening. I told Rosa this story. 'You're not out to get exercise—they say it's to digest your dinner, but at that pace it would do no good at all.'

But there was another ritual that satisfied many of the needs of the *passeggiata*. 'Mass every Sunday fulfilled the function of being seen, showing off your daughters and other elements of the *passeggiata*. It was an important ritual. We'd dress to the nines, and arrive early enough to have a get-together out the front. If you went to 10 o'clock mass, you'd get home just in time for lunch [which, we'll learn, was designed to cook in exactly that amount of time]. My mother still goes to the church, the Holy Rosary, now they have an Italian mass at 9.30.'

School was the Rosary in Prospect. 'It wasn't Italian, but there were a lot of Italians, so many that the headmistress was threatened by it. My first prickings of social conscience were when I was in Grade 5, and with another influx of Italian migrants—three or four families in the 1960s. They were just off the boats and the children found it much easier to talk in Italian—we felt comfortable with that. I remember Sister Rose Columba taking me into her office and saying she didn't think it was a good idea for the new girls to speak Italian because they'd never learn English. I said it's only at recess and lunch and she said, yes, well, would I just keep an eye on that for her and let her know if we were slipping into Italian? I said no in the only way I knew how as a young child overwhelmed by authority. She got the message. I've never forgiven her for that.'

Another problem—in addition to the inevitable school lunches—was milk. 'All the Italian kids found it very difficult to drink milk, especially when it was warm. The Anglo kids found it less revolting than we did, and they used to tell us how very good it was for us and how lucky we were to be in a country that gives us free milk—and you'd better drink it.'

I wondered what Rosa's parents thought about us Anglos at the time. What was revealed in her answers was a very complex—and uneasy—relationship on both sides.

On the one hand she told me 'My father didn't have a high regard for Australians,' on the other 'we had lovely Australian neighbours who became our friends, but we were almost always on the point of being patronised by them. For example, my father had a fabulous singing voice. We would be invited to a barbecue, and eventually, when they were all drunk—they'd have beerio, making us feel at home by putting an "io" on the end, Dad would have vino—they'd say, Albert—they couldn't say Alberico, or they'd try and make him feel more comfortable by saying Alberto and I'd say, Dad, tell them that's not your name and he'd say oh, don't make a fuss—they'd say Albert, why don't you sing something, and my brother would look at me and we'd cringe, and my mother would sit there sweetly as if she was terribly proud, and Dad would sing "O Sole Mio" and "Figaro" and all the standard tunes and they'd say oh, beautiful Albert, beeeuddiful. It was just excruciating.'

We now come to the forbidden potatoes. 'My father hated the smell of lamb roasts—a lot of Italians do—I love them. On Sunday morning, all of Prospect would have this smell. My father's usual habit was to get up in the morning, open all the windows and go into the garden. On Sundays, he'd get up at the usual time, and shut all the doors and windows tight—to keep the smell out. Our neighbours, the Greys—Aunty Bubs and Uncle Tom we'd call them—would always give me and my brother a roast potato which we thought was fabulous—my mother couldn't roast potatoes—but we weren't allowed to bring them inside, so we had to eat them in the garden.'

As a child, Rosa hated being different. 'I hated the way Dad gave us the impression we were better than anyone else when it seemed to me that we weren't at all because all the things I longed for and wanted were all Australian and Anglo-Saxon.'

How did he imply you were better? 'We were different, our morals were better, we had a higher standard of behaviour and we ate a good deal better. I agreed with that—except for roast potatoes. I felt sorry for fritz and sauce sandwiches and banana chopped up between two pieces of buttered bread, and later, when girls longed to have crisps on their rolls, I thought that was appalling. But all that was overshadowed by the fact that I wasn't blonde and blue-eyed. I had to have freckles—that was the big thing.'

And being Italian, life was very strict for the young Rosa. 'It was always a battle to go to netball and we couldn't play tennis because there was always something better to do like helping my mother or doing my homework. And I lost count of the parties I didn't even bother asking him if I could go to. I couldn't even go on retreat, for goodness' sake, where all we did was pray for two days because we had to sleep over. That's why when people roman-ticise about how wonderful it is to be Italian, and we mustn't lose our traditions, I'm a wet blanket and say I wouldn't keep all of the traditions.'

But she'd keep the culinary ones. What did the family eat during this period? 'Mainly things from the garden. *Melanzane* [eggplant] in summer, and tomatoes, but never enough to make the tomato sauce in the Cooper's beer bottle [an Adelaidean peculiarity of which more later]. We didn't eat a lot of meat, although, every Sunday, Mother would make a *braciola*, a very traditional dish from our part of Italy. It consists of a round or topside of steak beaten quite thinly, filled with chopped garlic, parsley and Parmesan cheese, rolled and tied with string. It's first browned in oil and then covered with a *sugo* [homemade tomato sauce] and simmered slowly so that there's an interchange of flavours. The *sugo* is served with pasta, and then the meat is sliced up and served with vegetables or a tossed salad. Sunday morning, you put the *braciola* on, and turn it right down to simmer. Then you go off to Mass, and it's ready in two or three hours, so you have a really rich, concentrated tomato sauce.'

'We never had dessert. In fact, I don't think my mother knows more than five cake recipes, she'd always buy cakes for special occasions. We'd have fruit and nuts and cheese for afters.'

'There were three or four local cheesemakers who'd work from their backyards—they'd make ricotta, bocconcini, fresh mozzarella, all fresh farm cheeses. We'd walk down and buy our cheese in the morning and have a salad with tomato and basil and oil.'

'We Mattos made wine until quite recently. We used to make our own olive oil, but that fell by the wayside because it got to be too much work. We'd all pick the olives, then take them to a plant in Thebarton and that would be a year's supply. But the men got too old and terrified they'd have a heart attack thrashing the trees. I'm reviving that now.'

'We had our own olive trees up at Morialta [they'd be wild offspring of those planted by Sir Samuel Davenport, see Chapter 6]. They have waterfalls there, so you can imagine the steepness of the slopes. We just knew that no-one else would be foolish enough to go up those slopes. We'd also pick cherries in the hills and Mum would put them in liqueur. We used to spend a lot of time in the hills. I think my parents felt comfortable there.'

Although a strict disciplinarian, Alberico very rarely hit Rosa, but she remembers one of those exceptions well. 'We were very poor and it was the end of the week and we had a soup. A lentil soup, with a boiled potato in the middle and my mother would pour olive oil over the whole lot. Delicious. But as an eight-year-old I thought this was the grossest, most disgusting thing on earth. And I said I'm not eating this, and my father took me outside and thrashed me and said you go inside and say sorry to your mother, and eat every last bit of that. Some years ago I asked my mother if she wouldn't mind making it again, and she refused. She said there was no need to eat like that any more. They'd grown up during the war, and they'd had to make bread from all sorts of things, like chickpeas, and that sense of their own grinding poverty was very real to them. Although we were poor, we never felt poor, because we always ate well and we always had nice clothes to wear, nobody would have known we were poor.'

But the most important food memories for Rosa are the celebrations. 'Wedding culture in early Adelaide was very interesting. I remember when everybody from Altavilla Irpina would be invited to a wedding. At the height of all the marryings, when I was five or six, there might have been two or three weddings a week that we had to go to—so the 200 of us would assemble in a hall, chairs would be set up around the edges of the hall, and they would pass around *panini* with prosciutto or provolone cheese and there would be olives and *lupini* [boiled lupins]. It was just an acknowledgement that this was our community. Gradually it got more sophisticated and there would be a sit-down meal.'

'The times I remember best were the celebratory times for our family, the day after the wedding when the extended family would get together. We would always sit down, we'd never have any food standing up, I still find this an unnatural act. Antipasto would be served—you know how we now have these very contrived platters, ours have never been like that. Depending on what was to follow, the antipasto would be really simple, maybe just a few slices of sausages and some olives that had been cured that year, or some-times a little *caponata* or *peperonata* [cold vegetable dishes]. That would be followed by pasta—for our family always fusilli, the speciality of our family—in Altavilla we make fusilli, the little spiral.'

'Women don't make fusilli on their own. They always call a friend or a sister-in-law or somebody to come and help. They say we need to make enough for twelve people, with 100 g each that's a kilo and a half of flour. You make pasta in the usual fashion, just flour, eggs and, depending on how the eggs are absorbing, a little water. Then you knead for a long time to get the elasticity, cut off a little strip and roll it around the rolling pin. I use my mother's rolling pin. She brought it from Italy.'

Rosa fetched it for me. It was more like a broomstick than a rolling pin, maybe a metre and a half long, and thin. She held it up for inspection. '42 years old. 42 years of constant rolling. She didn't know what she'd find here, even though my father would write and say you can get everything here, don't worry about it. She didn't believe that, so she brought her own rolling pin, two big white bowls, all the pasta goes into those, and twelve special dishes to eat pasta.'

'So you roll it out flat and thin, and as you keep rolling, you flip it around to get more air in it so you can roll it even finer and you make a big circle. Roll that sheet, fold it over and cut it into long strips, 10 centimetres long. Then, with the finest knitting needle—the one you use to make baby's clothes—put the needle across the end of the strip and then press it round so the rest of the strip rolls itself around the needle, and then you just pull it off.'

'When you start watching the oldies doing it, they go at such a cracking pace, they get it done in no time, whereas I'm sitting there consciously rolling and I do about three to their 30. It's a social occasion for them, they get together and they chat, they make enough to feed the gathering and some extra to take home.'

At twelve, Rosa left the Rosary school and went to St Dominic's. As she grew older, so too did she grow more comfortable with being Italian. 'I don't know whether I gave up the struggle in high school or I thought, no, I don't really belong there [with the Anglos]. I embraced Italianness in high school in a big way. It certainly was more tolerant. There were lots of groups—the girls who played tennis hung round together, the girls who liked horses, and then there was us, the Italians. We were very supportive of each other.'

After dutifully applying for, and getting, a job as a bank teller (what her parents wanted), she 'got cold feet and turned it down'. She matriculated and went to university to study teaching—something she had always wanted to do.

At university, she became the first female president of the Italian University Club. 'I felt I'd found a group of people with whom I was comfortable and to whom I belonged'—and then married an Australian, Stephen English, who she met on her first teaching job. 'I was sent off to Keith area school on the edge of the Ninety Mile Desert—and culturally on the edge is how it is. I was there three years and he was the only other interesting person on the entire staff. He could smell the coffee I was making from his house and he'd walk over and say I see you're making coffee, and it grew from there. It was the coffee really.'

It was only when she left home and set up flat on her own that she began cooking—her mother did most of the cooking at home, and not cooking was, she suspects, a part of her rejection of Italianness, 'but then when we sidled up to the table and ate all this delicious food it was no hardship at all.'

Living alone she found that 'cooking for yourself is so boring I'd invite people over to share with me. I worked my way through Margaret Fulton from fondues to Beef Wellington— there's nothing in her *Complete Cookbook* I haven't tried. Except I never really got baked potatoes right and decided I didn't like them. Then I went through a French phase.'

After thirteen years of teaching [English, history and drama] like a lot of teachers she began to ask herself what she was going to do with the rest of her life. 'The only other thing I could do was cook—and by that time people were asking me to cook dinner parties for them. So I thought I could make a living from this.'

All during this learning period, the telephone to her mother was running hot. 'She'd always say things like, why do you want to cook that for heaven's sake? Polenta, for instance, we make a lovely *pasticcio* [pie] with polenta, and my mother would say why do you want to make *pasticcio*, why don't you make something special, which for her would have been meat. Eventually she gave up and she'd ring me if she had a bounty of beans. Then I began to cook with her in the kitchen and she hasn't been able to get me out since. The first thing I do when I go to her place now is say what are you cooking Mum and look in her pots and pans. She'll always make something nice at lunch on the off-chance that my brother might turn up—which he often does.'

The next logical step for someone of an academic turn was to get formal training. 'When I started doing dinner parties people would ask me where did you train—in terms of credibility I felt I needed to do something. So I went off to Regency Park and that was an experience in itself. Remember this was ten years ago. We had the Swiss mafia there then. I did ice statues, margarine sculpture. It was an appalling time. I did very well because I knew how to study, so I used to get distinctions. It wasn't very challenging.'

On the positive side, 'I learnt classical French technique and lots of classical terminology. I did see some fantastic chefs with wonderful skills who were hopeless teachers. I also learnt what I didn't want to do. That's where my fascination with French restaurant food ended—and I realised I didn't want to be a restaurant cook.'

'I had to do a six-week placement with a restaurant, and I'd been to a dinner party catered for by [Algerian-born Frenchwoman, Adelaide caterer and food writer] Catherine Kerry. So I rang her up out of the blue and asked if I could do it with her. Two years later I was still there, learning the most extraordinary things. Above all learning that this was the kind of food I wanted to cook because this was the kind of food I loved to eat—Mediterranean, gutsy flavours.'

'She would say to me, here are some capsicums, do something Italian, do whatever you like. I'd cook them and we'd sit down and eat them and talk about them. She'd ask why did you put breadcrumbs on this, and I'd say, I don't know, that's just the way we do it. And that would send me back to my books and I'd work out why we did it. You see breadcrumbs were used a lot in the south of Italy, they were a substitute for Parmesan—breadcrumbs were the poor man's Parmesan, fried and sprinkled over the top of pasta and then toasted. It was a great way to learn.'

But she was also still learning from her mother. 'All the time she'd surprise me by doing something entirely new, and I'd say where did this come from? And she'd say, oh we always do that. I'm 40 for God's sake, why has it taken 40 years to emerge? Then I discovered my guru, Marcella Hazan.'

When Catherine Kerry went to take over the Bridgewater Mill Restaurant at Petaluma, Rosa took over her catering business, a lot of which was board-room lunches, which fitted in very well with motherhood—during this time she had Nicholas and Stephanie.

And then she bought the school. 'I always taught the odd class anyway—once a teacher, always a teacher.' The classes she runs are small, everybody sitting around the curved bench, watching closely the work of the cook. Her students are often professionals who come after work, 'and a few housewives who do a lot of entertaining' which can cause a few problems.

'Basically Italian food doesn't fit into dinner parties the way we give them in Australia. The Italian meal doesn't divide neatly into entree, main meal and dessert. We have a first course, and a second course—not necessarily smaller or bigger—the fusilli is always the first course—antipasto doesn't figure as a course—and it's followed by a smaller meat course. I always battle with people who want to divide their menus into three courses. And even though the three course structure is breaking down, we still have people coming to classes and saying but could you serve that as an entree? Or you serve something on a platter and it looks fantastic and they ask but could you plate it up for eight people?'

I told her that George Haddad bowed to pressure with Lebanese food and devised ways of serving it within the three course structure. 'I oppose that most strenuously. Especially with Middle Eastern food, part of it is the way it is eaten. You do no-one a service by teaching them something that's cul-turally wrong. There's a reason for pasta being the first course, so it fills you up, so that the second course, which might be a tiny bit of meat, can be divided between six people as a taste with a salad.'

I suggest that all this change is part of the new way we're doing things in Australia. Rosa doesn't accept that argument, and feels that in many cases 'the way we're doing things' is the wrong way.

'I'm sure you've noticed a cafe on every corner here in Adelaide.' I have. 'I think what that's done is set Italian food back about fifteen years. We'd just got to the point where people were beginning to understand there's more to Italian food than Southern Italian food—is there life beyond tomato sauces and fusilli? Well, of course there is. There are nineteen other regions who cook entirely differently and have a history and an integrity all of their own. These cafes have reinstated the notion that all Italians eat is tomato sauce and pasta. It might suit me but does it do any good for the rest of Italian food?'

Rosa has spent some time in Italy, and 'I feel very comfortable in Italy— but I don't feel comfortable in the village. I like wandering about in the hills and spending time with some of my cousins, but their world view is so constricted I get claustrophobic.'

When she went back did she recognise the flavours? 'Yes, there was no shock. They transported their cuisine intact. I think that's because they had no intention of cooking any other food. Witness my mother—she even brought her own rolling pin. She had no intention of falling into whatever the natives of the new land ate.' It is, of course, this culinary insularity that has brought us a new way of eating.

'In Italy, they don't eat anything else. They are so closed-minded it's ter-rifying. Here in Australia, we're so absorbent—we take things in and we change them. I don't think there'd be a household in South Australia that doesn't have a wok. Whether they know what to do with it is beside the point.' I ask why she thinks we are so open.

'We weren't threatened. Australians as a group are open to new influences. They don't feel they are going to be swamped—the majority of them—by any particular thing or group. They are ready and willing to absorb and learn. The trouble is we've got the smattering of all these little bits and pieces and we sometimes put them together in an appalling way.'

On the other hand, she loves the fact that in Adelaide's Central Market, 'we've got our little Chinatown cheek by jowl with all the European stuff— you get your eggplant and basil then whip over and buy some coriander.'

She thinks that 'our Central Market and our delis have done more to educate Australian palates than all the restaurants put together. We certainly didn't learn a great deal about Italian food from eating in Italian restaurants. But you can go to your local deli and say my recipes ask for *pancetta*—what is it? and he'll cut you a bit off and you'll say it's a bit fatty and then he'll explain you've got to have a bit of fat it's good for you.'

In many ways Adelaide is the most intriguing food city in Australia. Not only is there that astonishing roster of chefs whose careers began and developed there (see the Lew Kathreptis story, Chapter 6), there is a real culinary culture. In addition to the chefs, the city boasts two of Australia's most interesting food writers—Michael Symons (*The Shared Table, One Continuous Picnic*) and Barbara Santich (*The Original Mediterranean Cuisine*)—and it's the birthplace of the Symposium of Australian Gastronomy. And then there's tomato sauce in Cooper's beer bottles.

I first came across these big Cooper's beer bottles full of tomato sauce at the Wedgetail, a superior pizza joint in Newtown, Sydney. It's run by Peter Oxley, who insists that his entire staff drink only Cooper's, and only in the big bottles so that he can make tomato sauce every year. But it wasn't until I spent a little time roaming around Adelaide, and spoke to Rosa and others, that I discovered the extent of this Cooper's tomato sauce culture. All along the highway to Virginia, I ran into signs saying SAUCING TOMATOES FOR SALE and TOMATO CRATES HERE—and this in late March, beyond the official tomato saucing season. It is an extremely serious business. Rosa explained it to me, at least as practised by the Mattos.

'Any time after Christmas and until about early March you can make your own tomato sauce. You start by going off and picking your own tomatoes. They have to be uniformly ripe. We always start early in the morning because it doesn't matter what day we choose, it always turns out to be the hottest day of the summer. My mother washes the tomatoes and puts them in a copper to blanch them. Then you put them through a *spremipomodoro*, a tomato press—we've got an electric one but you can get little hand-cranked ones. You put the blanched tomato in, the juice comes out with no seeds and no pips, the flesh all pulverised. That goes into the bucket, and we put the skins back for a second run. The solid pulp is fed to the chickens.'

'Then you put three big leaves of basil into the bottom of each Cooper's bottle, fill them, cap them, boil them for 20 minutes in the copper, and let them cool. You end up with a delicious bottle of tomato purée.'

'We're doing what the restaurants should have done but have never done— beginning with the basics. I've always found that unless you make the tomato sauce in the Cooper's beer bottle, the finished product won't taste as good as ours. You've still got to work with that tomato sauce—you've got to fry off your onions and garlic, and reduce it a little.'

'We make it in the cooking class, there's a kind of co-operative. We also make our own olive oil and our own wine. It's called Our Own. My husband is taking the class off to pick the grapes next week. This year it'll be a pinot meunier.'

What Rosa Matto is doing with her classes and her olive oil, Cooper's beer bottle tomato sauce and winemaking activities is perpetuating and spreading this culture, in a lasting and tangible way, out into Anglo culture—beginning in the home. 'My husband,' she told me shaking her head, 'is more Italian than I'll ever be.'

# Fresh Cheese

This simple and quick-forming cheese can be made with cow's, goat's or sheep's milk. Most milks have been pasteurised which kills lactic acid bacteria, and this has to be re-introduced. This can be done with cultured buttermilk, rennet (an extract from the stomach of unweaned calves) or junket (a starter enzyme).

The baskets that we use to separate the curds and whey have given cheese its name. In Greek, a basket is 'formos' which gave rise to the French word 'fromage' and the Italian 'formaggio'. The Latin word for basket is 'caseus' which became 'cheese' in English and 'käse' in German.

The whey which results from this cheese is the basis for 'ricotta', which means 'to cook again'.

4 cups (1 litre) whole milk
2 junket tablets

With a fork, squash the tablets and dissolve them in a few drops of water. Meanwhile, in a saucepan over a medium heat, heat the milk until luke warm, stir in the junket, and stir until separated.

With a slotted spoon, transfer the curds to a basket lined with muslin or cheesecloth, sitting on a rack.

When set, in about 1 hour, serve with a tomato and oregano salad, or oily preserves such as *funghi sott'olio* (mushrooms in oil).

# Sugo alla Braciola
## Meat Roulade with Tomato Sauce

SERVES 4

**BRACIOLA**
250 g topside, beef or veal, sliced thinly
1 garlic clove, chopped finely
chopped Italian flat-leaf parsley
Parmesan cheese
salt and pepper
cotton thread or kitchen twine

**SUGO**
2 tablespoons olive oil
2 garlic cloves, left whole
1 bottle of homemade tomato sauce (see page 146 for method)
salt and pepper
a few basil leaves

To make braciola, beat the beef or veal gently until thin.

Scatter the garlic, parsley and Parmesan all over the meat, season with salt and pepper. Roll the meat to enclose all the seasonings, tie the roll with string as if it were a salami.

To make sugo, heat the oil in a saucepan over a medium heat, add the garlic and cook until it colours but does not burn. Remove and discard. Add the rolled up braciola to the flavoured oil and brown well all over.

Turn down the heat and add the bottle of tomato sauce all at once. With a little water, rinse out the bottle and add this to the saucepan. Allow the sauce to come just to the boil, turn the heat right down as low as possible and allow to simmer for about 1½ hours. The sauce should be rich and thick by this stage.

Season with salt and pepper and some torn basil leaves.

To serve: this sauce, which can be kept in the refrigerator for 3–4 days or even frozen, is now ready for use with pasta. Remember, toss the sauce through the pasta and reserve a little to finish off the top of the pasta.

The braciola will become the second course, with *spinaci al olio e limone* [spinach with oil and lemon] or green beans or a tossed salad.

Reserve a small amount of sugo to dress it; you will find it a delicious second course.

# Pasta con la Mollica
Pasta with Breadcrumbs

SERVES 4

I find this dish delicious as it is and often serve it as a first course at lunch. My mother finds this hugely amusing. She always jokes that I enjoy playing '*la contadina*' [the country peasant woman] in my comfortable suburban villa, making olive oil in winter, and bottling tomatoes in summer with my hair tied in a scarf.

She has eaten as a 'peasant' all her life, except now, as a pensioner, she can no longer afford to. Moreover, it is precisely because of people like me, she says, who have pushed up the prices of foods that were once condemned as 'wogfood'—foods like her beloved *baccala* [salted cod], or the humble rabbit, even polenta and macaroni are now sold as fashion accessories!

½ cup (125 mL) olive oil
2 garlic cloves
125 g anchovies
2 tablespoons chopped fresh parsley
3 medium tomatoes, peeled, quartered and seeded
salt and freshly ground black pepper
6 tablespoons white bread
350 g penne or spaghetti

Bring a large saucepan of salted water to the boil.

In a small saucepan, heat up half the oil with the garlic and cook until the garlic is brown. Discard the garlic and add the anchovies. Mash thoroughly in the oil, then stir in the parsley and tomatoes. Season.

Crush the bread into coarse crumbs and mix them with the remaining oil. Place on a baking tray and toast lightly in a hot oven at 200°C (390°F).

Cook the pasta in the boiling salted water until tender. Drain well. Pour the sauce over the pasta and toss together. Drain and transfer to an ovenproof dish. Scatter over the toasted breadcrumbs and return to the oven for 2 minutes.

## *Spinaci al Olio, Aglio, Limone e Peperoncino*

Spinach with Oil, Garlic, Lemon and Chilli

In my family we adore spinach, silverbeet, endive, dandelion—any green with a sharp, bitter flavour. We serve this dish with a twice-cooked polenta 'cake' or add the greens to a rustic 'zuppa'—a mixture of greens, potatoes, zucchini flowers, whatever is on hand, cooked at length in a single pot. This spinach dish is also good with a smoky, char-grilled steak.

1 bunch spinach
2 large garlic cloves,
  peeled and left whole
chopped fresh chilli to
  taste
½ cup (125 mL) best
  quality olive oil
lemon juice
salt and freshly ground
  black pepper

Wash and then blanch the spinach in a little boiling water. Drain well and squeeze out excess moisture.

Put the garlic, chilli and olive oil in a pan over a medium heat. When the garlic begins to brown, remove it and discard.

Add the spinach to the pan and warm it through in the flavoured oil, pour over the lemon juice and season with salt and pepper.

# Granita di Limone

Lemon Granita

When we spoke together in my kitchen, you asked me about my earliest food memory. Stupidly, after a lifetime of sustenance, I could remember nothing. All my memories are bound up with food. Perhaps the most enduring, most sensual and, because my father is gone, most emotive food memory is of the beautiful granita he used to make.

In the summer, the evenings would be spent on the raised back verandah, our very own piazza, trying to catch every breeze. The highlight would be Dad's granita—sometimes sticky and sweet espresso coffee, but more often lemon.

Apparently, it could only be made in the old-fashioned, tin ice-cube trays. Only Dad would know when it was just right to scrape the freezing mass into a sloppy mush, re-freeze it and repeat the whole operation several hours later.

I remember the mischievous gleam in his eyes as we danced around his feet, and his mock sternness as he returned to the verandah, shaking his head at our naughty impatience. When it was ready, we ate the granita with a teaspoon out of those unbreakable water tumblers that every Italian family owned.

Now I have an ice cream machine and can churn out utterly delicious sorbets in 20 minutes flat. Every time I do so, I think of him.

1¼ cups (310 g) white sugar
2¾ cups (700 mL) water
juice of 3 large lemons
finely chopped zest of 1 lemon

Place the sugar and water in a medium saucepan and bring to the boil, stirring until all the sugar has dissolved. Allow to cool and add the juice and zest. Allow to cool completely.

Spoon into freezer trays and, just before it sets, remove and break up all the large ice crystals with a fork. Put back in the freezer for another hour or so, then repeat this operation. The more times you break up the crystals, the finer the result will be, but always aim to do it at least three times.

Dennis Mifsud at his home in El Dorado, north-eastern Victoria.

*'You can take snippets from
different cultures, different
ingredients. Some things
work together.'*

# CHAPTER ELEVEN

# Dennis Mifsud

S OMEWHERE IN Burma. 1983. A young man with long black hair and big brown eyes is squatting beside a Burmese woman who's holding a cooking pot. He's chewing slowly and thoughtfully on something that looks like . . . it is, it's a grasshopper. She looks on apprehensively. He smiles a deep, slow smile and nods his head. He likes it. She beams at him. He pulls a notebook and a pen from his pocket and—mainly in mime—asks her how she cooked it.

The young man was Dennis Mifsud, who is, at the time of writing, the chef at the 100-year-old Vine Hotel in Wangaratta in north-eastern Victoria. The trip there was a long and circuitous one, during the course of which he picked up a heritage, a philosophy—and a style of cooking informed by influences as diverse as the Mediterranean—specifically Malta—Vietnam, India, Sumatra and Switzerland. In the techniques, ingredients and predilections that Dennis has brought back with him from his travels (and absorbed from his culture) he embodies the diversity that characterises the way we're cooking in Australia at the end of the twentieth century.

We spoke in the family home not far from Wangaratta. His partner Louise, a doctor, was pregnant at the time with their son Pepe. The house, right on the edge of the small hamlet of El Dorado (curiously and coincidentally where Sydney restauranteur Gay Bilson's father's family came from), had a calm and peaceful air about it, with Indian artifacts and fabrics scattered throughout. I wasn't surprised to learn later that on his travels, Dennis has embraced Buddhism.

Dennis Mifsud's parents Vincent and Doris are Maltese. Vincent came here as a 'ten quidder' in 1956 from the village of Qrenda (pronounced Rendi) on the southern side of this tiny (316 square kilometres) island, little more than a rock in the Mediterranean halfway between Sicily and Libya—

a geographical location reflected in the Maltese language, which is an Italian/ Arabic melange. 'The Qrenda side is very peasant,' Dennis told me, 'harsh, rocky, hilly, mainly a tomato-growing area. The other side, around St Paul's Bay, is the tourist side, the beautiful side.' Qrenda is in an area known as Ouid Ouseri, and this is also where the fishing boats are, the *luzzu*; like ornately painted giant gondolas, they go out with kerosene lamps into the middle of the Mediterranean.

Vincent was eighteen when he left, having served as a despatch motor cycle rider with the army, and worked as a mason, chipping away bits of the island for housing. He landed in Melbourne where he had brothers and sisters in the Richmond area. 'He was very homesick, and he didn't like it. He was also in love. That was one of the problems: he was in love with this woman in Malta and he left because he thought he was doing the right thing. He's always been a bit of a rebel, my father, and he didn't conform to the ideals of this girl's parents. And he wanted a bit of a change—so he came to Australia.'

'He got tired of Melbourne. He had one brother, Paul—his closest—in Perth and this brother said Perth was just like Malta, so he went there. Paul was married to Celia, and Celia had a sister—Doris. It went from there.'

Once again he joined the army as a despatch rider. 'He's always loved motorbikes. There's quite a story of him riding his motorcycle into one of the *gazeens* in Qrenda. A *gazeen* is a drinking house, and every village has two of them. They're politically oriented left or right, and they're usually across the road from one another. They brew beer there. There's a photograph of him driving his big BSA up the steps of the opposition *gazeen*— he rode into the hall, did a big wheelie, and rode out. The photo's still hanging in Qrenda.'

'Then he got into factory work, and ended up working for Vickers as a mechanical fitter, he went to school and did mechanics and hydraulics. Much later, he took a retirement package, and now works as a gardener with the council.'

Dennis was born in 1963 and has a younger brother David and a sister Leanne. He remembers his father coming home from work smelling of engine oil, and being in the kitchen with Doris 'licking the bowl—I've always had a good appetite. And I've always liked Maltese food, never went off it.'

Weekends were spent 'going down to Fremantle and pigging out on fish, and of course going fishing—we were Maltese. In those early days lots of

Italians and Maltese would fish off the wharfs at Fremantle, the Australians weren't into it. It wasn't such a big thing in their diet.'

The Maltese eat a lot of fish, game birds, goat—'not a lot of meat, mainly because the island isn't big enough—rabbit is probably one of the biggest meats. Italian food has been integrated into the Maltese diets, and lots of grains. There was a period when they ate a lot of couscous, and a lot of people still cook with it, but polenta has taken over—same basic idea, I guess.'

I remark that it's curious that polenta, a northern Italian dish, should be popular in such a southern part of the world. 'Probably because there's a lot of maize grown on the island,' Dennis suggests.

His mother was a good cook who cooked Maltese food 'four or five days a week, the other days she'd cook Australian, lots of lamb. I guess all of a sudden there was all the produce that wasn't available in Malta and she felt she had to use it or she'd never become an Australian. It was also because she was a true cook—always bringing new things into our diet. But deep down, she always cooked the Maltese things better.'

Because he was part of a large Maltese and Italian community—'the school was run by the Maltese and Italian kids'—there were no problems with prejudice when he was growing up. 'Everyone seemed to get along. There was friction, but there's friction everywhere. But not between the Maltese and the Italians. We befriended the Italians, at least in our area we did.'

Dennis starting cooking in secondary school. 'Basic home economics classes—that would have been the mid-70s. I never really got into football, but I always found food interesting. And, obviously at that age, women are not so much taboo as a mystery—they're things that you desire, but still a mystery. So I had two male friends and it probably started out as a joke—you know, what shall we do, let's do cooking—it had to have something to do with girls as well, getting involved in home economics, a way to break down barriers. And then after the first year, I really enjoyed it. But I was the only one who carried it through.'

'I started cooking at home. I'd go home with a hot cross bun recipe or something—we'd have them from one end of the kitchen to the other. Then I cooked through the next two years of secondary school. In year 10 we were making sauce Anglaise, emulsion sauces—it was a bit like Presbyterian women's cooking classes—you see the books lying around everywhere, Welsh rarebit and all that sort of stuff. It was good for me, I wasn't exposed to a lot of that stuff—the only Australian dishes we cooked were roasts and the barbecue. The Maltese community liked the barbecue, the blokes cooked and the women made the salads. That came from looking at their Australian neighbours.'

'At the same time a lot of Maltese food involves barbecuing—and stone oven cooking. That's been left behind, but it still exists in Malta—a lot of the houses haven't been modernised so the baker will have a huge oven and on Sunday everyone will go with their goat with potatoes or the big *lampuka* [dolphin fish or, more commonly in Australia, *mahi mahi*, *Coryphaena hippurus*—definitely not dolphin, *Delphinus delphis*] stuffed with garlic, onions and tomato and throw them in the oven.'

Young Dennis wasn't academically minded. 'I learnt things from being shown rather than reading. I didn't have the advantage of a mother and father helping me because they didn't understand the language well enough to help me. I thought I wanted to go into the metal industry—you always want to follow your father. So I left school in year 10 and—this was in 1978–79—I was after an apprenticeship, but the applications hadn't come out, I had six months to kill, so I worked in a restaurant. I had an aunty working in the European bakery in a smorgasbord place called Miss Maud's, run by Maud Edmonston. I started as a dishwasher. All of a sudden I had all this money coming in—about $40 a week—and I was meeting all sorts of people, chefs who had travelled all over the world, hearing their stories and adventures. Then I got accepted for an engineering apprenticeship.'

'I went to the manager, a strong Dutch woman. When I told her I was going to leave, she dragged me into her office, sat me down, and said, right, I'm giving you a quick lesson in life. You go into the metal industry, you're going to be dirty, you'll be doing hard physical work, and you'll be with men all the time. She talked me out of it.'

He did his apprenticeship at Miss Maud's, 'a year in patisserie, six months in butchery, a year in banquet.' Miss Maud's began life as a Swedish coffee shop, then provided open sandwiches, then opened a European à la carte restaurant and a banquet centre.

'It was good training. There were all these good European chefs coming through. I remember one, Wally, a Swiss German, a real authoritarian, seven of the twelve apprentices left the second week he was there. All of a sudden it became a brigade system. A very professional environment.'

When he finished his apprenticeship, the wanderlust that has been the constant in Dennis' life took hold. 'I'd had this fascination with Asia during my apprenticeship—hippie culture, marijuana, Indian clothes, all those things. A New Zealand friend was on his way to the UK. We were having a few drinks one day and he said, look, I'll make a deal with you, I'll come to Asia with you if you come to England with me.'

'Initially it was going to be a quick trip, with Bali first. We travelled through Asia experiencing all this food! A lot of places we stayed we had access to the kitchens, and we weren't moving too fast so we went to the markets—we were introduced to all these new things—rambutan, durian, mangosteen.'

They travelled on past Bali to Java and Sumatra, which in Dennis' opinion had 'the best food. The Batak people cook Padang food, lots of fish pâté and shrimp paste curries—I'd never experienced curries like that before.'

And he began to run out of money. 'We were only supposed to be away six weeks. Back in Perth I had this motorbike I'd restored, a '72 Supersport Ducati. Dad sold it for me. We flew out of Sumatra, and ended up in Penang. Wonderful food—we spent a month there eating.'

His friend went on to England, but Dennis kept on travelling—eating, collecting recipes and ingredients, talking to local cooks, generally absorbing the cultures, and laying the foundation for his lifelong love of this part of the world. He travelled through Thailand, and then on to Burma, where he discovered some of the more exotic ingredients. 'Pickled hornets, lizards, fried grasshoppers. I wasn't put off by them—I tried everything.'

Then on through Bangladesh, and, finally, India. 'I spent that whole year travelling in India and Nepal. I've spent quite a lot of time in India since then, it's my main focus.' The nineteen-year-old Maltese-Australian boy had found his spiritual home, but not yet his heritage. That was to come.

He didn't make it to London ('I lost the bet') and ended up back in Perth 'full of new ideas'. It was 1983, he had an apprenticeship in European cooking under his belt, and 'a massive overload of Asian cooking, Asian ingredients. I went away from my ethnic background. I knew how to cook those things anyway—I could do a rabbit stew blindfold—so a lot of the food I was experimenting with was Asian based.'

And in the kitchen of the restaurant at the Prince's Hotel he found a like-minded chef. 'Chris Hobin. He'd worked in Singapore and Hong Kong and had a fascination with Asian food too. We connected immediately. He gave me lots of room, I ended up becoming saucier there. He was getting some exposure at the time. I remember an orange roughie with a prawn and star anise mousse and a mandarin and ginger sauce.'

He lasted a year in Perth, then it was back to Asia—this time the east coast of Malaysia, Thailand and India—before heading over to London. By then his New Zealand friend had left.

Dennis landed a job at the Waterside Inn with the celebrated Roux Brothers, but it didn't suit his temperament. 'I had energy to burn and working there was too restrictive—you've got 35-year-old chefs wanting to work with these guys. I was in my twenties, no way was I going to get to chef de partie quickly enough.' He does concede that 'there was a discipline there, but you had to work for a year before they remembered your name.' Dennis lasted four weeks.

He went to the London International Hotel, a place that 'probably didn't fit the social scene after working for the Roux Brothers' but he'd heard the saucier was leaving and he wanted the job. 'They put me on as commis chef with a possibility of getting chef de partie sauce. The chef was worried by Australian cooks—he reckoned they worked the winter and when summer came around they were off. No, I told him, I'm not like that, I want to be a really good chef. After six months I got a letter from my father saying he was going to Malta. I did get the chef de partie job. It was really full on—a bit more than my capabilities. I could have stayed, the wages were good.' But he headed off to join his father in Malta.

'I didn't tell him I was coming—I still never tell them when I'm arriving.' Dennis hitchhiked through Europe, from Amsterdam to Switzerland where he worked for a while, and developed a fondness for *spätzle* [small dumplings]: 'it lends itself nicely to cream sauces, lovely just with a jus.'

He continued on down through Italy ('the women beautiful, the wine expensive') to Sicily, which he loved. 'It had a rawness about it, more peasant. I'd travelled through Asia so I didn't mind ratty old tables or chipped glasses, but the food was really good.' He spent time in Palermo and Siracusa, met a 'wild Sicilian woman with a Lambretta' who helped him talk his way onto a liner headed for Malta.

'And suddenly, right there in front of me, was this place I originated from. I got this overwhelming feeling—this is Malta, this is the place I've heard about all my life. There was ocean, ocean, ocean and then there was a rock. I couldn't wait to get off. I remember rabbiting away in Maltese to anyone who looked Maltese. I was so proud to be able to speak the language. You couldn't shut me up.'

He looked up the aunt whose address his father had given him. 'Long hair, unshaven, torn jeans, dirty backpack, knocked on the door of this marble palace. This is one of Dad's sisters who'd married into a wealthy family—there's a bit of animosity, he's a politician, she married into the opposition—the wrong *gazeen*. She opened the door, a look of horror on her face. I said I'm Vincent's son. She leapt out at me and dragged me in.'

He went looking for his father, who'd arrived five days earlier and hadn't been sighted since. 'We went looking for him. This guy staggering down the street—it was Vincent. He walked straight past me because I had long hair. He said gidday to my cousin Francis then saw me and said what the fuck are you doing here? For him it was like reliving his childhood. He took me everywhere. He caught up with the girlfriend he'd left behind. She'd become a nun because she couldn't love anyone else. It's a very passionate country, very emotional, they go by their word, die by the sword.'

Of course he cooked there. 'One of my uncles had a restaurant, Maltese food. Lots of rabbit stew, baked macaroni, char-grilled quail. I had a wild time. Picking tomatoes, drinking wine—the wine is like Cliff Booth's Taminick (a north-eastern Victorian wine), dirty, cloudy, gutsy.'

'I went out fishing for *lampuka* with my uncle. They take palm fronds, put out some buoys and make a canopy with the fronds on the water and they put a bit of feed under it. The fish think it's night-time, and shelter there. The fishermen go around with a net—the hardest part is pulling them up.'

His father left after five months, and Dennis didn't last much longer. 'Once Dad left I got a bit tired of lazing around.' He went back to England, then to Australia via Poland, Russia and Bangkok.

This time he went to Melbourne first, worked at Lynchs and the Rockman Regency, and then back to Perth and the late Laurie Connell's Mediterranean. He had it in mind to go to Sydney, but ended up in Adelaide, where he stayed four years and worked at Mistress Augustine and the Mandarin Duck Bistro. 'That was really great, I worked there with Cedric Eu, that was East meets West food' then at Jolly's Boathouse with Gordon Parkes—'a good duck chef.'

In 1989 he met Louise Marsh, then doing her internship at a Melbourne Hospital, having just finished medicine at Adelaide University. They met at a friend's house in Adelaide, and shortly after, Dennis moved to Melbourne to be near Louise, and there ran a Spanish *tapas* restaurant, Cha Cha's. '*Tapas* were all the rage, and I found it easy. Nice, simple food, provincial European food.'

He and Louise both made trips to India during this period, where Louise, now a doctor, worked in a hospital at Dharmsala in Himachal Pradesh, the centre for most of the Tibetan refugees in India. This time Dennis taught English, and continued his Buddhism studies, which he'd begun in 1983, and developed a taste for *chang*, the Tibetan barley beer. 'It's a bit like Cooper's. It would be more so if they roasted the barley; I suggested it, but they said no, no.'

During one of these trips they visited Vietnam, and he got a chance to try first-hand the food he'd been cooking for some time. 'I've always cooked it, it's simple food with great, clean flavours, you eat it and you feel like it's doing you good.'

And then, after a spell in England where Louise worked, they came back to Australia, and to Wangaratta, where Louise worked at the local hospital until they had Pepe. Dennis was thinking of leaving the kitchen for a while, and toyed with the idea of making furniture, when Paul Green, the licensee of the Vine Hotel, offered him the kitchen. He took over in February 1994. Wangaratta is not a name immediately associated with gastronomic adventure, but it's in this kitchen that Dennis has begun to develop his own brand of Australian food.

I remember the first time I was taken there by local cheesemaker David Brown of Milawa Cheese. The dining room at the Vine is a little like Dennis' food—conspicuously eclectic. The decor incorporates curious domestic artifacts from the early twentieth century to about 1965. Licensee Paul Green, who himself only took over the hotel in 1990, told me that he was shocked into inactivity by this room, which he was, initially, going to renovate before deciding that it was some sort of important archaeological site, and needed to be preserved intact.

I'd certainly never had a plate of baked goat's cheese (from Milawa Cheese) strewn with chunks of baked capsicum and cloves of garlic the size of elephant's toes in a country pub in Australia before. But somehow the food seemed to mesh perfectly with the huge red wines of the region—Cliff Booth's aforementioned Taminick a case in point.

Many of the locals were as shocked as I was at Dennis' food, but not so positively. 'I changed two-thirds of the menu when I took over here. It was a basic steak and schnitzel restaurant. When I wiped all that off, the people who came for that left and never came back. But as time has gone by, I've got the winemakers of the area coming in to replace them. I'm not denigrating other people and their palates, but I have to do something I like and believe in.'

Some items on the menu the day we spoke were: mussels steamed with

**Dennis in the dining room at the Vine Hotel, Wangaratta.**

chilli basil sauce; fetta cheese and vegetable salad; lamb roasted with eggplant, peppers, olives and a pesto sauce; steamed ocean trout with a ginger sauce; roast duck with black bean sauce; green chilli coconut curry.

Dennis sees his food as 'either provincial European or Asian influence—always the Asian influence.' But how do the two intersect? 'We've got access to all produce, right down to native Australian foods. You can take snippets from different cultures, different ingredients. Some things work together, it becomes very experimental and there's lots of scope for that—that's how we'll keep creating new dishes. But I think keeping the individual cuisines intact is a good thing too, with just a little interaction.'

One way in which cultures interact in Dennis' food is by introducing a European technique to Asian ingredients. 'With Asian sauces, to do them traditionally, you cook very fast and thicken with arrowroot or cornflour. But you can make these sauces in a classical French method, roasting bones and reducing the stock, adding ginger and tamarind and ending up with the same kind of sauce with more depth.'

For me, this brought to mind the moment—also in Dharmasala, where Dennis and Louise had lived—where I first understood the reasoning behind the stir-fry. A woman was preparing a meal on the street outside her home. She had prepared all the ingredients on a tray. Beneath a wok-like cooking vessel on a stand was a bunch of thin twigs. She lit the twigs, they flared up, she threw in the ingredients. By the time the twigs had died down, the dish of finely chopped vegetables was cooked. How much was a cuisine dependent on the availability of fuel?

At the time of writing, Dennis is still in the kitchen at the Vine. How long he'll stay there, given his peripatetic habits, is anybody's guess. But he's one Australian cook who I don't think we'll see in a city restaurant. As I left he was speaking of a small guesthouse on the Margaret River in Western Australia as one possibility. 'I've never wanted to be a public figure. I just don't want that life. Cooking is to a great extent something I do for myself, to the best of my ability.'

# Rare Fillet of Kangaroo on Steamed Tatsoi with Lime and Chilli Sauce

SERVES 4

4 pieces of kangaroo fillet (about 220 g each)
300–400 g kangaroo trimmings
2 cups chopped onions, carrot and celery
2 × 2.5 cm ginger pieces
a few peppercorns
1 piece galangal
1 bunch coriander with roots
⅓ cup (90 mL) good quality soy sauce (not too salty)
2 tablespoons honey
2 limes, zest and juice
chilli to taste
2 tablespoons clarified butter
black pepper
8 bunches baby tatsoi or 2 bunches large tatsoi

Trim any sinew from the kangaroo fillets and set fillets aside.

To make sauce, roast the trimmings, onions, carrots and celery until golden. Deglaze the pan with a little water, then transfer the mixture to a heavy-based pot, and cover with water. Add one piece of the ginger (roughly chopped), peppercorns, galangal, coriander roots and soy sauce.

Simmer for about 3 hours, then strain through a muslin cloth. Return the liquid to the pot, add the honey and turn up the heat to reduce the stock. It should be thickened slightly, but still quite thin. Add the lime zest, juice, ¼ bunch chopped coriander leaves.

Blanch the other pieces of ginger in boiling water for 1 minute, then thinly slice and chop them and add them to the sauce. Add chilli as desired.

Sear the kangaroo fillets in a heavy cast-iron pan with some clarified butter. Season with coarsely ground black pepper. Remove and keep warm.

Steam the tatsoi until it is just soft.

To serve: slice each kangaroo fillet into three or four pieces and place on top of the tatsoi. Pour over some of the chilli lime sauce. Serve with a big bowl of steaming hot rice.

# Maltese Provincial Rabbit Stew

SERVES 4

Doesn't everybody have a favourite dish that Mama makes?

12 hind legs of rabbit
1 cup (250 mL) olive oil
3 onions, chopped
2 medium carrots, chopped
2 celery sticks, chopped
2 bay leaves
a few peppercorns
6 pimentos
6 garlic cloves
1 cup smoked pork belly
  or smoked pancetta,
  chopped
4 cloves
1 teaspoon ground
  cinnamon
½ teaspoon ground nutmeg
½ teaspoon allspice
1 cup (250 mL) red wine
2 cups seeded and peeled
  tomatoes
2 tablespoons tomato
  paste
3 bay leaves
2 rosemary sprigs
3 cups (750 mL) chicken
  stock
1 cup (155 g) shelled
  peas
salt and pepper to taste
flat-leaf parsley

Marinate the rabbit legs in a mixture of the olive oil, 1 chopped onion, the carrots and celery, a couple of bay leaves, a few peppercorns, the pimentos—and leave for at least 2 hours (preferably overnight).

Remove the rabbit from the oil but retain the oil marinade. Fry the rabbit in a heavy-based pan over a medium heat until golden, then remove.

Add to the pan the olive oil from the marinade then fry the remaining chopped onions, chopped garlic, pork belly and spices. Fry (without burning) the spices then add the wine, tomatoes, tomato paste, bay leaves, rosemary and rabbit. Cover with chicken stock and cook over a low heat until tender, about 1½–2 hours.

Alternatively, the stew can be placed in a deep dish, covered with greaseproof paper and a lid, and baked in the oven at 175°C (350°F) for about 1½–2 hours.

Add the shelled peas when nearly cooked and season to taste.

To serve: sprinkle over roughly chopped parsley. Serve with a grilled polenta cake or potatoes (boiled or mashed). A crusty loaf of bread—broken at the table—a green salad and a good bottle of red are prerequisites to fully enjoying this meal.

# Milawa Mountain Goat's Cheese Souffle

SERVES 4

40 g butter
200 mL milk
40 g plain flour
1 whole head garlic,
 roasted then puréed
2 hot chillies, finely
 chopped
¼ cup roughly chopped
 flat-leaf parsley
¼ cup (45 g) roughly
 chopped black olives
5–6 large eggs, separated
300 g goat's cheese
black pepper

Melt the butter in a medium saucepan. Add the milk and the flour. Bring to the boil, stirring, until the sauce thickens.

Stir in the garlic purée, chillies, parsley and olives. Then add egg yolks, one at a time. Crumble the goat's cheese into the mixture.

Season with pepper then allow the mixture to cool.

Brush four individual soufflé moulds with olive oil and flour.

Whip the egg whites to soft peaks and then fold them into the cooled goat's cheese mixture, adding a half at a time.

Spoon the mixture into the moulds and bake in a preheated oven at 200°C (390°F) for about 25–30 minutes.

To serve: serve with crusty bread and a green salad.

Mietta O'Donnell.

'I don't feel very Italian because
of the way that I was brought
up. But then I feel a foreigner
here too.'

# CHAPTER TWELVE

# Mietta O'Donnell

**M**IETTA O'DONNELL is a paradox. Her maternal family, the Viganos from Milan, leading lights in the pre-war Italian restaurant aristocracy of Melbourne, owned a pub: a real pub with real beer served in real Aussie bars. Possessed of both Scottish and Italian grandmothers, she claims to have been influenced more by the food and recipes of her Scottish grandmother than of her Italian grandmother—who, it must be said, was more often to be found at the easel than the stove.

Although my favourite instruction from any cookbook ever comes from *The Scottish Rural Women's Institute Cookery Book* ('warm slightly over the fire 2 pints of milk and carry it to the side of a cow'), Scotland is not a name that springs to mind as a centre of culinary inspiration.

To get this complex story into perspective, we have to travel to Vancouver before the First World War. It was there that Maria Teresa Ferrari (known as Teresa), Mietta's grandmother, met and married Mario Vigano. Curiously, both were from wealthy Milanese families. Maria Teresa, having studied art at the Brera Academy in Milan, took a job as a display artist in a department store in Vancouver. Mario was an adventurer travelling the world. They married, had two children in Vancouver (including Mietta's mother) and, when war broke out, Mario joined the 29th Vancouver Battalion and was awarded the DMC.

After the war, they returned to Milan, but almost immediately they had to flee in fear of their lives in the face of fascism—the Viganos were not only wealthy, and so natural targets for brownshirt thuggery, but were strongly anti-fascist. A story is told of Mario's mother meeting Mussolini and saying, haughtily, 'so you're Mussolini,' before turning her back on him.

They arrived in Melbourne penniless, having been stripped of their family properties. 'My grandfather always said,' Mietta told me, 'that he arrived with nineteen shillings and six pence in his pocket.' If it was difficult for the later post-war Italian immigrants, it is easy to imagine how it was for these fore-runners. 'My mother grew up in Milan, she was thirteen when she arrived in Melbourne. She tells the story of being sent out to buy some bread, she was told the words to use, which she did, and was shown something which she didn't recognise—a strange looking rectangular object.'

The early years were also a struggle financially—Mario worked as a waiter at Scotts Hotel and Teresa scrubbed floors. But they began working together as caterers and, by 1932, with some help from the Bourke family, were able to lease the old Melbourne Club Hotel on the corner of Little Bourke and Exhibition Streets. This was to be the site of Mario's, one of the grand Melbourne Italian restaurants, until the death of Mario Vigano in 1968.

Mario's was by no means the first Italian restaurant in Melbourne. In the 1890s, Vincenzo Fasoli, a Swiss-Italian and an ex-associate of Garibaldi's, opened Fasoli's Cafe in Lonsdale Street which remained there until he retired in 1905. Fasoli's was the centre of Bohemian life in Melbourne at the time, establishing a tradition of connection with artists and writers (C. J. Dennis, Hal Gye, Bernard O'Dowd) which has carried on down the years in Melbourne, and has continued at Mietta's until recently. The Cafe Latin was opened by Peter Navaretti in Exhibition Street in 1919, the same year in which Ernesto Molina opened the Cafe d'Italia in Lonsdale Street. The two other great Italian restaurants of Melbourne were the Society, opened by Guiseppe Codognotto in 1925, originally in Little Bourke Street, and Rinaldo Massoni's Florentino in Bourke Street, dating from 1928.

It's interesting to note that, for no reason I can discern, these culturally enriching Italians were more likely to settle in Melbourne than in Sydney. Before the Second World War, Sydney had Azzalin Romano, and little else in the way of prominent Italian restaurateurs. As we have seen, from the turn of the century, Melbourne had a rich and diverse range of restaurateurs.

According to Mietta, in those early days, Mario's was 'more of a cafe, it catered to a lot of students. But when they grew up and became more "estab-lishment", Mario's grew with them.' Eventually it became 'the largest and grandest of that group of Italian restaurants. Practically everybody in Melbourne went there at least once, usually for celebrations.'

Teresa set up a studio on the roof of the hotel, and began to establish a reputation as a painter. She became a close associate of the artists Jock Frater and Arnold Shore, and her portrait of Frater is one of three of her works owned by the National Gallery of Victoria. She painted many portraits, most notably of the ballet master Edouard Borovansky who 'came for lunch every day' and of another customer, Richard Bonynge. Today, many of her portraits and still lifes hang at Mietta's Queenscliff Hotel.

All these pre-war restaurants were clustered around the theatre district of Melbourne—Mario's was opposite Her Majesty's Theatre—and the post-theatre crowds were important to them. But the timing of this custom ran foul of the antediluvian Victorian liquor laws of the day. Hotel bars stopped serving at 6PM and all glasses of alcohol had to be off restaurant tables by 8PM—unless there was a 'special occasion'. Mietta takes up the story. 'My grandfather had trained as a lawyer in Italy, and was very proud of waging battles with the licensing commission.' To get a special occasion dispensation, you had to sign a statutory declaration and obtain a permit. 'He used to send my mother down to the court every day. Every day was a special occasion.'

Over the years, the Viganos expanded their business, first buying the hotel from the brewery, and then acquiring an adjacent building. As business expanded, so did the capabilities of the kitchen. Initially, according to Mietta, it was 'very much standard Italian fare; minestrone, veal and chicken dishes, the *costolette alla Milanese* [Milanese veal chops] was obviously a standard as was risotto Milanese. But as it developed over the years, my uncle Tony—there were two brothers and a sister, my mother, who was in the middle—who was very ambitious, went back to Italy and recruited some good chefs from the Veneto region, who subsequently moved on and opened their own businesses. He went to the extent of getting pasta specialists and he also brought back an ice carver. There was a grand central table where they served buffets and there would be an ice carving.'

And, always, the bars were kept open. 'There was a bar on the corner when it was the original hotel, a saloon bar, then later they added what they called a public bar, and there was also a lounge bar.'

Initially, Teresa, although deeply involved in painting, worked full-time at the restaurant as the maîtresse d', but then, as the years went by, she moved behind the scenes and retreated to her painting. She used to make up little bouquets of flowers and give them to the customers.

Little Bourke Street at this time was frequented by prostitutes. Mietta's grandmother would make up huge bell-shaped glass jars (the originals of which contained preserves from Italy) of minestrone and give them away 'to all sorts of people, including the prostitutes, who she was convinced would die from lack of nourishment'.

Mietta's mother, Maria, married Donald James O'Donnell, who, although a customer at the restaurant, could not have been further removed from the Viganos in background or profession. He was an industrial chemist of Scottish-Irish ancestry, and he regarded the restaurant, where Maria continued to work in the office, as an 'alien world'.

By the time Mietta arrived, the Viganos were prosperous enough to have bought a farm property at South Morang, north of Melbourne, near Plenty. Her childhood memories are of growing up at home in Glen Iris, with her Scots grandmother, and of weekends spent on the farm at South Morang, with her Italian family and a mixed group of Italian, Australian and even Spanish farmworkers. Two of her earliest memories are of Angelina, a Sicilian maid, and the 'vivid red tomato sauce she made, and the way she squeezed and peeled the tomatoes to make the sauce' and a Spanish girl, Josefina, who made *tortilla* (Spanish omelette). And there was always Mario's, as later became clear, an indelible and powerfully formative memory for the young Mietta. 'We used to eat there frequently. As a child I had very boring tastes, always choosing the same things, much to my regret today: *costolette alla Milanese* was a big favourite. But my grandparents also had big Sunday lunches at the farm. In many ways it was more interesting seeing the whole entertaining process there.'

It's no surprise that Mietta began to develop a feeling for hospitality at a very early age. She can't remember the exact age but knows that 'before I was ten, and when I was left alone, I'd go through the kitchen cupboards and leaf through my Scottish grandmother's recipe books and try things out. I remember doing something that I did later at [the first] Mietta's, a sausage and tomato casserole. One of the first dinners I remember doing was for my grandmother when she was quite old. She wanted to—or I probably talked her into it—invite a Greek friend who ran one of the shipping lines and who was regarded as a very fussy eater. I convinced her I was capable of doing a proper meal for him—I was about thirteen at the time. He could only eat things that were lightly cooked. I did veal, I think, lightly braised on a purée of carrot and leek.'

School was the Sacré Coeur Convent in Glen Iris where she learnt 'French but not Italian, which was a great pity. I had to learn Italian later at Perugia University,' and where 'I hated my name. I felt it was unfair that my sisters had ordinary names (Patricia and Robin) and I was odd because I was third and supposed to be a boy, and because they hadn't decided they called me Maria, which my grandfather changed to Mietta.'

Her father didn't want the children to have anything to do with the restaurant life, 'He wanted us to go to school, go to university and lead what
he regarded as an ordinary existence. And very early on, I wanted to do
exactly that. On leaving school, I started a cadetship with the (Melbourne)
*Herald*, and did a part-time arts/law degree at Melbourne University. I loved
cooking, and loved entertaining, but I never thought then of doing it
professionally.'

In her first year of study, she won an essay competition (run by *The Australian* newspaper and judged by Manning Clark) whose prize was a trip to
Indonesia 'just after the coup in 1969, a very interesting period', and on her
return she changed subjects to political science and Indonesian. After a period
of full-time study ('boring') and as a stringer for *The Australian*, she finished
her cadetship, was graded, and was preparing to go and work with the United
Nations in Indonesia when, suddenly, she decided to go to Italy. 'A bizarre
choice, I know. But a friend, Joanne Molina [grand-daughter of Ernesto
Molina, the original owner of the Latin in Lonsdale Street] had been trying
to persuade me to go and I thought, what the hell?' This was the trip to
Perugia where she did a three-month language course, extended this to eighteen months, 'tried living in France, couldn't, and ended up living and cooking
in Greece.'

When she came back to Australia, Joanne Molina suggested they go into
a restaurant business together (they never did, as Mietta says Joanne 'never
liked food, wine or cooking, she prefers horses'). She then met someone—
Tony Knox— who wanted to start a restaurant, and so began the first Mietta's
in an old butcher's shop at the top of Brunswick Street in 1974. 'The name
was very much last choice—we tossed around lots.'

The partners were Jules Lavarack, who had been a second chef to Tony
Bilson (at time of writing chef at The Treasury in the Sydney Inter-Con-
tinental Hotel) and her current partner Tony Knox, son of the celebrated
Eltham mud brick architect Doctor Alistair Knox, who converted the shop.
'Actually Tony Knox and Tony Bilson knew each other from Eltham, and
they were going to start a restaurant together. Then Tony went to Sydney,
and that's how I came into it.' At that stage, Mietta was also working full-
time as electoral-cum-press officer for the Labor politician (former Treasurer
in the Keating Labor Federal Government) Ralph Willis, 'which was fulfilling
my political science and journalism background. I used to cook on Jules' day
off and on Sundays. But I gave up my job before Jules left in 1975.'

How to explain such a complete turnaround from her father's (and her) desire for 'an ordinary existence'? 'There's no rational path through that. I suppose we all underestimate the influences of growing up that stay with you.' And with the whole family. Patricia O'Donnell currently runs the Queenscliff Hotel; her other sister, Robin Moser, worked at Mietta's for many years.

It was an exciting time for Melbourne restaurants. The changed licensing laws saw a rash of BYOs. Melbourne was the site of the first radical experiments with food that have been, ever since, at the centre of the development of Australian cuisine. Hermann Schneider of Two Faces had been using Asian ingredients in his western dishes since the mid-sixties. Mietta's was in the thick of it—Stephanie Alexander cooked there before opening her own place nearby.

'Jules and I were very much in the rebellious school at that stage. We wanted nothing to do with anything that was happening in other restaurants. We had a menu that changed every week—four or five entrees, mains and desserts—madness. In any one menu you could have an old English dish, a Chinese dish, an Italian dish and a French dish. The French food had nothing to do with Melbourne French of the time—it was Escoffier, not provincial. One of the things we said was that we weren't going to have oysters or steak on the menu.'

She felt that Chinese and Italian were the strongest influences on Australian food at the time. 'I began thinking we should be cooking what was available at the markets, which was Chinese and Italian, so I recruited a Chinese chef and an Italian chef. We ran straight Chinese and Italian menus parallel for a while. I sent Winston (the Chinese chef) to Italy for three months, but not the Italian to China—there are more good Chinese restaurants than Italian.' In its final stages in Brunswick Street, the restaurant went through what she calls her 'European period' with German, Austrian and French chefs.

In its last guise in the old Naval and Military Club in Alfred Place, in the distinguished end of Melbourne (off the 'Paris end of Collins Street'), it reverted, to a degree, to what I imagine the old Mario's would have been like in its heyday—another example of the persistence of childhood influences? As a Sydneysider, my reaction was—what a pity we don't have restaurants like this in Sydney any more.

The 1886 colour schemes of the builder, John Augustus Bernard Koch, had been reproduced, and the litter of years of neglect and disinterest swept away under the supervision of Suzanne Forge, herself an owner of a Koch house and an aficionado of the style.

Mietta in the main dining room at Mietta's in Melbourne.

It had a plush, red velvet, grandiose style, the main room punctuated by early Victorian statues of women holding lamps aloft, gleaming damask napery and glinting glasses, an environment that brought a sense of occasion to the dining experience. Downstairs, there was a less formal area, known as the Lounge, as well as a bar area. Mietta (in partnership with Tony Knox) had continued her familial connection with the arts. While we were there a song cycle of C. P. Cavafy's poems entitled 'When the Lips and the Skin Remember' was being performed in the bar as part of the Antipodes Festival, performances and concerts being a regular feature in the restaurant's various spaces. In celebrating its 21st anniversary, O'Donnell and Knox made the following statement about the restaurant: 'Few such places ... have succeeded in the remarkable and stylish mixture of cuisine, concern and connections that has come to mean Mietta's.' The entrance, with its glass-fronted office and grand staircase, actually looked more like the entrance to a theatre than a restaurant.

Is it any surprise, though, that Mietta's was never all that Italian? A menu during my visit featured such dishes as tian of crab with avocado and a gazpacho sauce and sautéed breast of duck with apple champagne sauce. She called the food 'Melbourne Classical'. The *1995 Age Good Food Guide* called it 'French in bias' (although Mietta's was not reviewed for that guide, at her own insistence, to do with a fundamental disagreement with the way in which the reviews are carried out, she was still listed). Mietta may well be half-Italian, but, as she points out, 'I don't feel very Italian because of the way that I was brought up. I'd like to live there for a while, but I still feel a foreigner there. But then I feel a foreigner here too. I feel neither Anglo-Saxon nor Italian. I feel, more than my sisters, a bit of an outsider, I suppose.'

This is, it could be argued, the fate of the cosmopolitan Australian. And if Melbourne, as has been said, is the most cosmopolitan of Australian cities, then Mietta's was Australia's most cosmopolitan restaurant—offering us our (and her) diverse roots rather than concentrating on their 'Italianness'. With her willingness to accept a multitude of influences—Scottish, Italian, German, English and French—Mietta O'Donnell is perhaps pointing clearly to that (so far) mythical Australian cuisine at the end of the rainbow.

But it could also be useful—in its failures—in pointing out the dangers of such a 'bastard' cuisine when poorly assimilated. Towards the end of our time together, we spoke of the lag between what people are eating in restaurants, and what is being eaten in the home. Mietta reported a conversation she remembered with the owner of the property that was to become the first Mietta's in North Fitzroy. 'He told us his Mum used to be a good Australian cook, but now she "mucks around and makes all this rubbish with satay sauce", the implication being that she doesn't know what's she's doing, so makes a mess of it. But when she did roast lamb, it was delicious.'

*Postscript*: Mietta's closed on New Year's Eve, 1995—or 1 January 1996, if you like. In an article in the *Melbourne Age* (14 November 1995) about its impending closure, Mietta was quoted as saying that the closure was part of a plan by her and Mr Knox to 'explore new opportunities'. The article went on to say, 'For a time, Ms O'Donnell and Mr Knox spoke of the importance of traditional European dining. More recently, however, they said there was not much place for such a style.'

Whether this is fashion, or the genuine passing of an era, it's hard to say right now. But pendulums swing. And I am doubly sad that we've lost Mietta's. Because now, there is nothing like it in either Sydney or Melbourne.

## Scallopine di Vitello alla Cacciatora

Veal slices
Hunter style

SERVES 2

250 g veal
flour
oil or butter for frying
1 cup (90 g) mushrooms
1 onion
butter
1 cup (250 mL) sweet
 white sherry wine
1 tablespoon tomato purée
a few parsley sprigs
1 teaspoon butter

Cut the veal into slices, beat until thin and flour them. Brown the veal in oil or butter. Place the veal slices on paper or bread to drain.

Finely chop some mushrooms and an onion. Fry them quickly in butter then add a glass of sweet white sherry wine and continue to fry quickly. Add some tomato purée, chopped parsley and about a teaspoon of butter.

To serve: pour the sauce over the veal and sprinkle with chopped parsley.

## Marinated Mushrooms

This is an early first course from Mietta's in Fitzroy. The quantities given are to feed a restaurant full of people.

1 case mushrooms
4 pints (2.5 litres) vinegar
1½ pints (875mL) olive oil
10 garlic cloves
3 bay leaves
peel of 4 lemons grated
 coarsely
2 teaspoons ground
 coriander

Blanch the mushrooms in boiling water for 5 minutes (if desired). Mix together the remaining ingredients and place in a large saucepan. Bring the marinade to the boil and simmer for 10 minutes. Season to taste. Pour the marinade over the mushrooms.

# Chou Farci with John Dory

Stuffed Cabbage with John Dory

SERVES 4

(From chef Romain Bapst, Mietta's 1990–93.)

1.5–2 kg John Dory
bouquet garni
carrots, leek, shallot and
 garlic for stock
200 mL chardonnay
1 large green cabbage
salt and freshly ground
 black pepper
4 shallots
300 g butter
¼ pumpkin
50 g caviar

Fillet the John Dory and reserve the bones.

Make a stock with the bones, bouquet garni, vegetables and wine. Reduce the liquid over a high heat down to about half a cup. Strain. This is the sauce.

Blanch eight big cabbage leaves in boiling water for 10 minutes then refresh in cold water.

Slice the John Dory fillets into 5 mm thick pieces, and season with salt and pepper.

Chop the shallots and sweat them in 100 g butter until blonde in colour.

Place a cloth on the table and layer the cabbage leaves, shallots, and John Dory fillets and form into a big big ball then tie it up with string. Steam the ball for 30 minutes.

Finish the sauce by stirring through the remaining 200 g butter.

Dice the pumpkin into five 5-mm pieces or into small balls and cook for 10 minutes in boiling water.

Place the John Dory/cabbage package onto hot plates and pour around the sauce with caviar spooned through at the last minute. Dot with pumpkin balls and serve immediately.

# Sausage and Tomato Casserole
SERVES 4

An adaptation of my Scottish grandmother's dish. I made this for lunch at Mietta's, Fitzroy.

1 small onion
1 kg thick pork sausages
2 large tomatoes, skinned and sliced
500 g potatoes, boiled
butter

Peel, slice and fry the onion in a little oil.

Bring a large saucepan of water to the boil. Add the sausages and boil for 5 minutes, then skin them and cut them in half lengthwise.

Put half the sausages in a pie dish, cover with the cooked onion and the sliced tomato. Place the remaining sausages on top.

Peel and then mash the potatoes with a little butter and milk. Spread the mashed potato over the sausage layer. Dot with butter.

Bake in a preheated moderate oven at 180°C (355°F) until brown, about 10–15 minutes.

# Spumone
SERVES 6

From *Nonna*, my Italian grandmother. The original recipe specified two glasses liqueur and six sherry glasses of white wine.

6 egg yolks
3 cups (750 mL) white wine
6 tablespoons sugar
2 cups (500 mL) whipping cream
125 g nuts
125 g peel (orange, lemon and banana)
1 cup (250 mL) liqueur (any according to taste)

First make a zabaglione—beat the egg yolks with the white wine and sugar. Continue to beat in a double saucepan over a pan of boiling water and cook until thick (do not boil). Allow to cool.

Whip the cream and then mix in the chopped nuts, peel, and liqueur. Stir this into the zabaglione. Place in a large rectangular mould and freeze for at least 5 hours before spooning it out.

Michael Platsis.

'I wasn't interested in the
tips ... I wanted people to
be happy.'

# CHAPTER THIRTEEN

# *Michael Platsis &*

# *Dean Merlo*

**M**ICHAEL PLATSIS is leaping nimbly over boxes of wine, scaling ceiling-high racks, searching for a magnum of 1958 Chateau Margaux—first growth—eyes gleaming, fingers brushing lovingly over dusty labels. The cellar is beneath his restaurant, Michael's Riverside (actually, restaurants: we're also below Marco's, Rivers Cafe Bar and Eagles Coffee Bar) in Brisbane. It's not your traditional dank, stone cellar with candles and cobwebs in dimly lit corners, but a series of rooms off the carpark in the Harry Seidler-designed Riverside Centre—the walls are cinder block, the floors concrete—in the heart of boomtown Brisbane's CBD.

I ask him how many bottles of wine he has stored here. He tells me he's not sure, but thinks about 80,000, and that his accountant is always trying to get him to sell the collection. An accountant would. This—one of the most extensive collections of wine in a restaurant anywhere in Australia—is about passion, not profits. His hands flit from bottle to bottle, pulling them out, displaying them briefly: a 1975 Watervale DW13 Rhine Riesling; a 1980 Grange Hermitage; a Reynella made by John Reynell in 1950 'probably of cabernet sauvignon and shiraz' according to the new label. Mr Platsis is displaying the feverish restlessness of the collector surveying his collection. Accountant indeed.

80,000 bottles of wine beneath three bustling and successful restaurants. In the carpark, a red 500SL Mercedes Benz ('my toy'), and an elegant old Rolls Royce Silver Shadow for VIP guests—like Count Freddy Chandon, who Michael entertained on the roof of his riverside home: 'There were magnums of Dom Perignon, buckets of Beluga. His wife is the daughter of the writer Somerset Maugham.' We're a long way from the village of Gennadi on the Greek island of Rhodes, and his Uncle Klimi's fish cafe on the water's edge.

And yet, in spite of the extravagant strelitzia and turpentine arrangement in the foyer, the American Express Awards plastered over the walls, the empty magnums and jeroboams of Moët and Pol Roger on display, there is still something Mediterranean about Michael's Riverside: the blue, grey and white colouring, the water outside the floor to ceiling glass, maybe even the cut velvet chairs with the strange clasped hand device on the seat.

But it's the Mediterranean of Onassis, not Zorba, in spite of the woodfired oven in Rivers, the bistro attached to the main restaurant. 'I said to Mum you can come in and bake your bread in the oven. She said do you do it with wood, and I said, yes, in exactly the same way you did it in the village. There was a big smile because she makes the bread for the church, for Father Gregory.' She hasn't taken up the offer.

Brisbane is the odd place out in this book. More than anywhere else we went in search of wogs and Wogfood, Brisbane is about success and money before food. Brisbane is about making it. And Michael's Riverside is one of the power centres of the city.

Michael Platsis tells his story: 'I was born in the village of Gennadi on Rhodes, about 70 kilometres from the capital, past Lindos. My father worked in a brick factory, and he was a charcoal burner. We had no power.' Michael is referring here not to social or political power, although this is also true, but to the age old use of charcoal around the Mediterranean as a fuel in regions with no electricity or gas. Walk through forests, and you will see the raised black circles, the remnants of the charcoal burners' slow fires.

'Each family in the village was self-contained. We had a few olive trees, we grew tobacco, which we picked and dried for the buyers. We grew grapes for winemaking, picked them, put them in containers on the donkey, took them home and trod them to make the juice also to sell. Mum would keep the skins to make vinegar and sweets. We grew our own wheat, there was a miller in the village, we'd harvest it, thresh it, then let it dry and grind it with the neighbours. There'd be enough for the season.'

The Platsis family ate what is today being heralded as the life-saving, health-giving Mediterranean diet. 'Octopus, the small fish called *barbouni* [rouget or red mullet], you can't give them to people here but in Greece they're the most expensive fish. We didn't have a lot of meat, mainly vegetables, cereals, fresh and dried beans—a bit of lamb—we had three goats, Mum would make cheese. We'd pick *horta*, the spicy wild greens, cook them in a pot, put a little onion and garlic over the top with a squeeze of lemon and olive oil.'

As a boy, he worked in his spare time at Uncle Klimi's waterfront cafe, 'in the school holidays I'd clean up, serve and clear table.' He didn't develop any early feeling for the business then, it was 'just pocket money'. The cafe is called, naturally enough, Klimi's, and it's still in Gennadi which has become a popular tourist village. 'My uncle came out here a few years ago and saw this restaurant. He thought it was amazing.'

Michael's father Emmanuel came to Australia in 1955, stayed with a relative in Brisbane and worked for the railways and at nights as a kitchen hand in Lennon's hotel. In 1959, the rest of the family arrived—mother Anastasia and Angela, Michael, at ten, the oldest boy, Vasilis and Sávas. 'We went to the city of Rhodes to have photos taken, then to Piraeus for a couple of days, and caught an Italian ship, the *Aurelia*, to Sydney. I cried when I left home, it wasn't my choice. It was all very strange to come from a small village to a big city. We had relatives who met us in Sydney and put us on the train. We spoke no English at all.'

Michael started at school where he had left off in Greece—in Grade 4— at Dutton Park State School. 'There was one other Greek kid there, but he was born here and couldn't speak a word of Greek. Then I went to South Brisbane State, there were a lot more Greek kids there, and we had a very good headmaster.'

There was a small Greek community in Brisbane then, 'nothing like Sydney or Melbourne', but enough so that his mother never learnt a great deal of English. 'She used to go to the butcher to buy meat and point to a part of her and say 'I want some from here.' There was this Italian, Bruno his name was, he used to come around to Greek and Italian homes in an FJ ute and knock on doors and sell pastas, cereals, lentils, olives and cheeses. There were a few importers—Samios in Woolloongabba, and the Greek Club in Charlotte Street had an importer in the basement.'

Michael's mother had problems here in the first years. 'She started getting quite sick, she was used to working in the fields—all day long, morning till sunset in the fields and then come home to prepare the food. Over here she started putting on weight and she had heart problems. She's fine now.'

The family lived in Highgate Hill, then mainly a Greek area. 'Now they've moved out to the suburbs and the Vietnamese have moved in. The little shops once owned by Greeks are now owned by Asians.' And the cycle continues.

'Halfway through Grade 8,' Michael continues, 'I asked for a special permit to leave school and start work. My headmaster said, well, you can't do that, it's against the law. I said if you don't allow me I'm going to go.' He had to work. With six in the family, even with his father's two jobs, and Michael catching a tram to the city to sell newspapers (outside the Bank of NSW, an important detail), there wasn't enough to pay the rent, or to buy furniture, clothing and food. 'Being the oldest boy, I had to start work. I was thirteen.'

In 1961 Michael started work with a friend of the family who was a tailor, then got a job as a presser in a factory, 'but it wasn't my scene.' Then he was offered a full-time job at the restaurant in the Valley called the Cortina Bar (owned by Sam Vico's father, see Chapter 16) where he'd been working part-time in the coffee shop. 'At the factory my pay was four pounds five shillings and threepence. In the Cortina Bar they said the first month we'll pay you nine pounds a week, the second twelve and the third fifteen pounds a week. It was a lot of money—but twice the hours of the factory job. I wasn't quite fourteen.' He took the job. Next door to the Cortina Bar was Florentino's, a white tablecloth restaurant with a function centre upstairs.

'I started washing up, making coffees, then making the lemon gelato— we'd squeeze the lemons and then use the skins and the sugar and the water and with your hands break the skins and massage the lemon skin through the water—you'd get all this acid under your fingernails. I worked seven days a week for five years.'

When he was sixteen, he was charged for selling liquor without a licence. 'There were only one or two licensed restaurants—the Camellia was one of the first. If a client wanted a glass of beer or wine we'd take his money, run down to the pub, buy it, bring it back and serve it to him. At that time, the owners being Italians used to buy Stanthorpe wines [Stanthorpe is just past Toowoomba, they no longer make wine there]. We'd serve a glass of wine to the Italians with lunch and sometimes the Australians would say what are they drinking over there, and they'd try it and they'd say awful stuff, I'll have a beer instead. But slowly they'd get more educated, then they might take half a glass. We served pastas, lasagne, ravioli, fettucine, linguine, also on the menu were T-bone steak, chicken in a basket, whole chicken—you could have your T-bone with chips, onions, a couple of eggs, sauce, the works— the plate was just piled up.'

The clientele was mainly Australian, except for 'the Italian bludgers who'd hang around all day drinking one cup of coffee, we'd have to kick them out at lunchtime. I still have clients I served there 30 years ago. Jim Kennedy is one [he owns Daydream Island]—we raced a horse together. And Sir James Killen [retired Federal Liberal politician and Minister] who bought my house at Chapel Hill.'

'I bought a house for my parents in Highgate Hill when I was sixteen years old. I paid 4200 pounds.' He borrowed the money from the Bank of NSW. His guarantor was someone who worked at the bank, and used to buy papers from him when he sold them outside the bank as a schoolboy. 'He said you got no problems with this kid—look at his bank account. I paid the house off before I was 21.'

He began at Florentino's, the white tablecloth restaurant next door to Cortina, and was taught service by a Swiss-Italian waiter. 'I started to take an interest in food, they had an Italian chef and a French chef. I'd go home and cook a *scallopine* the way I saw them prepare it. I knew I'd have my own restaurant one day.'

His next job, in 1969, was as caterer on an oil rig. 'I was earning $220 a fortnight. Twelve hours a day—8AM to 8PM. I was cooking and serving. It was quite an interesting job. We served good food—in quantity. Break-fast—bacon and eggs, lamb's fry; morning tea—biscuits and cakes; lunch—steaks and roast dinners or chicken. I remember I caught 70-odd kilos of jewfish once but they were too lazy to clean it.' He was only on the rig for four months, and his number came up for National Service.

Michael went back to Brisbane, and took a job at Milano's—then Brisbane's top restaurant—while waiting to be called up. It took twelve months. 'I did my basic training in Singleton and at Victoria Barracks in Sydney. I used to stay with relations and drive to the officers' mess each day—of course I was in the catering corps, an instructor.' He managed to be posted back to Brisbane to look after his mother, and took over the officer's mess. 'I used to look after them. I still get quite a few of them here. I ran it not as an army catering mess, but as a restaurant.' He was also working at Milano's at night. 'I told them it was my uncle's restaurant—Gino Merlo [the owner] was Italian and I was Greek!' He left the army as a sergeant.

Michael then went to work at Milano's full-time, and eventually became the manager. There were two licensed restaurants in Brisbane at the time, Camellia, owned by Michael Kahlos, and Milano's. 'Milano's was the first—it was bigger than Camellia. There was the Terrazza, the coffee shop, the Bistro and the Galleria—the white tablecloth room. Gino had all three. He did very well. It was just what the market wanted. He served the lawyers, the judges, all the legal people.'

After managing Milano's for twelve months, Michael went to see Gino Merlo with a grievance. 'I was getting about $15 a week more than the waiters. I said to Gino, look, I'm not happy with what I'm doing. Well, he said, I could see you couldn't handle it, he said I don't want to lose you, would you like to go back to being a waiter.'

This was a seminal moment in young Michael Platsis' life. He was deeply hurt by this comment. 'As a waiter I could earn $200 extra a week in tips. But I wasn't interested in the tips. I was interested in looking after people. Even if there was a non-tipper who left me 20 cents—I wanted people to be happy. If Gino had given me an increase in salary, I would have stayed on as manager. But he said I couldn't handle the job. That hurt. His wife, whenever they went on an overseas trip, would say, "Michael, you've done a great job," and give me a pat on the back.'

'On the first of April 1975 I bought Camellia—a basement restaurant in Queen Street.' It was the first step in his plan to overtake Gino Merlo. 'I bought it from Michael Kahlos' sons-in-law—Michael had retired. At this time they were doing five or six for lunch, the same for dinner. They'd pulled out the pages of the reservation book so I wouldn't see that. But the piano player told me the secrets.'

He went back to Westpac (formerly the Bank of NSW) to borrow $25,000. They would only lend it to him if he mortgaged both his houses—each worth $25,000–$30,000. He was furious—this was the bank that had lent him 4200 pounds when he was sixteen—he immediately withdrew all his money and went elsewhere.

'I made a complete change in the kitchen at the Camellia, a new menu and fresh produce. They were selling frozen vegetables, frozen fish. I threw everything out. This was the garlic prawn era. The three oyster dishes, the coquille St Jacques, champignons with white wine and cream—but very good food for its time.'

On a 1975 Camellia menu are listed seven seafood dishes—including the inevitable lobsters mornay and newburg—and twelve beef dishes, including an alarming tropical steak, 'eye fillet pocketed and stuffed with banana and garlic butter'—which is either a nod in the direction of nouvelle cuisine or an instance of what local food writer Jan Power terms the 'mango fever' that can cloud the judgement of Brisbane folk. But he must have been doing something right. 'From doing six for dinner and lunch I started filling it every day. I kept the name Camellia at first, then changed it to Michael's Camellia, then eventually to Michael's.'

It was during this time that he began his cellar. 'While I was working for Gino I saw him buying wines and watched his cellar grow. Now I started to buy wines for myself, putting them away, and developing my own palate.'

Between 1977 and 1979 he also opened Brisbane's first licensed Greek restaurant in Albert Street, called Rhodes. Again, he designed it himself. 'Greek food, Greek music, Greek dancing. I sold it in 1979 because my brother who was helping me went back to Greece.'

Unable to extend the lease on the property in which Michael's was housed, he left in 1981, and opened another Michael's, upstairs in the City Centre Arcade on Queen Street in an old Coles cafeteria. 'I built the whole restaurant—demolished the kitchen, designed a new interior with big comfortable tables, good silverware and china—I was going to build a better restaurant than Gino Merlo's. I started taking a lot of customers away from Milano's at the time, because I had a better ambience, more of the style of the 80s—not the food, I never went for fashionable food. I kept it fairly simple and I served large portions.' For this he was criticised by a local critic.

In 1982, in a review in the Brisbane *Courier Mail*, Des Partridge wrote that while 'Michael's . . . probably could claim to be Brisbane's swankiest restaurant . . . the ambience . . . is jarred by the curiously old-fashioned menu items. I don't believe anyone would be offended if the Australian habit of big servings—proper enough in truckies' cafes—was abolished immediately in these health-conscious times.'

In Michael's defence, It should be pointed out that in 1982, the nouvelle cuisine, which had passed through the southern states like a miniscule but oft-repeated dose of salts, with its snowy expanses of almost—but for a couple of perfect snow peas—empty plates, had by then travelled north, and was being promoted by those feverish followers of fashion, the tribe of food writers. It would also have gone against Michael's native Greek sense of hospitality ('I wanted people to be happy') to skimp, as he would have seen it, on servings.

As for an old-fashioned menu. Well, from the menus I have in front of me, I think even that's a little unfair. I'm pleased to note that tropical steak has disappeared, to be replaced by a navarin of lamb, described as 'loin of lamb lightly braised with prunes, apricots, almonds and steamed couscous'. Notwithstanding the misuse of the word 'navarin', which is defined as 'a ragoût of mutton with potatoes and/or various other vegetables . . . more than likely named after the *navet*, turnip' by *Larousse Gastronomique Cookery Encyclopedia*, which goes on to say that 'some chefs therefore use the word navarin quite justifiably for other types of ragoût'—but certainly not a braise, and absolutely not with fruit. But what is really startling is this first recorded use of couscous on a menu outside a specialist restaurant in Australia. Peter Koch, still head chef with Michael Platsis, told me that he discovered couscous as an apprentice working with the French Algerian Luc Turschwell at Belmondo's in Noosa between 1989–91, and that it used to come up from Sydney in sacks.

Adelaide food writer and chef Cath Kerry came to Australia from Algeria in 1959. Within months, her mother had found couscous at the Star Grocery, something which always puzzled her: as far as she knew, there were no other North Africans living in Adelaide. Even with this background, when Cath took over the restaurant at the Petaluma winery in the Adelaide Hills, she didn't put couscous on her menu until 1984, and only then as part of a special North African menu. 'Even as an evangelical caterer,' she told me, 'the occasion to use couscous didn't arise until relatively recently.' So what with this early appearance of couscous, the *carpaccio* of beef and the fried baby calamari, it is hard to pin the label 'old-fashioned' on this incarnation of Michael's.

In 1985 Michael beat 42 other applicants from around Australia for the tender for what is now Michael's Riverside. He opened in 1986, not a great time for restaurants (the year of the introduction of the Fringe Benefits Tax), but as he puts it, 'I was full every day.'

Also in 1985, Gino Merlo sold Milano's, whether because he felt outdone by Michael, or, as recounted by son Dean, 'he'd been at the top for 25 years ... there were no challenges anymore,' we shall never know. Gino's not talking to anyone (see Dean's story, page 191).

In 1994, Michael opened Marco's, his Mediterranean restaurant, named after his son Mark (he has two marriages behind him, and two children from the second marriage, Mark and Michael, the eldest), who said to him, 'Dad, Michael's got a restaurant named after him, why don't you buy another restaurant and call it Mark's Riverside?' And then, in 1995, the sleek and stylish New York brasserie-style Rivers Cafe Bar, complete with woodfired oven (still waiting for Mamma's bread) just across the courtyard from the other two. The ingredients on the menu at Rivers—pizzas, focaccia, homemade pies and salads—are a collection of the buzz ingredients of the day. A random sampling: kangaroo, sundried tomatoes, Kalamata olives, Roma tomatoes, bok choy, gnocchi, virgin olive oil, *melanzane* (eggplant), Parmesan. And a couple that have, perhaps, crept in from Gennadi; *kourapiedes* and *koulouria*, two varieties of Greek biscuit.

At the end of the interview with Michael, during an excellent lunch (wild barramundi and a bottle of that 1975 Watervale DW13 Rhine Riesling), I mentioned that the idea of 'looking after people' cropped up often in our conversation, and asked him if he had any idea why the idea of service was so important to him. 'I think because I'm a servant. We are peasants, and we come from a little village. I've learnt to look after people. I want to give my customers what they want. I even say that on my menus: Michael welcomes you to his restaurant and if we don't have your favourite dish on our menu, please ask and we shall be delighted to prepare it for you.'

This raises an interesting point—one that underlies the enormous changes in restaurant culture in the last twenty years. I remember my mother (a very early restaurant critic, for the Sydney *Daily Mirror* in the 1960s telling me that the sign of a great restaurant was that, whatever was on the menu, they would make you a perfect omelette if that was all you desired.

This was all very well in the days when chefs were mere technicians. But somewhere between nouvelle cuisine and 'modern food', chefs became artists working with a palette of ingredients and flavours, the very best of them creating an individual style of food which could be recognised and attributed. In a restaurant such as this—as examples I offer Rockpool, Cosmos and Restaurant Manfredi in Sydney; and O'Connell's, Marchetti's Latin and Stephanie's in Melbourne—you don't go if you don't like the style of the artist in the kitchen.

Michael Platsis comes from the old school. He told me a story about a chef no longer working for him. 'The second chef said he needed to talk to me. He said the waiters are coming into the kitchen and ordering fish deep-fried in beer batter with chips and this is not a fish and chip shop. I said listen, these people are paying your wages, my wages and the rent. If they ask for hamburger you will make the best hamburger you have ever made in your life. If you don't like it, you go.'

It was late afternoon, and the sun was going down on the Brisbane River, casting a bronze glow over the water. Local writer Des Hart may be going a little too far when he says that this is one of 'the most exquisitely positioned restaurants in Australia' but right now one would have to say, not too far. One of Erik Satie's Gymnopedies drifts languidly over the half empty room. 'This is a special restaurant,' Michael says firmly, 'people come here, you've got to spoil them.'

We've learnt about a lot more than food from this post-war Mediterranean invasion.

## Sardelles Tiganites

Grilled Sardines

SERVES 6–8

The last time I visited my village, some of the locals were on the beach with their young children, and I saw how they were catching sardines. They had a clear plastic bag with some pebbles and dried bread inside and a couple of holes in it. They submerged the bag in the water and the little fish swam into the bag and they lifted it very quickly out of the water, and when they had caught 2 kilos of these tasty little morsels I took them to my uncle's cafe and had them deep-fried in oil.

800 g fresh sardines
plain flour
olive oil

Wash and pat dry the sardines, then place them on a tray of flour.

Dust off all the loose flour. Pour olive oil into a cast iron pan over a high heat, add the sardines and fry until golden and crisp.

To serve: serve with olive bread and a *khoriatiki salata*—a village salad of fresh tomato, olives, fetta, cucumber, onion and capsicum dressed with extra virgin olive oil.

## Snails in Conchiglie Pasta (from Michael's Riverside)

SERVES 2 AS AN ENTREE

250 g conchiglie pasta
  shells
2 garlic cloves, crushed
pinch of cumin
½ onion, finely diced
50 g butter
2 dozen canned French
  snails
25 mL Pernod
½ cup (125 mL) chicken
  stock
2 cups (500 mL) pure
  cream
salt and pepper
1 bunch English spinach,
  washed and dried, stems
  removed
25 g butter
½ cup julienne of leek,
  deep-fried until crisp,
  drained well

Cook the pasta in a large saucepan of boiling salted water until *al dente*, about 10 minutes. Drain and set aside. Crush the garlic with a pinch of salt and a pinch of cumin and set aside.

Sauté the onion in the 50 g butter. Add the snails, and heat through with the garlic and cumin mixture. Flambé with the Pernod. Add the stock and cream to the pan and reduce by half over a medium heat. Add the cooked pasta and heat through. Season to taste.

In another pan, sauté the spinach in 25 g butter.

To serve: arrange some spinach in the centre of each plate. Spoon the pasta shells in sauce around the spinach. Dividing the snails between the two plates, place a snail in each pasta shell and top with any remaining sauce. Garnish with the julienne of fried leek.

# Pintarde Maleny
# (From Michael's, on the Mall)

Roast Stuffed
Guinea Fowl

SERVES 2

1 × 1.4 kg guinea fowl
salt and pepper
butter
olive oil
2 carrots
2 onions
1 celery stick
a few sprigs thyme
2 bay leaves
2 cups (500 mL) white
  wine
150 g fresh ripe figs,
  diced
1 tablespoon cream
2 tablespoons Cointreau

STUFFING
1 onion diced
a few sprigs thyme and
  rosemary, chopped
1 bay leaf
butter
½ cup day-old-bread,
  crumbled
1 cup (155 g) dried figs,
  chopped
½ cup (75 g) roasted pine
  nut kernels
salt and pepper
zest of 1 orange
1 nip of brandy

To make stuffing, sauté the onion with the herbs in a little butter. Add the remaining ingredients and stir over a medium heat until a firm, moist stuffing is achieved. Allow the mixture to cool.

To prepare birds, trim the neck, wings and giblets from the bird. Force the stuffing into the carcass. Season the bird with pepper and salt and rub with butter and olive oil.

Place the bird in a roasting pan with the carrots, onions, celery, thyme and bay leaves.

Roast in a moderately hot oven (180°C/355°F) for 45 minutes then pour off the fat and add the wine to the pan, cover with foil and braise for a further 20 minutes.

Remove the bird from the pan and transfer the vegetables and pan juices to a saucepan, add 2 cups water and simmer for 10–15 minutes, meanwhile keeping the meat of the bird warm in foil.

Strain the sauce and then pour it back into the pan. Add the figs, Cointreau and cream and stir gently.

To serve: carve slices of guinea fowl breast, place them on individual serving plates and pour over the sauce.

Dean Merlo outside Bar Merlo.

# Dean Merlo

**A**S NOTED in the Platsis story, Brisbane is the odd place out in this book. Besides being the only place where I got the feeling that the money outranked the food, it was also the only place where I was refused an interview. By Gino Merlo. But I did manage to meet up with his son, Dean. And when I told him the way that his father had refused my interview, he laughed hugely, and said, 'That's the old man. Are you going to print that?' I told him I was thinking of it. 'You've got to,' he insisted, 'you've got to, it's too good.'

When I was planning this book, I made up a list of the people I wanted to interview, and sent those I didn't know a letter containing an outline of the book, and a request for an interview. Some replied, others I had to chase. Gino Merlo proved very difficult to find.

When I did track him down, he declined, claiming that he was too old—which he certainly didn't sound on the telephone, nor was this the impression of him I'd picked up from his friends. So I pushed it a little. Then followed this exchange.

'There is a time to pick a flower,' he said in a voice full of melancholy and finality. Nonplussed, I attempted to pick up on the donnish mood.

'But often, Mr Merlo, the older the flower, the more powerful the scent and beauty.'

'Perhaps. But only if it comes from a healthy branch.' I know when I've been out-metaphored.

So I'm forced to tell the story of the father—a very important figure in the history of Wogfood in Brisbane—through the son. But that, as it turns out, is fortuitous. The son had recently turned his back on the law, and opened Bar Merlo, fashioned after a Milanese coffee bar, in the heart of Brisbane (up the hill from Michael Platsis), and owns the first outdoor seating permit in the CBD. 'They wouldn't let them do it 25 years ago,' Dean told me, 'they reckoned dust would get in the food.'

'We had to struggle to get this outdoor area here,' he continued, 'it's in the Lord Mayor's plan to have more al fresco dining, but when I put in the permit, they said no, so I had to convince them.' Once more, it's these blessed wogs we have to thank for forcing the joyless Anglo bureaucratic hand.

And Dean—lawyer, and now coffee entrepreneur—is here because his father came here. Gino Merlo arrived in 1953 with his mother Maria, father Luigi and two brothers Gian and Lou from the mountain village of Tirano, one of the northernmost points in Italy—it's just 50 kilometres from St Moritz—on the Swiss border in the province of Lombardy. 'I've been there,' Dean told me, 'and it's a very hard living.' So it [coming to Australia] wasn't much of a choice. The whole family said, let's go. They worked their farms, and they played around with food in the trattoria style.'

They came to Australia and headed straight for Mackay, and Gino—a strongly built man—took a job as a canecutter. In the off season he would work at Hayman Island, and it was here that he began to foster a feeling for food.

In Mackay, he met Dean's mother, Mary de Pinto, Australian-born of a family from Bari in Puglia. In 1958, the young couple moved to Brisbane with the money Gino had earnt in the canefields, and began work at Milano's, then owned by Onorato (Cicco) Vico (also the owner of the Cortina Bar (see Chapter 16), as a dishwasher, according to Cicco's son Sam.

It was a coffee bar in those days, on the ground floor at 78 Queen Street. He soon bought out the owners, and continued it as a coffee bar serving cafe food. But Gino was 'hungry for knowledge about restaurants. He went overseas, went to all the fine restaurants, and picked up what he could.' He came back and, in 1969, moved Milano's upstairs—and upscale. 'It was an incredibly brave move—not just an enormous amount of money, but putting a restaurant on the first floor of a building—something which had never been done before in Brisbane.'

Young Dean had come along in 1962, so his earliest memories of his father were as a successful restaurateur—and someone he didn't see much of. He was educated by the Christian Brothers at St Joseph's, Gregory Terrace, where he 'copped a bit [of anti-Italian feeling] at school. But my cousins, who were five years younger than me, didn't. In fact, by then it was very trendy to be Italian. You could see the change.'

Young Dean was proud of his father. 'It was such a well-known restaurant—you'd meet your friends' parents and they'd all know it. I used to go with my mates and we'd sit around the table and have the best time. Dad'd come and say—what are you having, boys? All the boys had menus, and some would order fettucine, and some *scallopine piccante*, then Dad would look at me and say, five specials it is, then walk away.'

But it was his mother's food that he ate the most. 'You're always brought up with your mother's cooking, but I never tasted cooking like my mother's until I went to Florence when I was 23. Soon as I had the ravioli bolognese there I said, Jeez, it tastes like Mum's. A good bolognese is a wonderful thing. She's given me the recipe, and I've tried to make it the same but I can't.' (When asked to supply his mother's recipe for bolognese sauce, the reply was 'you've got to be joking.')

Gino's interest in wine was fuelled by his friendship with Len Evans, and the Merlos would often visit the Evans in the Hunter Valley, were Dean has fond memories of Evans cooking 'so quickly, so easily and with so much flare', and where Welsh/Italian connections were forged.

Dean Merlo didn't follow his father into the business, although as the only son he could so easily have done so. 'I thought it [running a restaurant] was great, but it looked like a hard slog—and also as time went on, and the option was there, I could see fine dining was struggling.' He took up the law, and finished his degree in 1983. He worked for a while for a Supreme Court judge, practised as a solicitor. Then he went overseas, where he worked in a merchant bank in England for a while, then in advertising and tourism in America. In America 'I saw this idea in Los Angeles—a coffee shop like this but takeaway, catering for the CBD. The Italian side of Dean Merlo loves the idea of the Italian coffee bar. 'There are people who'll come in, have a short black, and leave—it's a Roman idea. They've got a wonderful attitude— the espresso bar operator will never look at you—and if he does he's got a half snarl on his face, because the man's busy and you've got to know that. That's the attitude, it's brilliant. The people who come in there, they just gesture, they don't need to say anything, they come in every day—they get their *panino* [small bread rolls], they get their short black, and they like it real short. I wanted to duplicate that, but you can't do it. You're trying to duplicate a culture. We get some Italian guys in here. One guy comes in five times a day—short black—he doesn't say anything.'

Bar Merlo is a smart, slick operation, way ahead of anything else in the centre of Brisbane in 1995. He has a short, cafe menu of pasta, frittata and focaccia and cake with very good coffee. He understands the importance of having a dedicated machine operator, and chose the coffee he uses after 'intensive research with Dad looking for the right blend—he's got a great palate'. Neither will he reveal the source of his coffee to me, it's part of 'the mystique'.

When Dean decided against carrying on the family business, Gino sold Milano's in 1985. When asked why, Dean shrugs and replies, 'I believe there was nowhere else for him to go. He wasn't going to open another restaurant. All the challenges had gone.'

He even sold off his fabled cellar. 'He really went into wine in a big way. His was voted the best and biggest wine cellar in Australia every year. He had to get the building engineered so it could take the weight.' When it went to auction he did 'tremendously well out of the wines. He got the idea that 70–71 were going to be great years. They turned out to be two of the biggest years of the century. I think he realised 1000 per cent profit on the wines.' Sanctuary Cove bought about one-third of the collection, two-thirds went to private collectors . . . and its memory spurred on Michael Platsis.

Dean Merlo is happier with coffee than he was with the law: 'I've always liked coffee.' As far as he's concerned, the restaurant business is too much of a risk. 'That's why I was happy to open an espresso bar. Coffee's a drug.' So is the restaurant business.

# Dean Merlo's Zucchini Frittata

SERVES 6

30 g butter
1 onion, chopped
1 garlic clove, chopped
3–4 large zucchini, sliced
1 red capsicum, chopped
¼ cup fresh basil leaves
10 eggs
¼ teaspoon salt
a sprinkling of freshly
 ground black pepper
2 tablespoons freshly
 grated Parmesan cheese

In a large frying pan—you need a pan which can be placed under the griller, a heavy iron pan is best—melt the butter and sauté the onion and garlic until clear. Add the zucchini and capsicum. Stir until cooked, about 5 minutes. Add the basil.

In a bowl, mix together the eggs, salt, pepper and Parmesan cheese.

Add the egg mixture to the pan and reduce the heat.

When cooked, place under a griller to brown on top.

To serve: the frittata can be eaten hot or cold, cut into slices.

Beppi Polese in the cellar room at Beppi's in East Sydney in front of the *Bissietta* fresco.

*'It's not the ingredients that make the cuisine, it's the cuisine that makes the ingredients.'*

# CHAPTER FOURTEEN

# *Beppi Polese*

**C**ROSSING THE old Spit Bridge in 1956, you may well have come across an unusual sight. A rowboat bumping against the wooden pylons, in it a young couple, obviously of 'foreign appearance' (this is 1956), one with a knife, collecting something from just below the surface of the water. It was the young Beppi Polese and his new wife Norma, gathering mussels for the restaurant they had recently bought from a Yugoslavian.

Across the harbour in Double Bay, in the same year—maybe even on the same day, who knows?—the eleven-year-old author of this book and a mate standing under the wharf, up to our thighs in pristine harbour water (this is 1956), with bent forks stolen from home lashed to broomsticks, could be found spearing baby octopuses and throwing them into little plastic buckets. When we had a bucketful, we'd sell them to the wogs for sixpence.

'What do they want them for, bait?' my mate asked one day.

'They eat them,' I replied, mine being the more sophisticated household. My mother cooked spaghetti bolognaise.

'Aw yuck!' his face screwed up in horror and revulsion.

These two activities reveal a lot about the times. The Italians we sold the octopuses to would have taken them home and eaten them in private, amongst their own kind, often in a furtive and even frightened manner: these aliens they found themselves amongst (us) just wouldn't understand.

But Beppi and Norma Polese were about to change all that. And the mussels were the among the first shots to be fired in a gastronomic revolution that is still being fought—if on different fronts.

Beppi would take the mussels back to the kitchen at Beppi's, then as now on the ground floor of the St James Building on the corner of Yurong and Stanley Streets in East Sydney, and have them cooked up as *cozze alla marinara*.

And then, in those early days, he'd give them away. 'The mussels I used to put on the table,' Beppi told me, 'the same with the calamari, and say, go on, try them. They had to acquire the flavour.' Earlier on, he said something that was repeated time and again in the interviews I have done for this book: 'I find Australians very interesting because they're willing to try anything.' And in 1956, when Beppi and Norma opened the doors of Beppi's, there was an awful lot we hadn't tried.

'Beppi's was the sun coming over the horizon,' reports Max Lake, then a member, along with Rudy Komon and Neville Baker, of the Wine and Food Society, 'because although we knew Australian-Greek food and Australian-Chinese food, the first taste of really authentic Italian food we had in Sydney was at Beppi's.'

Sydney had had French food for many years—Jeanne and Henri Renault's Hermitage restaurant and Walter Magnus' Claremont and Coq d'Or were both open during the war years. But that early French food was not as democratic as Beppi's. I remember walking, with my father, down Elizabeth Bay Road when I was very young, and he pointed out a beautiful two-storey Victorian house set back from the road in a lush garden. 'That was a restaurant during the war,' he told me, 'for officers only.' That was Kenneil. But Beppi's was more than a revolution in food (Jeanne Renault told me that Henri Renault was serving mussels to the members of the Wine and Food Society before the war), it was a revolution in egalitarian eating, one of the first restaurants in Sydney where everyone was welcome, from Sir Frank Packer and his boys Kerry and Clyde, to the lowliest D grade journalist on Sir Frank's *Daily Telegraph*.

Beppi's has been renovated recently—crisp white walls inside with a smart black cotton awning out front, shades of Milan, where Beppi learnt his craft. Large windows have been let in to the front, and the barber shop next door has finally been moved down the street to make more room for tables. But Beppi chooses to speak to me in the cellar room at the back of the restaurant, unchanged from those days, except for the gradual accretion around the walls of what is currently around 10,000 bottles of wine. On the one wineless wall is a fresco, inscribed '*Tofontanelus alias Bissietta Miniatensis pinait*' (as far as I can ascertain a dog Latin private joke whose meaning is lost in the mists of time) by one Professor Bissietta, another Sydney Italian, brought to Sydney to paint murals and frescoes by the Hordern family who set up an art gallery, and who taught art and Italian (to, among others, the young Norma Polese, then Zaccaria, before her first trip to Italy) in Pitt Street between the wars.

The room resonates with almost 40 years of good food, good wine and good conversation. I can almost see Max Lake ('I was looking up girls' legs in those days') and the late Rudy Komon (who somehow was never young) sipping and chomping. If there were gastronomic heritage listings, Beppi's would be an early nomination.

Norma Polese's parents were unusual immigrants. First, her father came from Sandrigo in the province of Vicenze and her mother from Toppo in the province of Udine in 1929, before the post-war immigration boom. And, secondly, they were relatively well off. Norma's father was a furniture manufacturer. Her parents met and married in Sydney in 1932, lived first in Earlwood and moved, when their Olympia Cabinet Company was doing well, to Bellevue Hill.

Growing up at that time, without the support of other Italian children, Norma had worse than normal childhood experiences of feeling different—'I hated my mother speaking to me in Italian in public'—and the usual cruel schoolyard taunts: 'they'd say look at Norma Zaccaria, she's got a dirty ear.'

Unlike many Italians, (father) Zaccaria wasn't interned during the war, although the police did come around looking for firearms, and Norma finished school, went to St Patrick's Business College, and began office work. In 1954, the family went on an extended trip to Italy, spent the summer in San Remo, celebrated her twenty-first in Venice, and returned in 1955.

Her mother's brother Roberto had opened a restaurant called Milano's in Edgecliff. The family went one afternoon, and that's where she met young Beppi Polese.

'You said, I've been to the beach,' she reminds him, 'and I said, why don't you take me next time.'

'She picked me up,' he shrugs, and, to my incredulity at such behaviour from a nice young Italian girl in the fifties, he adds, 'you have to remember Italians from the north are more liberal.'

Beppi Polese was born in San Giovanni di Polcenigo, a village about 100 kilometres from Venice. His father was a small landholder, and, as a boy, Beppi worked with him tending the land. In 1939, at the age of fourteen, his mother packed him up and sent him to Milan where he worked in a factory for a year. But what he earned was not enough to live, so his sister found him a job as an apprentice in the Albergo Doria 'in Via Pisani' he remembers, 'in front of the railway station.' No-one could accuse Beppi Polese of not starting at the very bottom: 'I used to rub the parquet floors with steel wool, then I worked in the kitchen, the dining room and finally serving.' At the end of a year and a half, he'd found his metier, and began amassing experience.

When Beppi was learning to be a waiter during the Second World War in Italy—and, indeed, after the war—the training in the kitchen and on the floor of the restaurant was French, and rigid. 'First you're an apprentice,' Beppi explained, 'then a *commis*—a busboy who does the service between the dining room and the kitchen. Then a waiter, then a *chef de rang*—in Australian terms a station head, in charge of five or six tables, then chef, or head waiter. Before advancing to *chef de rang*, you have to be able to dissect, for example, ducks and pigeons at the table, to carve—I did a course in carving—and to be able to peel fruit in the old style.' By 1950, Beppi was working in Florence as a *chef de rang*. But first there was a war to attend to. Beppi Polese had an interesting war.

From Milan, he went to Venice, and worked until 1943 at both the Danieli and the Gritti Palace as a *commis*. 1943, you might remember, was a bad year for Mussolini. The war was going disastrously, his followers melted away, he resigned on 25th July, and was thrown into gaol by Vittoria Emmanuel, then, when liberated, formed a brief and futile government he called *La Repubblica de Salo*. He needed an army, and a healthy eighteen-year-old *commis* waiter in Venice looked like good material. But, by this time, Italy was fighting against Germany—Beppi's brother's parachute corps had joined the 8th army in Sicily. It was a confused and dangerous time. Beppi takes up the story.

'Three of us—the others were Cipollato, a head waiter, and Giacomelo, a fellow from a village not far from Polcenigo—decided to escape. I couldn't imagine myself as a fascist, we'd always been against this. The Triparti Embassy—the Japanese, Germans and Italians—were stationed at the Grand Hotel. There was a minister there we knew (from the dining room) and he gave us a letter of recommendation so that we could go to Austria. When we got to the Italian-Austrian border, they tore it up and put us in a train with Russian and Croatian prisoners. They took us to a concentration camp in Vienna near the *Riesenrad* [the huge ferris wheel made famous by the film *The Third Man*, in the Prater, Vienna's amusement park]. I remember American planes dropping bombs. The Germans would let us out of the concentration camp and we didn't know where to hide.'

After a dispute over labour conditions, Beppi was sent to dig anti-tank trenches on the Hungarian-Austrian border, but he escaped and walked the 120 kilometres back to Vienna, with the idea of getting back to Italy. He stowed away on a train to Villach on the Austrian-Italian border, crossed the border safely, secured a passport, and went back to Polcenigo. When he did, he found the Germans already there. 'I joined some partisan friends in the mountains. We used to come down in the night to put mines on the freeway.'

We spoke about food during this period on the run. In the cities it was a matter of scavenging—they ate orange peel, and stole bread from the bakery. 'But you know, when you live in the country, you always have potatoes, sweet corn, vegetables—you survive. When you only have limited things, you make the food taste and you experiment to find the best way to give it flavour. In the country, we learnt to go around the fields and pick the greens from the ground. We call it *radicchio bottonéra*.' Today, it's fashionable, and it's called *cucina povera*. But then, on the run from the Germans, or surviving in a remote village, it was this need to make a luxury of necessity that was all that was left of civilisation.

After the war, ironically, Beppi was drafted into the army for national service. Then he went back to Venice, and a couple of years of working the seasons around Europe—the Baglioni in Florence (where he first achieved the rank of *chef de rang* in 1950), the Regina and the Excelsior in Rome. He applied for a job in London (at the Savoy), and, thankfully, didn't get it, applied to come to Australia, and did so in 1952, paying his passage to Melbourne in the *Neptunia* with money he'd earned during a season at the Excelsior de Lido in Venice.

Once in Melbourne, he activated contacts within the already extensive Melbourne Italian community. His friend Cipollato, with whom he had been in the concentration camp in Austria, had a brother who worked at Mario's and knew the head waiter at Romano's in Sydney, and recommended Beppi for a job there as a waiter.

Romano's, run by the flamboyant racehorse owner and (self-confessed) sly grogger Azzalin ('the Dazzlin'') Orlando Romano, was one of the two great restaurant/nightspots of its time in Sydney—the other being Jim Bendrodt's Princes—and had been since the 1930s.

Romano got on well with the handsome young waiter from the Veneto, and, in 1953, sent him to run the restaurant in his hotel in Wagga Wagga, also called Romano's, which he had bought (as The Commercial) in 1946 for fifty thousand pounds.

'I had a lot of problems,' Beppi recalls. 'They wouldn't wear ties in the dining room,' explains Norma, 'he thought that was terrible.' We can only imagine the impact of Wagga Wagga in the 1950s on the elegant *chef de rang* from Florence, Venice and Milan.

'God, I mean, these people would come to the restaurant [with their clothes] full of mud. I nearly fainted.' And what did they eat? 'Beef and lamb mainly. But we used to cook some pasta—lasagne—the chef was Italian, the menus were very good. I used to cook steak Diane in the old Romano's style, at the table.'

This dish—steak Diane—was supposed to have been invented by Tony Clerici, who worked as head waiter at the first Romano's in York Street. But Beppi maintains it was an example of the English 'continental' style food that passed for both French and Italian food in Australia in this period—Clerici (like others) was recruited from London.

Eventually and inevitably, the clash between Polese and Wagga came to a head. Wagga lost. Polese left. 'I used to refuse people [entry to the dining room], the manager said you'd better stop doing this, so I gave in, but I wasn't happy.'

After Wagga, a period of disenchantment set in. He worked casually at Romano's and at the Australia Hotel, but he also applied for a licence as a taxi driver. 'Our game is very demanding, you work every night and Sunday, it was a terrible life in the beginning. I didn't have any friends.' But it was this stint of taxi driving—and meeting Norma—that eventually led to Beppi's.

'I gave up driving a cab [unable to cut his ties with the restaurant world entirely, he was also working at Milano's at night] because once when I was driving on a Sunday—I was in Double Bay or somewhere—bang, all of a sudden I woke up. I'd been sleeping at the wheel, the car went against a tree. It was then I decided to open my own place.'

My first taste of Italian food in Sydney was at La Veneziana in Stanley Street, which later became Mario's (if you looked down as you entered the first Mario's you could still see the name La Veneziana in mosaic on the floor). This was a little later than the opening of Beppi's—six or seven years—but little had changed in that time. Here, and at the other Italian restaurants round at the time, like Lorenzini's, Florentino's and Chianti, we ate what we thought—and the people who cooked it told us—was Italian food. You can still find this 'Italian food' in some places; there were usually three veal dishes—*piccata*, *limone* and *marsala*; a chicken cacciatore, and a handful of spaghettis (and, later, fettucines).

After a bowl of spag bol, accompanied by a bottle of Cawarra claret, you'd be handed a card from a commercial gelato company (like Mr Pisa) with lurid coloured photos of the various offerings: a real treat was the ball of chocolate ice cream dusted with cocoa and a maraschino cherry in the middle called a *tartufo*. This, with minor variations, was Italian restaurant food in Sydney (and all over Australia) in the 1950s and well into the 1960s. Until the arrival of Beppi Polese, who didn't want to open a cheap Italian restaurant, but a good Italian restaurant, serving the kinds of dishes he remembered from Italy.

This, in itself, was unusual for the time. Beppi had been trained in the French tradition. The great hotels of Italy—the Gritti Palace and the Danieli in Venice, the Regina and the Excelsior in Rome—where he had worked as a waiter were, up until well into the 1970s, in the grip of French classical cuisine.

In 1995, I interviewed Doctor Natale Rusconi, the managing director of the Hotel Cipriani in Venice, and someone who had worked for many years in the hotel and restaurant business. He told me, 'When I began my career in the Palazzo in Venice in 1970, all the menus were written in French! If you had dinner in a grand hotel and asked for a pasta or a risotto, it was a scandal.' For a professional of Beppi Polese's level to even consider real Italian food was extremely daring.

At Milano, for example, the restaurant run by Norma's Uncle Roberto, the chef was an Egyptian by the name of Saheed, whose training was French, and whose menu was, as outlined by Beppi, '. . . Italian with a bit of French— pasta, steak Diane, chicken Kiev, chicken chasseur (cacciatore in Italian).' The standard restaurant fare of the period: where did it come from?

It was, according to Beppi, 'the sort of cuisine that came to Australia with Clerici and Romano, because they had all come here via London. In London you worked in a hotel or restaurant where the basis [of the food] was French, or even French/English, and there is a kind of involvement with Italian cuisine at the same time,' because they themselves were Italian. 'They came over because Dawson was the fellow who got Romano and Clerici from London for a nightclub and they cooked this food in his nightclub. And they cooked *coq au vin* and things like that which come from London.'

But Signor Polese had different ideas. 'I came over here and my idea wasn't involved with French at all. I wanted to cook Italian food.'

The Yugoslavs who had run the cafe which became Beppi's had a system of luncheon vouchers. For four shillings and sixpence, you had a three-course meal and a cup of tea. That was the way Beppi's started. They didn't change the menu straight away, but kept doing the stuffed cabbage, the stuffed capsicum and the schnitzels.

'Gradually, I changed the menu to an Italian one,' recalls Beppi, 'calamari, artichokes, mussels. Nino Ruello [Nick Ruello's father, see Chapter 15] remembers me because I used to go to the fish market myself.'

Produce was hard to come by back then. As well as gathering mussels, they recruited Norma's mother to grow radicchio, and friends of hers to grow artichokes. The pasta was, at first, imported Barilla, then local, although the problem with local pasta was the grain, because at first they didn't use the hard grain, *Triticum durum*, needed for dried pasta, *pasta asciutta*. 'We used to get olive oil from Fiorelli and Cantarella [both companies still around today]—good olive oil, mostly from Tuscany, but it wasn't yet much in demand here.'

There were two events that changed the course of events for the better for Beppi—and for Sydney. A restaurant needs an audience. And Beppi and his first chef, Guiseppe Arena, finally found one. 'The word went out, and then I had some of the members of the Wine and Food Society here every Friday. Rudy Komon walked in with a bottle of wine wrapped in newspaper under his arm. Rudy had come from Yugoslavia, he was experienced in cheese but not so much in wine. He brought Neville Baker, Max Lake, there were twelve or fourteen of them. They used to say to me, Beppi, just cook what you want and bring it over. I was in my glory!'

Early typical menus for those Friday lunches might include, depending on the season, those mussels, stewed artichokes, *polpo in umido* [octopus stew] with polenta. 'We used to use rice at the time, you couldn't find polenta. We made polenta in the beginning with semolina, the Roman way. I had the time to do risotto for them. By the time they'd tasted the wine and talked about it, they could wait for the risotto. We used to use Chinese rice.'

By 1960, Beppi's was doing well. At about this time, another Italian from San Giovanni di Polcenigo came back from a stint working in Surfer's Paradise to work with Beppi, once more, as a waiter. Aldo Zuzza, who was himself to be influential in Italian food in Sydney in his own right, had worked with Beppi at Romano's, and, back in 1955, Beppi and Aldo had even spoken of a partnership in a restaurant venture. This was not to be, and for now, Aldo was working for Beppi.

In 1963, to establish themselves in Australia, Alitalia Airlines held a competition to ascertain the best Italian restaurant in Sydney. 'By then there were about twelve of us. We had to produce a four course meal, balance it properly, and suggest wines to go with each course. We won the first prize—a gold fork. Then the place started to take off very quickly.'

Thirty years on, what does Beppi Polese think of the food being produced by this new generation of Australian cooks? As you would expect, the old general is critical of the young Turks. But not unreasonably so. 'I find a lot of young chefs, they haven't had the experience, they read a few books and they start cooking. Fine, you have to read the books. But you have to have the experience too. What I don't like is when I go to places—I won't name them—and they have, for example, gnocchi or risotto, and it's not. To me it's a sacrilege. I've had gnocchi served to me in a soup plate with broth, call it *zuppa di gnocchi*, but don't call it *gnocchi di patate al sugo di funghi* [gnocchi in mushroom sauce].'

'These young fellows come out with some wonderful ideas, but they make mistakes—they are wild on flavours. They don't know that each particular flavour belongs to a particular type of dish, because not every flavour belongs with everything. For instance, I had a ravioli with crab sauce and balsamic vinegar. OK, balsamic vinegar, yes, but a drop! That's where the experience comes in.'

On the birth of Australian cuisine, as one of its—if he will forgive me the appellation—godfathers, he has much to say. 'With all these different nationalities, we are going to create an Australian cuisine. But this is the first generation of chefs. The next will improve it.' And of the oft-asserted notion that we have a cuisine because we have the ingredients, he says, with profundity, 'it's not the ingredients that make the cuisine, it's the cuisine that makes the ingredients for your imagination, and the dishes you cook.' He goes on to explain.

'Dishes. That's important. Let's go back to the Roman times. Rome was such a small city. Any idea they picked up in a country they conquered, they'd bring it back to Rome. Rome was only Roman, but [they would say] that's a good idea, we'll have that. Like the snail from Africa. The mandarin from Persia. And that is how Italian cuisine was built. They brought back the ingredients and they used them in a Roman style. And then the Romans had their own cooks—slaves, the slaves of the countries they occupied, and they cooked the original dishes from their countries. That is what happened.'

A quick glance through the recipes of Apicius, an Imperial Roman cook, yields such ingredients as 'Aethiopian or Syrian cumin', 'a pinch of ginger'.

We also find sausage from Epirus, cherries from the Pontus and oysters from England. As eclectic a list of ingredients as you will find at a modern Australian providore's—but awaiting a repertoire of dishes. Flour and water are the ingredients. Pasta makes it a cuisine.

The latest chapter in the Beppi and Norma Polese story is Mezzaluna, a new restaurant (relatively, it opened in January 1991) run jointly by Norma and their son Marc (a veterinarian, a profession that makes some customers wary of the osso buco, according to Norma). The building is owned by the Poleses, and was let to restaurateur and chef Mogens Bay Ebersen, who ran Butler's there very successfully for many years. When Butler's closed, Norma persuaded Beppi to allow her to take it over.

'When I said how about if I give it a go?' Norma recalled, 'Beppi and Marc looked at me and said—what would you know about running a restaurant?'

Beppi demurs. 'What I said was we need another restaurant like we need a hole in the head.' In theory, he was right. 1991 was the middle of one of the worst recessions Australia has ever had. It was not a propitious time to open a restaurant. But Norma prevailed—as I suspect she has often in the past—and Mezzaluna opened. This is their avant garde venture. Once a year, Norma, Marc and Beppi return to Italy, and pick up recipes from the more unusual restaurants, bring them back and work on them with their Australian chefs.

Beppi's today is an institution. Which doesn't mean what that word usually means. The food is still of a high enough standard to place it in the top echelon of Italian restaurants in Sydney—or in Australia for that matter. But what it does mean is that over the almost 40 years of its existence, Beppi's has been the kindergarten, the training ground for an astonishing number of successful Italian restaurateurs and chefs.

In 1983, David Dale wrote a Walkley Award-winning story for the *Sydney Morning Herald* entitled 'The Italian Waiter Conspiracy'. In it, he meticulously unravelled the network of relationships between Sydney's Italian restaurateurs. At the centre of the web sat Beppi Polese. As anyone who has had anything to do with Italians would suspect, he is not universally liked. Statements recorded by Dale include such as 'Beppi's problem is that he thinks he is God'.

Nevertheless, it was at Beppi's that Aldo Zuzza (Darcy's) and his brother and sister-in-law Guiseppe and Antonietta Zuzza (The Mixing Pot), Lino Mascolo (Lino's) and his brother Guiseppe (Mariu) to name only the most prominent few, made their mark. Of any criticism, Beppi has only this to say: 'I know food. I know flavours. I know my training. I know what works. Sometimes I get upset because I can't get the message through to other people.' If we are eating better Italian food in Sydney today than we were ten, twenty, thirty years ago, it is largely due to Beppi and Norma Polese.

## Polenta con il Muss
### Polenta with Salami

SERVES 4

butter
50 g lean pancetta, cut
 into small pieces
8 slices of fresh
 homemade salami, cut
 3 cm thick
4 sage leaves
6 tablespons plain flour
1¼ cups (310 mL) milk
teaspoon of ground pepper

POLENTA
4 cups (1 litre) water
4 cups (1 litre) milk
2 tablespoons salt
900 g polenta

Brush a frying pan with butter. Fry the pancetta with the salami and sage until the pancetta is crisp, about 2 minutes. Remove the salami from the pan.

Add the flour slowly to the pan, mixing with a wooden spoon until it is amalgamated. Add the milk, stirring continuously until the sauce is thick.

Replace the salami in the pan and set aside.

To make polenta, pour the water and milk into a large saucepan (preferably copper) and bring to the boil over a medium heat. Add the salt and then add the polenta flour a little at a time, mixing constantly with a whisk.

When all the polenta has been added reduce the heat and simmer while mixing continually with a wooden spoon. Cook for approximately 30 minutes or until a thick consistency has obtained.

To serve: soak a tea towel in water and wring out the excess water. Lay the tea towel on a tray and pour the polenta onto the tea towel. Cover the polenta with the four corners of the tea towel and place the tray with polenta in it in the middle of the table. Portion out the salami mixture and sauce onto individual plates. Allow guests to serve themselves the polenta using a wet wooden spatula.

# Anguilla dell'Alto Livenza in Umido con Polenta
Eel stew with Polenta, Alto Livenza style

SERVES 4

['In Umido' is a method of cooling in a very small amount of liquid, literally 'sweated'. The closest term in English is 'stewed'.]

1.25 kg freshwater eels
juice of ½ a lemon
2–3 rosemary sprigs
salt and freshly ground
  black pepper
2 medium onions, cut into
  small pieces
olive oil
8 very ripe pear tomatoes
  cut into small pieces
4 tablespoons sun-dried
  tomato paste
150 mL white wine
plain flour for coating the
  eel
Polenta (see previous
  recipe)

Wash the eels well and dry them with a cloth. Cut into 8-cm long pieces, discarding the internal organs, head and tail and place in a bowl. Sprinkle with lemon juice, add rosemary, salt and pepper and leave to marinate for 15 minutes.

In a large frying pan, pan-fry the onion in a little olive oil until brown. Add the tomato and tomato paste and wine and cook for 30 minutes over a low heat.

Flour the pieces of eel and brown in another frying pan with olive oil. Add the pieces of eel to the pan containing the sauce and simmer for another 15 minutes.

Prepare the polenta as for previous recipe.

To serve: portion out the eels and sauce onto individual plates, and allow guests to serve themselves with the polenta using a wet wooden spatula.

## Risi e Bisi
Rice with Peas

SERVES 4

This dish is served moister than most risotto dishes, somewhere between soup and risotto.

1 medium onion
1 celery stick
⅓ cup (90 g) butter
400 g fresh peas
2 cups Arborio rice
3 litres chicken stock
grated Parmesan cheese

Finely chop the onion and celery. Melt the butter in a large saucepan over a medium heat. Brown the onion and celery in the butter. Add the peas and the rice and stir briefly to coat the rice. Add enough stock to cover the rice and simmer slowly. Keep adding the stock until it evaporates and the rice is *al dente*, about 15 minutes.

Serve in a large soup plate and sprinkle with grated Parmesan.

Nick Ruello at the Sydney Fish Markets.

'He'd obviously never seen anything like it. All this black stuff coming out of our mouths!'

# CHAPTER FIFTEEN

# Nick Ruello

ONE OF the first conversations I had with Nick Ruello was about the size of a prawn's penis. It may intrigue you, even amuse you, to learn that the animal with the largest penis (in relation to its size) in the world is Sydney Harbour's own greasyback prawn (*Metapenaeus bennettae*).

Now, if you're like me, you see a pile of cooked prawns glistening pinkly in the fish market and say—yes, they're prawns; the big ones are king prawns; the little ones are schoolies (harbour prawns). But when Nick Ruello, MSc Marine Biology, son of a harbour prawn fisherman, prawn biologist with the NSW Fisheries Department, and seafood consultant to industry and government scoops up a handful, it's a biology lesson.

'Right,' he says, fanning them out like a poker hand, 'three species here. There's an eastern king, a red spot—see the red spot on the shell? And a blue leg—you guessed it, blue legs. The red spot comes from north-eastern Queensland; the blue leg runs everywhere except Victoria and NSW; and the eastern king runs off the NSW coast. And this lucky little bloke is the greasyback.'

It's no wonder that this man knows more about prawns—and just about everything that swims, floats or scurries around the ocean bed—than most living Australians. Both sides of his family have ancient connections with the sea, and fish; his wife Judith (nee Woods) began her working life as a marine biologist; he was, for some time, the only Japanese speaking fish merchant in Sydney (perhaps the world?) with a degree in marine biology. It's a wonder he hasn't got fins.

But the Ruello story starts for us with Nick's father, Nino. Nino Ruello was born in Sicily in the village of Ganzirri about 8 kilometres outside Messina. A fish merchant, he bought job lots of fish from around the Sicilian islands.

He would cruise the islands in a 20-metre launch, and sell them in various local markets.

Nick's mother Melina (nee Zappala) is from a family of swordfishermen on the Italian side of the Straits of Messina, near the rock called Scylla, of Scylla and Charybdis fame.

It's the current—called Charybdis—that brings the rich marine life to this area, and, as Nick told me, 'That's why the swordfish migrate through there. The last time I was there they were harpooning the swordfish. There were high lookout towers on the boats, and a guy with a hand harpoon.'

Nino and Melina were married in 1944, Nick was born in 1945, his younger brother Tino was born in 1947, and they decided to migrate to Australia. 'My mother's family were relatively well off, but my father had been in the war and had been a prisoner of war of the Germans for a while, and even though the fishing was terrific after war [no-one had been fishing commercially for five years], I imagine he wanted a break. He was 27, he'd heard that everyone had jobs galore in Australia. I suppose he wanted to show [his wife's family] he could do it on his own. He wanted to take my mother away from her family and not be in their shadow.'

Nino came first, arriving in Sydney in 1949 (the rest of the family came a year later), went to join relatives in Innisfail, and tried his hand at canecutting. This was not a good idea for a fisherman. He developed allergic rashes, so he came back to Sydney and worked as a labourer in the inner-city areas. In those days, there was no shortage of factories and jobs for unskilled men. CSR at Pyrmont, Cyclop Toys at Annandale. Nick says, 'My old man told me he used to walk past and they'd grab him and offer him a job. He couldn't speak a word of English but all he was doing was pulling levers or loading bags of molasses, he didn't need English.'

Soon after the rest of the family arrived—they first lived above a shop in Annandale—Nino became involved in harbour fishing. And Nick was out there helping. 'I recollect as a kid in fifth class at Holy Cross College helping him haul in bream and whiting and trevally, whatever was going. All we had was a hauling net and a little rowing boat. I was scared shitless, up to my waist in water, hauling in the net, thinking—what am I doing, there are sharks out there, this is night-time! I was ten or eleven. I remember taking home the baby stingrays that popped out of the female fish. Everyone thought I was a weirdo.'

But how could he possibly escape an obsession with fish? 'My earliest rec-ollection of fish was collecting a series of tropical fish cards in Weet-Bix packs.

I must have been eight. And bringing home *gambusia* [mosquito fish that live in shallow ponds] in a jam jar.'

Later, Nino bought a trawler and trawled Sydney Harbour and Botany Bay, mainly for prawns. 'One year I remember, one of the wet years, big floods, working 24 hours a day up around Homebush Bay—after rain you get schoolies so thick you wouldn't believe it.'

Eventually the Ruellos moved to Cleveland Street, not an Italian neighbourhood, but with a few Italian families around. Times were tough. 'We were poor. Even among our neighbours. My mum will kill me for telling this story, but I remember in those days the Italians used to buy pasta by the case from a deli in Cleveland Street run by the Bambagiottis, a French–Italian couple. At one stage my old man was between jobs—or maybe we were just always on the borderline in those days—some visitors came and my mother said, oh what a shame, we've just had lunch, and I piped up, what do you mean, we haven't eaten since we ran out of pasta yesterday.'

Aside from poverty, getting the food they were used to eating was not all that easy for the Italians in Sydney in those days. Although in his book *Correggio Jones and the Runaways* (a history of Italians in Australia and Australians in Italy), Desmond O'Grady notes a macaroni factory in Hepburn Springs, Victoria, in the 1860s, it wasn't until the establishment of Nanda by Frank de Pasquale in Brisbane in 1948 that pasta was being made in any big way in Australia—and even then it was not being made with the hard wheat *Triticum durum*, essential for *pasta asciutta*, dried pasta. In Sydney, there were a few pioneering delis, like Bambagiottis, and Toni's, run by Toni Peruch from the Veneto and his Australian wife Fay in Glebe until 1994. Toni first imported pasta from Italy, and then began bringing down a semi-trailer load every week from the Nanda factory. He was also one of the first, in the 1950s, to begin selling Italian coffee, and olive oil in 44-gallon (200 litre) drums from Umbria, and cheeses like pecorino and Parmigiano. But mostly, it was a matter of scrounging.

'As a kid,' Nick told me, 'we had relatives and friends who worked on ships and they all used to smuggle in food and clothing, things like pointed shoes, and delicacies like Italian nougat, salamis and cheeses.'

But the Ruellos, while never rich, soon escaped from poverty. Nick again. 'My old man was a real entrepreneur with seafood. He was the first in Australia to farm mussels—they hadn't invented the word aquaculture then—he'd put out the spat on chicken wire in Botany Bay, harvest them and then pickle them, which is the only way the Australians would eat them. The problem is in those days, Botany Bay was full of bream—still is—and bream love mussels.'

'He got into salted fish early, and canned tuna—Italian style in oil. The brand was called Aurora. He got successful and was bought out by one of the big companies to get him out of the business. But he never became really wealthy. He never did things to build an empire, he never invested to make a fortune. He just sort of did things. We share that in common.'

By this time Nick Ruello was around fifteen, and still helping his Dad, 'I finished my intermediate certificate and everyone else is out chasing surf and sex and I'm filling cans of tuna at Bankstown thinking life's a bitch. That's one Christmas I remember.'

Nick did his leaving certificate at Cleveland Street High, a school he describes as 'segregated, there were the wogs, the Chinese and the Aussies'. He didn't get into much trouble for a couple of reasons. 'I got the usual taunts—wog, garlic smuggler, garlic muncher. But I was smart enough to know when to run and when to fight—and most times I elected to run because I'm too small to fight. Also, I always went to schools where there was a fair mix of new Australians. The Australians had to be careful about taking you on when there were 20 wogs.'

Cleveland Street at that time also had a fair mix of pupils from affluent Strathfield, and one of these boys became friendly with the young Ruello. 'He wore tailor-made grey suits and used to talk about having a freezer chest full of chickens at home. I couldn't understand why you'd want to keep a freezer full of chickens.'

The gap between the food 'we' ate and the food 'they' ate is no better illustrated than by a story from Nick's later teenage years, by which time the family had moved to Brighton. 'We had a kitchen built out on a verandah, and the baker used to bring the bread to the back door. We were eating spaghetti with cuttlefish sauce, and the baker came to the door and we could see the look on his face. He'd obviously never seen anything like it. All this black stuff coming out of our mouths. He mightn't even have been a spaghetti eater in those days.'

They ate a lot of seafood at home. Nino would bring home the less popular fish. 'What fishermen tend to do is sell the big value stuff, the bream and the whiting, and bring home the odds and ends; the soft shell prawns, the odd crab, all the big ugly rock fish, and make big hearty things like *cioppino* [fish soup, sort of an Italian bouillabaisse, see recipe], or a sauce for pasta.'

Meanwhile, Nino had traded his small trailer for a bigger one, and later began retailing fish in the old Haymarket fish markets. A bad accident (he was hit by a taxi outside the market) put him out of work for a few years—and meant more hardship for the Ruellos. But he came back, first mending nets, then, once more, as a fishmonger.

After school, Nick went to Sydney University and studied science. Marine biology wasn't an option then, so he majored in biology, and studied zoology, biochemistry and histology. He also got into the prawn business.

'I had to work my way through uni. One of the things we (brother Tino was by now also at university) did was buy prawns from the harbour fishermen. We'd meet the boats at 5AM, load up with prawns, and take them out to Lilyfield where we'd cook them, then deliver them to customers like Victor's in King Street and David Jones in the city. We took about a ton a day, and we had to get to uni by 9AM.'

'We'd change out of our smellies in the car and whip into lectures, and sometimes we were late. I had a professor called Cleland. He got the shits with me for being late. But when I told him why, he said, fair enough, and he told me he used to work at the market when he was a student. He said look at the literature and you'll see two papers on whiting by K. W. Cleland—that's me. So we didn't have any more hassles coming in late.'

After graduation, his first job was with the fisheries department. Although he hadn't studied marine biology then, he got the job because of his family business, his obvious interest, and because 'they took a punt on me. The director at that time was a bit of an odd character, Don Francois. He's now got a little vineyard in the Hunter Valley. He had a liking for Italians and we got on well in the interview.' This put an end to his prawn retailing activities. What he and Tino had been doing was 'borderline, basically black market, but the fisheries turned a blind eye to it. But when I went to the department, I kept right away from the family business. I never knew what the old man was up to.'

One of the things he was up to in 1967 was moving into the new fish market at Pyrmont, where it is today. There were only two retailers who went across to the new market, Ruello and Arena—Manettas paid rent for a couple of months, saw Ruello and Arena losing money, and pulled out. There was one more, Whiteman, in another building but outside the main market area. Where Ruello was then is where the De Costi shop is today, but it was less than half its current size.

It was a very primitive affair. 'In those days, there wouldn't have been wharves. Most of the trawlers unloaded by truck—they still do. Firstly, it's cheaper, secondly it allows them to sell a little bit on the black—and thirdly, in those days with crews living on the boats, it [Darling Harbour] was closer [to leave their boats there] if they wanted a night out. They could talk a girl into coming down to the trawler at Darling Harbour, but not Pyrmont.'

Nick was with the Fisheries Department for ten years. During that time, he completed his MSc in prawn biology and married Judith Woods, whom he met at university (on a study trip to Heron Island with the biology department), and who later took a job with CSIRO involved in prawn handling and processing, and later with the Commonwealth Government working around Australia on the food side of prawns. Pretty soon, they were known in the industry as the prawn king and queen. 'There was a national prawn conference in Maroochydore in 1973, and there was a photograph taken of us alongside this big fibreglass prawn that made it into the national media.'

Around this time, Nino was considering retiring and Judith was at a crossroads with her career. Their eldest son, also Nino, was born. And Nick was getting restless. He'd gone as far as he could with the department. It was a series of meetings that Francois sent him to in Canberra that made up his mind for him. 'They were going to re-organise the department and put me in charge of marine fisheries research. I sat in those meetings and thought—this is not for me. It all started to fall into place. I thought—why don't we buy the family business and put our ideas into practice?' Both the Ruellos felt that the fish industry could do a lot better with its stock—and that meant retailing.

By the time the Ruellos moved into Pyrmont, Musumeci had joined the market, so now there were three. The Ruello shop was next to Noel Arena's outlet. Nick and Judith started learning how to be aggressive retailers. The fish market had taken a big dive when first they moved to Pyrmont. At Haymarket, it had been part of a fruit and vegetable market, and behind the old Paddy's Market. But Pyrmont then was in the middle of nowhere. They still had their ethnic clientele—with Asians and especially Japanese becoming more and more important—but if they didn't entice the Anglo-Australians, they couldn't make enough money. Nick soon learnt important lessons in publicity and customer cultivation.

'Cliff Ryan used to write the shopping column for *The Sun* in those days. When I was 21 and fresh out of uni, I met Cliff and I said why do you write such rubbish? He obviously didn't have the time to research his stuff.' When Nick had his own shop, he soon learnt the difference between good research and good copy. 'I'd tell Cliff it's so dry up in the Gulf of Carpentaria, the

Aborigines are doing rain dances, so Cliff'd write a great story about it.' From Noel Arena he learnt how to cultivate the media. 'Noel used to cater to the celebrities. He had the gift of calling people into his little cubbyhouse and giving them a drink. These were the days when the media were just beginning to get interested in food, and Noel was a great mate of John Laws, he used to deliver cases of stuff to him, so Laws would promote him. I built up my connections with Brian Bury and Malcolm T. Elliott. I learnt what the media wanted—they wanted something new. That's what the word means, news.'

It wasn't long before the marketer had won out completely over the scientist. 'When I repainted the front of the shop, I took the liberty of calling it "Australia's Leading Fish Market". Who cares? In a couple of years it was.' But the scientist occasionally came in handy: he built a little museum where people could see all sorts of piscatorial curios. Anything strange from the sea that came up in the auction, he'd bid for it. 'I've got pictures of myself with a 400 kg swordfish. When the first live Tasmanian crabs came to Sydney, Ruello's was the first to put in glass tanks. We were innovators.'

In the mid-70s the Anglos started coming to the market—Nick's estimate was that the dollar value was still 80 per cent ethnic market, 20 per cent Australians: 'They [ethnics] eat more seafood, and eat it more often.' It was the early days of the raising of food consciousness amongst, at least, middle-class urban Sydney. Nick shows how the prawn tells the story of our development.

'In the fifties and even into the sixties outside the cities, we were all eating boiled prawns, schoolies were cheap, people would have prawn nights. When I was a biologist on the Clarence River in 1967, they used to put schoolies on the bar instead of peanuts. Then we started to fish offshore, so prices went up and we started getting into bigger prawns. This is the era of the garlic prawn. Then we developed overseas markets which siphoned off the bigger prawns and forced up the price domestically even higher. It wasn't until relatively recently when they started to freeze green (uncooked) prawns on the boat that you got good quality green prawns in Sydney. Today it's the era of the Thai prawn.'

But Nick was getting bored with retailing in the late 1970s, and so began to develop a business selling to restaurants. 'We started doing what the Flying Squid Brothers and Martin's Seafoods (two quality Sydney seafood brokers) are doing now. Ruello's was the forerunner of the white tablecloth fish merchant.' In those days he was supplying restaurants like Darcy's in Paddington and the Mixing Pot in Glebe.

In 1978 he went to Japan on a fishing industry trading mission. It was the beginning of the worldwide 200 mile fishing zones, and the Japanese could no longer fish anywhere they wanted, so they had to look for importers. This was a real eye-opener for him. 'Before I went to Japan, we'd have tuna in the shop, and I'd cut it into cutlets. The Japanese would come in, and point to the belly of the tuna, which I now know is called *toro*, and ask me to cut it for them, and I'd almost tell them to piss off. If you don't like it, go somewhere else. So when I went to Japan, and learnt the way they handle fish, it blew my mind. In Japan, fish merchant is an honourable profession— the kind they put an "o" for honourable in front of. Later, back in Australia, I was making a delivery in the back of a Japanese restaurant, and I heard the guy call out "o sakanaya is here". I thought, that's nice, honourable fish merchant, not the smelly bloke from the market.'

When he returned, he did two things. Enrolled in Japanese classes at Macquarie University. And chased the Japanese market—both retail and restaurant. 'We got ourselves a little sashimi counter in 1979, and I repainted the front of the shop and put up "Fish Market" in Japanese.'

By the early 1980s, Nick was supplying just about every Japanese restaurant in Sydney, and all the way to the Gold Coast, as well as forging strong links with the stars of the new Sydney food scene. 'I had Patric Juillet and Damien Pignolet as customers. I first met Patric when he was at Hyde Park, and Damien bought fish from me when he was at Butler's [now Mezzaluna]. We used to do a bit of business with the Bilsons [then Berowra Waters Inn]. The restaurant scene was growing and I was growing with it. I was doing business with what I call owner-drivers. My attitude was we could never beat Poulos and Manettas on price, but we could beat the arse off them on quality and service.'

By 1982, the restless Ruello was sick of being a fish merchant. He was ready to become a consultant, and Judith felt the same way. 'It was all resolved when George Costi [De Costi's] came along and just on spec asked me if I wanted to sell. As it turned out on the day he asked me I would have given the business to him. George and I've joked about this.' He sold to George and his then partner, Harry Demetriou (the 'de', no longer in the business) and settled down to consulting, and writing his PhD thesis.

This is a sore point with Nick. The thesis was on the ecological impact of Munmorah Power Station on the prawns of Tuggerah Lakes. 'One examiner passed it, one didn't. I later discovered [the examiner who didn't] was dependent on the Electricity Commission for research grants. The story's out now because he's done the same thing to other people.'

But the bitterness is over, and today Nick is consulting for government and industry, writing for *Seafood Australia Magazine* and *Australian Gourmet Traveller*—and eating as much fish and seafood as he can. I once rang him to tell him of a restaurant that had shark carpaccio on the menu. He rang me the next day to tell me he'd tried it and it was 'terrific'.

Nick Ruello is currently interested in aquaculture, and it would be in character for him to take a more active role. 'The future for fish is that it's going to get dearer. We're not going to get more John Dory out of the ocean, so if you want it you'll have to pay for it. We're going to get more farmed fish. But Australia is not the cheapest producer in the world because of the cost of land, labour and feed. In twenty years time, fresh fish, wild fish will be the domain of the better off.'

And what does Nick Ruello like to eat? 'Flounder, flathead, shark. I like it fairly simple—the best way to eat fresh fish is raw or barbecued. Even a so-called ordinary fish—a mullet—is great barbecued. I've been

**Nick Ruello examines the evidence.**

to beaches as a poor young biologist trying to save a quid, and we'd get a couple of mullet and barbecue them. Any fisherman will tell you can't beat a mullet, a shark or a flathead. If you can get them fresh.'

# Yuki's Japanese Sauce

1 cup (250 mL) bottled
tomato sauce
¼ cup soy bean paste
(*koshi miso*)
1 tablespoon finely
chopped onion
1 teaspoon crushed garlic
I tablespoon soy sauce
1 tablespoon white wine or
sake
small pinch black pepper
pinch chilli powder

Place all the ingredients in a saucepan over a medium heat and bring to the boil, stirring to combine. Simmer for 15 minutes.

Allow to cool to room temperature. The sauce can be stored in the refrigerator for up to 1 month.

# Sepia Ink Pasta

Ruello's method

Carefully squeeze the ink from one or two ink sacs which have been removed from inside undamaged cuttlefish into your favourite tomato-based pasta sauce to give it a piquant flavour and a remarkable black colour. The sauce is great served with fettucine.

# Lazy Man's Cioppino

Fish soup

olive oil
½ onion, chopped
1 garlic clove, minced
1 bay leaf
1 pinch oregano
1 pinch sage
2 × 410 g cans tomatoes
1 tablespoon tomato paste
¼ cup (60 mL) water
salt and pepper to taste
750 g crabmeat, cooked
4 large oysters
8 scallops
8 prawns, shelled and de-
veined

In a large saucepan over a medium heat, sauté the onion and garlic in a little olive oil until soft. Add the spices and cook for 5 more minutes.

Add the tomatoes, tomato paste, water, salt and pepper and simmer for 1 hour.

When ready to serve, add the seafood to the sauce and cook for about 5 minutes.

The sauce can be stored in the refrigerator for several days or frozen for later use.

To serve: serve with plenty of good crusty sourdough bread.

# Nick Ruello's Barbecue Hints

Roll your fish fillets in flour before cooking them on a barbecue plate. Have the plate hot and oily just before you add the fish—a hot, oily plate gives floured fish a lovely crisp golden skin.

Large whole green prawns are mostly frozen at sea these days and are best bought frozen and thawed as required in a few minutes in running water. Just cut the shell down the middle of the 'back' (tail segments) with scissors but leave the shell on while cooking. Barbecue for 1 or 2 minutes per side. These are ready to peel after cooking and delicious dunked in teriyaki or Yuki's Japanese sauce (see recipe).

Sam and Olga Vico with their daughters Sofia and Giulia outside the original Pasticceria Bassano in Griffith.

'When we were in Italy,
we realised we're now
Australians—with a bit
of Italian mixed in.'

# CHAPTER SIXTEEN

# Sam & Olga Vico

'**M**ATE, THE** bacon and egg focaccia is a ripper!' Now, you wouldn't get a wrap-up like that in any old NSW country town. Especially not from a solid young blond bloke in work boots and tats. But this is Griffith. And Griffith is different, because of what my young mate tucking into the focaccia would probably call the 'eye-talians'. How they got there and what they're doing now is a story that starts with the century, and one that must be told before I begin talking to Sam and Olga Vico.

Griffith is at the heart of the Riverina—land brought to life by one man's vision. A land written off—a little prematurely as it turned out—by surveyor John Oxley as 'country that would never again be visited by civilised man'.

This is the Murrumbidgee valley, a wide flat land (known as 'the Bland' in the nineteenth century) bounded by the Murrumbidgee and Lachlan Rivers. Its original vegetation was low, impenetrable native pine and mallee-clad sandy ridges with no ground water. In the Cocoparra National Park, you can see how it looked to Oxley and, later, Major Mitchell. Aside from the McPherson Range (and La Collina, of which more later), it's flat as far as the eye can see—140 metres above sea level, all the way.

The idea to irrigate the valley had been canvassed as early as 1891. Then, in 1906, an Irish visionary by the name of Samuel McCaughey made a magnificent speech to Parliament, convincing them that ' . . . gold will eventually become exhausted, while water will continue as long as the world lasts.' Work started almost immediately. By 1912 the first farms became available. Government advertising attracted farmers from all over the country, but most especially Italians, who recognised the intensive agricultural methods being used.

And that's why you'll find the Trimbole family making superb bread in wood-fired ovens in south-eastern NSW, and why the wines are made by people called Calabria and de Bortoli and Fiumara, and why there's a Pasticceria Bassano on Banna Avenue, the main drag.

There's a murky side to Griffith too. It's hard to miss as you drive in, and see the name NUGAN written in huge letters on the side of the group's fruit and vegetable packing plant—even the name of that family of innocent bakers, Trimbole, sets up nervous reverberations until you learn that in Reggio Calabria, Trimbole is a bit like Smith. Most of this is unfair. Griffith is a prosperous town of mainly hardworking people—but it's the only town in Australia where there's a non-Anglo-Saxon/Celtic majority.

I tasted Sam Vico's food before I met him. I'd been invited to lunch with winemaker Darren de Bortoli in the company's boardroom on my first visit to Griffith some years ago. I can still remember what we ate: *vitello tonnato* [cold veal with tuna mayonnaise]; zucchini marinated in de Bortoli's red wine vinegar; fresh borlotti bean salad; roast peppers in olive oil; and a fresh fruit tart—accompanied by a selection of the world-famous de Bortoli botry-tised semillons. I'd never really had food like that in a country town in Australia before. I had to meet that cook, if only to get the recipe for the marinated zucchini.

This time I spoke with Sam and Olga in their new house in the area known as La Collina (the hill), named for a nearby escarpment, the only bump for miles around. The interview is delightfully interrupted by Giulia, their four-year-old (Sofia, their eldest, is nine) who is home with a cold. I soon found out why it's called the Bassano, but only later why a cafe is called a Pasticceria.

'My parents are from Bassano di Grappa,' Sam tells me. 'Dad [Onorato Vico] was born in a stable in a village called Belvedere. There were eleven brothers and sisters. My mother, Lina Gastaldello, was born in Rossano Veneto, close to Bassano, a beautiful region near the foot of Monte Grappa, and famous—of course—for its grappa [Italian spirit]. The Nardini Grapperia has been making it there since around 1730. It's also well known for white asparagus—the speciality is risotto with white asparagus and porcini.'

As much as they loved their country and their countryside, the Vicos had to leave to find work. Onorato—universally called Cicco—came to Australia on the *Achille Lauro* in 1955. Lina came later—'they were sort of betrothed, they knew each other in Italy'—with her family.

Cicco Vico was a restless adventurer and an entrepreneur. Of his father Sam says that he was ' . . . a wise man rather than an educated one . . . it was the poor who came to Australia . . . they had a lot of courage and they learnt through their mistakes.' Wherever Cicco Vico went, he left behind businesses—mainly food—that continued to prosper with their new owners.

First stop for the Vicos was Brisbane. And the first business Cicco opened in 1958, after a stint spent canecutting, was the Cortina Bar, the Italian coffee shop where Michael Platsis began his career as a restaurateur. It was also Cicco Vico who opened Milano's in 1960, later to be Brisbane's leading restaurant under the supervision of Gino Merlo, who bought it from Vico, and employed the young Michael Platsis.

When Sam was four (he was born in 1960) the family moved to Melbourne, to Carlton, where Cicco opened a 'gambling den' in a building which today houses a cafe called Sabatini's, then a small pasta and gelato factory—Sam used to sell ice cream after school at St Ignatius in Richmond—then a pizzeria in St Kilda called Osteria, and finally (although with all this moving around, the chronology is a bit hazy), he opened a cafe, also called Cortina, in Bourke Street across the road from radio station 3KZ in Melbourne. This was before television, and the big stars of the day, Phillip Brady and Graham Kennedy, adopted the Cortina as their bar.

The next move was to Griffith in 1969 where he opened the first Italian restaurant in town, the Belvedere. 'Back in those days, it was a ghost town—they used to call it chook town, because only the chooks were awake at night. But after a few years, we had to tell people to get out at 3AM—they were lining up for pizzas and coffee. Mum made ravioli by hand, Dad was still making his ice cream. After a while we went into partnership with another uncle, Saverio Gastaldello. Now he's one of the top Italian chefs in Canberra.'

And then, in 1974, after five years in Griffith, Cicco again became restless, and decided to return to Brisbane and buy back the Cortina Bar in Fortitude Valley, the same one he'd opened 20 years before. 'Things didn't turn out too well in Brisbane. Dad's like a lot of Italians—TAB, gambling, you know. And Brisbane had changed. The valley was becoming more of a Chinatown. I was fourteen, working, I couldn't fit into school. So I left. I was pretty grown up.'

In 1976 the family (which included Sam's brothers, the older Robert and the younger Renato, 'my real name is Secondo,' he told me, a little sheepishly, half way through this interview) returned to Griffith, this time opening a restaurant called La Scala, where it is today, on Banna Avenue, two doors up from Bassano, in partnership with Angelo Guidolin.

Now Sam Vico began working in earnest, trying every job in the restaurant until deciding that he wanted to cook. La Scala opened as a pizzeria, like the old Belvedere (also, incidentally, still there) but later developed into an Italian restaurant (and a very good one—on my first visit to Griffith I had an excellent dish of grilled quail on polenta there, a dish I later found out was introduced by Sam).

And it was here that the Vicos, finally, decided to stay—well, Sam and his brothers at least, Cicco and Lina returned to Bassano in 1988. I asked Sam was it difficult growing up with such an adventurous father?

'He wasn't difficult, he was always joking, very tricky. He was like one of the boys more than a father to be feared.' But surely this Gypsy existence had left him feeling a little insecure? 'Yes,' he admitted, 'it's not easy making friends, especially as you get older. But I was busy working, always in the restaurant.'

One thing his early peripatetic life did was to give him an insight into a number of Australian cities. Of all the places he has lived in, he prefers Melbourne. 'I feel I belong more in Melbourne, there are more diverse cultures there. Every city has a different feel to it. Brisbane is very Aussie. Sydney's getting more Asian—the Italian restaurants will disappear in a few years. We've always had a passion for Melbourne.'

By 1976, young Sam Vico was pretty set in his future plans: 'I always knew I'd be involved in the food industry, from an early age being in a restaurant—all the smells, all the memories.' And then he met Olga, who became his wife, best friend and partner. Her father was (and still is) the landlord of the building in which the Vicos built La Scala.

Olga Vico is the daughter of Antonio and Lina Battaglia. Her father's father, Francesco, came to Australia in the 1920s, went sugarcane-cutting in Queensland, sent for the rest of the family, and came with them to live in Griffith. Olga tells the story of the family's arrival:

'I still remember Dad telling me with tears in his eyes that when he arrived at the airport in Sydney, my grandfather wasn't allowed in to see the family, I think because he was Italian. Dad would have been 21. He hadn't seen his father for 15 years.'

Olga is the perfect mix for Griffith—half northern Italian, half Calabrian. 'My Mum is from Cavazzo del Tomba near Bassano, and Dad is from Petrizzi, a mountain village. They met here in Griffith.'

With the money he'd made in the canefields, her grandfather, in partnership with another Italian, opened a supermarket, Tom's and a liquor store next to Bassano (still there). 'Dad was one of the first barbers in town.'

When she was about eleven, she noticed the handsome young Secondo Vico. 'He made friends with my brother. Every time he looked at me I'm sure I'd go red as anything. It was terrible.' When she was sixteen, and he was eighteen, they started going out, and in 1984, they married.

But before he got married Sam left La Scala. 'I said to my younger brother, you're in the kitchen—goodbye. I went to Queensland, worked on Green Island for a while, came back and got married. Then we went to Bassano di Grappa for a year. We didn't travel as much as we would have liked— Olga was pregnant with Sofia—but it was a real eye-opener.'

Deciding he didn't know much about making cakes and pastries, he apprenticed himself to Bassano's most famous pastry chef, 76-year-old Osvaldo (Aldo) Sciamoncin.

'We used to walk along the Via Roma and see all the pastries sitting up there in one of the *gastronomias* [cafe/delis]. There was a *tavola calda* and a *tavola fredda*, antipasti, cakes, it was like a miniature foodhall with a wonderful window display.' Sam found out who made the cakes, and begged for a job with him. 'I used to kiss arse and sweep the floors—I just walked in off the street, I didn't want any money, I said please, please give me a job. Eventually we became great friends. He was the father of pastrycooks in Bassano. At one stage, he had twelve pastrycooks working for him. His father was a pastrycook in Venice, and in those days, pastry cooking was considered a noble thing—the pastry cooks would work for the rich people, they were the only ones who could afford this fine expensive food.'

'He was the king of the *sfoglia* [puff pastry]. But I had to change his recipe when I came back here. Butter was different, the flour was different—you can bring some aspects back, but you have to change. But what I did bring back was an attitude.' An attitude that persists to this day. After dinner one night in the Vico home, we ate some almond biscotti. They were exceptionally good. Sam told me he uses ground apricot kernel instead of almond, because the Australian almonds, predominantly the soft shell American kind, don't have enough flavour.

After Sofia was born, they came back to Griffith. I asked why they came back. 'There's more opportunity here,' Olga told me. 'And the space. There's not enough space for me there. And over there all the jobs are taken by *Marocini* (Moroccans). Italians study until they're 32 and then they don't have a job to go to.'

'We came back in April of 1987,' Sam continued. 'We opened the

Pasticceria Bassano in September. There was just me and Olga and a part-time worker. Now (eight years later) there's something like fifteen people on the staff. It's started to happen in the last two or three years. In the early days, when we opened as a cake shop (a pasticceria), people would look in the window and think, oh, no, it's too nice in there, it must be expensive. Country people are reserved and shy. So we started making lunches, and it's moved from there, we're progressing. Now we've reached the stage where we want to streamline the pasticceria and incorporate it into a *gastronomia*.'

Having decided to stay in Griffith—the old wanderlust habits die hard, a couple of years after they returned in 1994, they sold up and thought for a while about moving to Melbourne and made another trip to Italy—they've also decided to expand, to separate the cake shop and the cafe, to take over the liquor shop next door and make that the cafe, and even to export the Bassano idea to other large regional centres. 'There's nothing like this in Shepparton, Albury or Wagga Wagga.'

There are three very good things about Pasticceria Bassano. The food, the cakes, and the coffee. And if that sounds self-evident, you haven't tried all three in small Australian towns. On the day I ate there, I tried the *farfalle* with salmon and vodka; an *involtini* [stuffed rolls] of prosciutto with polenta; and garfish baked with fresh thyme, white wine, tomato and pine nuts. The meal would have been noteworthy in Sydney or Melbourne: in an Australian country town, it was astonishing. The *sfoglia* filled with cream, fresh grapes, candied fruit and amaretto was sensational, and was made by a young woman then working for Sam, Tanya Schubert, who he believes has a real gift. Aldo Sciamoncin, the king of *sfoglia* in Bassano di Grappa, has left a legacy in southern New South Wales.

Sam's food comes from all over Italy. He reads Italian cookbooks, has a pile of the Italian food magazine *Cucina Italiana* in his house, and borrows and experiments like any good chef. But I was interested to know whether a Griffith regional style had developed. I asked this question after dinner. Olga left the table for the kitchen.

'Very peasant,' was Sam's judgement. 'Some people make the most beautiful preserved fruit. They do eggplants and red pepper under oil, dried tomatoes—home-style peasant food.' Olga returned with bottles of delicious preserved eggplant and capsicum from the mother of a woman who works at Bassano. 'Locally there are quail, rice, oranges. And they do the pig slaughter here every winter. There's a bit of a competition. Everyone says they make the best salami, so we go salami hunting in the season after the slaughter. Our new partner, Vince Ferraro, the chief surgeon at the local hospital, he made one of the best last year, but we ate it all. I wish we still had some for you.'

The story of the pig slaughter sparks off a childhood memory from Olga. 'When I was a little girl I used to watch my Dad and my uncles make the salamis. I'd go down to where the pigs were. They'd hang the pig up and split it down the middle and all the guts'd fall out and I'd be standing there, just watching it. But before that they'd cut the neck and Dad would collect the blood.'

'My grandmother would take some of it and make a little bar with it. She'd boil it, I think with sugar, put sesame seeds in it, let it cool down and cut it into cubes. Sometimes she'd put nuts in it too. We'd eat it like a muesli bar. It was called *sanguinazzo*, candied blood.' This is not as unusual as it sounds to the Anglo. Rosa Matto (Chapter 10) is from Adelaide (her family from the region of Campana near Naples) told me that as a child, 'We were very wary of accepting "chocolate pudding" from an ancient relative in the months of June to August—there was every chance it had been thickened with pig's blood.'

But in Griffith, there is nothing that could be called a regional cuisine, nor even, as far as the Vicos know, a regional dish. That is yet to come, and it may even be, as in the rest of the country, the professional chefs, like Sam, who create it. He wants to encourage the use of regional products, to sell the preserved fruits and vegetables made by the local women. 'My father-in-law's got a bit of land, a couple of acres, and I'm going to grow artichokes. I want to experiment.'

Pasticceria Bassano is one of the rare places outside a major city where you can get a well-made cup of Italian coffee. It was late in the afternoon, and Sam was fading when I suggested we talk about coffee. He came alive. I asked the difference between a good cup of coffee and a bad one.

'There are three important things to watch for. Firstly, you've got to have good quality water. The water here in Griffith has a lot of chlorine, so we filter it—and we keep the machine clean. Then you've got to have the machine running at the right temperature—it varies, especially if it's working hard, when it seems to pump out a lot of hot water and burns the coffee. Then there's the grinding. Coffee changes according to the humidity. On a hot day, it runs quicker, you have to pack it in tighter, grind it a bit finer. On a cold day, you have to open it up, grind it a bit coarser.'

'Each cup I make, I empty the group [the reservoir that holds the coffee], and I run the water from the machine and rinse it. In the morning, when the machine is a bit putrid, you've got to waste coffees—run it for a while, run a few coffees through the machine to clean it out.'

'And most importantly, you can't get a good cup of coffee if it's boiling hot. Sometimes the hardest thing is, when you make someone a beautiful cup of coffee, and they bring it back and complain that it's not hot enough. You can't taste coffee when it's hot. You've got to explain that.'

Finally, we spoke about the relationship between Italy and Griffith. 'We have Italian newspapers here,' Sam said, 'but they're not that interested in what goes on in Italy. A lot of the farmers renounced Italy when they came here. Italy never gave me a living, they say, Italy never put food on my table. On the other hand a lot of them—like my parents—went back. And then their sons and daughters go back to find their heritage. Like us.'

He stopped and thought a moment. 'It's funny,' he said, 'because before we left to go to Italy, we thought, oh, we're Italian. And when we were in Italy, we realised, no, we're not, we're Australians—with a bit of Italian mixed in.'

Just out of town, a bit beyond the huge de Bortoli operation, you'll come to the West End Winery, one of the smaller local wineries, owned by Bill Calabria. Bill is about ten years older than Sam, a friend of his, and obviously someone he admires. He's a nuggety kind of bloke with a well-broken nose and a good, slow smile about whom stories are told. 'He was a pretty good boxer when he was a boy,' Sam tells me later, 'and that's how he got his nose broken. I'm not sure,' he said, 'but that's what they say.'

Bill's father came out in 1921. 'He came straight from Italy to Griffith, with a friend. As soon as they got here, the other bloke got on the first train out, and went straight back to Italy. This is a desert, he said. Dad worked on a farm for a while, then with McWilliams, then he bought this land—it was cheap then. This property was 150 quid in the 1920s. It's six acres.' Then he started making wine for himself 'because he was thirsty,' Bill adds with a grin, and then he began making it by request for friends, until one day he found he had a reasonable business. Later, he changed the name from Calabria Wines to West End because Australians could neither pronounce nor spell Calabria in those days.

When the business began to grow, Bill's father employed a young wine-maker just out of college. The first vintage, they made 4000 gallons of wine, and lost the lot. It turned to vinegar. 'That was a big setback. He virtually hit the wall. He started slowly climbing back.' One way was that he managed

**Sam Vico, Tony and Franca Trimbole in the bakery at Franca's Traditional Bread, Griffith.**

to sell the 4000 gallons. 'He told people the wine wasn't really vinegar, it was just the style. The reds were pretty rough in those days.'

And winemaking was hard work in those days. 'You were shovelling the grapes with a pitchfork. Everything was horse and cart. There were no machines, no nothing. I unloaded a lot of grapes with a pitchfork. We had a small crusher and a must pump, but there was a lot of hard work.'

Bill began running the winery when he was fifteen. 'I was running it but I wouldn't say I was running it.' He had five brothers, and one of the elder brothers was the salesman for the wine in Sydney. In those days—the 1950s—a lot of wine was sold in bulk, and people bottled it themselves.

Bill remembers his father with fondness—and regret. 'The thing about the old Italians is they didn't know how to read or write, but they could tell you what the phases of the moon meant. You can imagine how much he knew about making wine. He went by all the old traditional things, that's how they did it. Sometimes I look back and think, gee, it'd be nice to have him here now to explain it all. You'd listen now you're older, because when you're young you don't listen at all.'

Today West End makes a fine cabernet sauvignon, a chardonnay and sometimes a barbera. Bill also owns a big bottle shop in town, with the very Italian name of Billabong. One more thing. He doesn't drink. Never has. 'Don't like the taste of the stuff.'

Early on the morning I left Griffith I paid a visit to Franca's Traditional Bread, a bakery in a back street in Griffith on the edge of a canal. Out the front, great stacks of red gum and apple wood ready for the oven. Out the back, a nanny goat for milking. In between, the heady, yeasty smell of real bread baking in two Calabrian woodfired ovens.

Franca Trimbole is the baker. She makes that very clear from the outset. She is following the family trade—her grandmother was a baker in Plati in Reggio Calabria, where they came from 30 years ago. She's helped by husband Sam, and son Tony. Last year they bought an electric dough mixer. Before that, Franca had done it by hand, for seven years, seven days a week. They still knead by hand, all three of them. About 30–35 minutes of kneading for the dough from a batch of 30 kg of flour.

Nothing could be simpler than this delicious crusty bread they make. I asked her for the recipe. She handed me one of their paper bags. It reads 'Ingredients: flour, yeast, salt, water added.' They make 300 big round loaves a day, and then smaller loaves, buns, olive focaccia, and round, thin pizzas with tomato, thyme and olive oil on top.

When I left, Tony thrust a bag at me with two small loaves, two olive breads and two pizzas. I'd almost scoffed the lot by the time I got to Goulburn—the Caltex Quickbite on the Old Hume Highway—another outpost on the Wogfood map—real coffee made by ex-Chilean Guillermo Olmos and his Aussie wife Barbara Maclean. About as good as Sam and Olga's.

Postscript: Don't look for that Caltex Quickbite. Just before finishing this book, two things happened. It was given an entry in the country section of the 1996 Sydney Morning Herald *Good Food Guide*—and Caltex announced it was to be closed. A spokesperson for Caltex said the company wasn't interested in food, just 'pumping petrol'. We still have a long way to go.

# Zucchini al Lime
Zucchini with Limes

SERVES 4–6

350 g young zucchini with
 flowers
3 limes
plain flour
extra virgin olive oil
salt and pepper
10 basil leaves

Pull the flowers from the zucchini without breaking them and throw away their internal stalks.

Wash the flowers rapidly and delicately and pat dry on paper towel or clean towels. Dust with flour and shallow-fry in hot oil until golden.

Cut the zucchini into thin rounds and dress with a mixture containing the filtered juice of 1 lime, 70 g extra virgin olive oil, salt and pepper. Sprinkle chopped basil on top.

Peel the remaining 2 limes and cut into segments. Place a segment on top of each zucchini flower.

To serve: arrange the zucchini flowers around a large plate with the sliced zucchini in the middle and serve immediately.

# Gelato alla Lavanda con Anguri Marinata
Lavender flavoured Ice Cream
with Marinated Watermelon

MAKES 1 LITRE ICE CREAM

½ watermelon
50 g sugar
fresh mint sprigs

ICE CREAM
400 mL fresh milk
100 g sugar
1¼ cups (310 mL) fresh
 cream
dried lavender flowers
1 vanilla bean

Remove the seeds from the watermelon, and cut it into regular triangles. Place the pieces in a deep dish, sprinkle with sugar and fresh mint sprigs, add 100 mL cold water, cover with plastic wrap and place in the refrigerator for 1 hour.

Meanwhile, prepare the ice cream.

Mix the milk with the sugar and 200 mL cream, add a pinch of lavender flowers and the vanilla bean and warm in a saucepan without boiling. Set aside and allow to cool. When cold, filter the mixture and place it in an ice cream churner. When the ice cream starts to solidify, add the extra 110 mL cream and churn until ready, then place in the freezer.

To serve: place scoops of ice cream on top of the watermelon triangles. Garnish with fresh mint.

# *Crostata di Semolino*   Semolina and Fruit Tart

SERVES 6–8

### SHORTCRUST
1¼ cups (310 g) unsalted butter
4 cups (500 g) soft biscuit flour or plain flour
1 whole egg
3 egg yolks
200 g icing sugar or caster sugar
pinch of salt
rind of 1 lemon
flour and butter for mould

### CAKE
1 apple
2 pears
3 peaches
1 tablespoon white sugar
40 g butter
2 cups (500 mL) milk
100 mL fresh whipping cream
⅔ cup (150 g) caster sugar
80 g semolina
5 egg yolks
1 sachet Bertolinni vanilla
30 mL Grand Marnier
1 punnet (200 g) raspberries
icing sugar for dusting

To make shortcrust, soften the butter. Mix the butter into the flour with your fingertips, then make a well in the centre. Add the whole egg, egg yolks, the sugar and a small pinch of salt and the lemon rind.

Rapidly mix with your hands until the mixture is amalgamated. Don't overmix. Set aside in the refrigerator wrapped in plastic wrap for 30 minutes.

To make cake, peel the apples, pears and peaches and cut into cubes. Place in a large saucepan over a medium heat with a little sugar and butter, and half cook them or at least until they have lost some of their juice. Put in colander and set aside to cool.

On a lightly floured work bench, roll out the shortcrust to 4 mm thick and then place it in a 24-cm spring form tin which has been lightly floured and buttered, so that the pastry covers the base of the tin. Cut off the trimmings, flatten them to a ball and set aside in the refrigerator.

In a saucepan, bring the milk and cream and 100 g sugar to the boil over a medium heat. Sprinkle over the semolina, whisking it over a low heat for at least 10 minutes. Lastly, incorporate the egg yolks, vanilla and Grand Marnier.

Spread all the fruit (reserve a few raspberries for the top) over the pastry in the cake tin, cover with the hot semolina mixture, and spread it over uniformly.

Finish the tart by using pastry cutoffs to make a grid pattern on top of the tart, and placing remaining raspberries in between the spaces.

Cook in a preheated 180°C (355°F) oven for approximately 1 hour 10 minutes.

To serve: allow to cool or eat just warm, dusted with icing sugar.

# Bibliography

Alexander, Stephanie. *Stephanie's Seasons*, Allen & Unwin, Sydney, 1993.

Apicius, *Cookery and Dining in Imperial Rome*, edited and translated by Joseph Dommers Vehling, Dover, New York, 1977.

Barron, Rosemary. *Flavours of Greece*, Penguin, Harmondsworth, 1994.

Beckett, Richard. *Convicted Tastes*, George Allen & Unwin, Sydney, 1984.

Bernal, Martin. *Black Athena, the Afroasiatic Roots of Classical Civilisation*, Vintage, London, 1987.

Carluccio, Antonio. *A Passion for Mushrooms*, Pavilion, London, 1990.

David, Elizabeth. *Italian Food*, Penguin, Harmondsworth, 1987.

Donnini, Tiberio. *Donnini's Pasta*, Viking O'Neil, Ringwood, 1988.

Germanos, Irini. *A Taste of Greek Life and Cooking*, self-published, South Australia, 1992.

Grey, Patience. *Honey From a Weed*, Prospect Books, London, 1986.

Johnson, Hugh. *Hugh Johnson's Wine Companion*, Mitchell Beazley, London, 1991.

Kremezi, Aglaia. *The Foods of Greece*, Stewart Tabori Chang, New York, 1993.

O'Grady, Desmond. *Correggio Jones and the Runaways*, Cardigan Street Publishers, Melbourne, 1995.

Roden, Claudia. *A New Book of Middle Eastern Food*, Claudia Roden, Penguin, Harmondsworth, 1986.

Sluga, Glenda. *Bonegilla, A Place of No Hope*, History Department, University of Melbourne, 1988.

Symons, Michael. *The Shared Table*, Australian Government Printing Service, Canberra, 1993.

Waines, David. *In a Caliph's Kitchen*, Raid El Rayyes Books, USA, 1989.

Wolfert, Paula. *Good Food From Morocco*, John Murray, London, 1989.

# Index

Italic page numbers refer to photographs

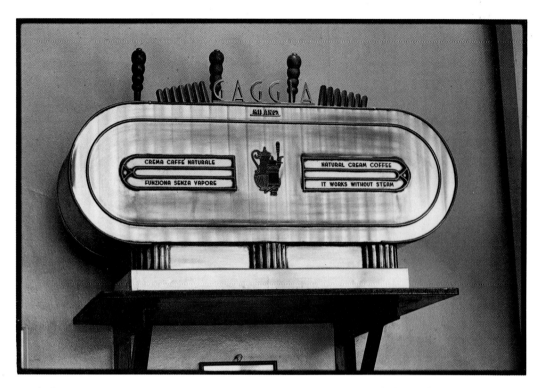

The first licensed espresso machine in Australia, still on the wall at the Universita Bar Restaurant (formerly the University Cafe), Lygon Street, Carlton.